THE
"MR. BIG"
STING

THE
"MR. BIG"
STING

THE CASES,
THE KILLERS,
THE CONTROVERSIAL
CONFESSIONS

MARK STOBBE

This book is also available as a Global Certified Accessible™ (GCA) ebook. ECW Press's ebooks are screen reader friendly and are built to meet the needs of those who are unable to read standard print due to blindness, low vision, dyslexia, or a physical disability.

Purchase the print edition and receive the eBook free. For details, go to ecwpress.com/eBook.

LIBRARY AND ARCHIVES CANADA CATALOGUING IN PUBLICATION

Title: The "Mr. Big" sting : the cases, the killers, the controversial confessions / Mark Stobbe.

Other titles: "Mister Big" sting

Names: Stobbe, Mark, author.

Identifiers: Canadiana (print) 20210210869 | Canadiana (ebook) 20210210923

ISBN 978-1-77041-612-3 (softcover)
ISBN 978-1-77305-827-6 (ePub)
ISBN 978-1-77305-828-3 (PDF)
ISBN 978-1-77305-829-0 (Kindle)

Subjects: LCSH: Undercover operations. | LCSH: Undercover operations—Canada. | LCSH: Confession (Law) | LCSH: Confession (Law)—Canada. | LCSH: Police questioning. | LCSH: Police questioning—Canada. | LCSH: Criminal investigation. | LCSH: Criminal investigation—Canada.

Classification: LCC HV8080.U5 S76 2021 | DDC 363.2/32—dc23

Published by ECW Press
665 Gerrard Street East
Toronto, Ontario, Canada M4M 1Y2
416-694-3348 / info@ecwpress.com

Cover design: David Drummond

This book is funded in part by the Government of Canada. Ce livre est financé en partie par le gouvernement du Canada. We also acknowledge the support of the Government of Ontario through Ontario Creates.

PRINTED AND BOUND IN CANADA

PRINTING: MARQUIS   5 4 3 2 1

This book is dedicated to the memory of the
following victims of homicide:

Chelsea Acorn
Mr. Argent
Amanpreet Bahia
Dexter Bain
Jack Beauchamp
Karrissa Beaudreau
William Bedford
Fribjon Bjornson
Keith Black
Mark Bonkes
Daleen Bosse
Kevin Bowser
Myrol Brock
M. Marc Brûlé
Florine Brun
Cynthia Burk
Joleil Campeau
Catherine Carroll
Adam Cavanaugh
Erin Chorney
Shannon Collins
Sylvia Consuelo
Bruce Crawford
Vaughn Davis
Juan Dequina
Judy Dick
Darcy Drefko
James Dubé
Helen Dunlop
Evelyn Ellision
Adela Etibako
Benedicta Etibako

Edita Etibako
Stephane Etibako
Jo Anne Feddema
Alexandra Flanagan
Robert Forgan
Audrey Foster
Jodi Franz
Victor Fraser
Kulwinder Gill
Anthony Gordon
Connie Grandinetti
Raymond Graves
Santo Graves
Gwenda Gregory
Raymond Greenwood
Heather Hamill
Barry Head
Landis Heal
Olive Hill
Premier Hoang
Jenny Holtham
Leonora Holtham
Monica Jack
Lionide Johnson
Earl Jones
Roy Jones
Meika Jordan
Ryan Kam
Cindy Kaplan
Ali Khamis
Daryl Klassen
Theresa Klassen

Gordon Klaus
Monica Klaus
Sandra Klaus
Stacey Koehler
Theodor Keeper
Carol King
Carmela Knight
Douglas Kuntz
Laura Lamoureux
Gordon Langmead
Nick Larsen
Daniel Levesque
Robert Levoir
Keitha Llewellyn
Otto Loose
Clara Loski
Glen Martin
Luis Martins
Lyne Massicotte
Dylan McGillis
Monica McKay
Tiffany McKinney
Terry McLean
Joy Mendoza
Lisa Mitchell
Gloria Mott
Victoria Nashacappo
Zaher Noureddine
Melanie O'Neil
Bill Palmer
Brenda Pathammavong
Jaclynn Patterson

Shayne Preece	Jeffry Sabine	Judith Thibault
Basma Rafay	David Sanha	TM
Sultana Rafay	Peter Sciemann	Ed Vetere
Tariq Rafay	Gordon Seybold	Gladys Wakabayashi
Isabella Rain	Ashley Singh	Alyssa Watson
Susan Reinhardt	Billy Smith	Joshua Williams
David Roberts	Julie Smith	Elizabeth Zeschner
Josiah Roberts	Angela Steer	Anonymous
Susan Roberts	Beverly Taylor	[Publication Ban on Name]
Derk Roelfsema	William Terrico	
William Rudy	Mr. Thandi	

These are all victims of homicides. Their killers would not have been brought to justice without Mr. Big. This list is incomplete — it includes only cases identified in researching this book.

ACKNOWLEDGEMENTS

Writing a book is a solitary activity, but it is not possible without help from many other people.

This book would not have been possible without support from family members — most importantly, my wife, Marilyn Totten, who patiently listened to far more accounts of vicious crimes than she wanted to hear about. My sons assisted both emotionally and practically. Nicholas Stobbe provided guidance on my discussions on legal issues and Jacob Stobbe provided many useful editorial suggestions. My parents, Margaret Munro and the late John Stobbe, helped instill both intellectual curiosity and determination to complete tasks.

Other people also played an important background role. Tim Killeen, Sandra Chapman, and Shannon McNicol provided me with role modelling in a commitment to making the criminal justice system deliver justice. Judge Jim Jacques provided a wise way to operationalize the concept of reasonable doubt. Professors Harley Dickinson and the late Joe Garcia provided me with a similar model for seeking truth in academic research and writing.

The professionalism of the staff at ECW Press made the publishing process a pleasure. Jack David was helpful and insightful in keeping the manuscript focused. Sammy Chin, Cat London, and Adrineh Der-Boghossian edited the manuscript with an eagle eye and a gentle pen. Any mistakes or problems are my responsibility.

This book was written with great respect for the police officers who have conducted Mr. Big operations with integrity in the pursuit of justice. Most of these officers are members of the RCMP. However, the book was written without the cooperation or support of the RCMP as an institution. Not only did the RCMP refuse to assist with allowing officers to share their insights and experiences, it failed to meet its legal obligations in providing basic information about Mr. Big operations in response to Access to Information requests. In November 2020, the Information Commissioner of Canada informed Parliament that "the RCMP's inability to meet statutory timeframes under the Act is the norm, not the exception." The RCMP was described as having a "culture of secrecy." This is problematic because it undermines accountability mechanisms for Canada's national police force. In the case of Mr. Big, it also has the perverse effect of hindering the ability to tell a positive story about the dedication, imagination, and skill of investigative officers.

TABLE OF CONTENTS

CHAPTER I

An Introduction to Mr. Big

Susan Roberts was tired but happy on the evening of July 18, 1995. As she drifted off to sleep, her loving husband massaged her back. Her three children were in their cribs. Three-year-old Jonathan was hers from a previous relationship, while the eighteen-month-old twin boys (David and Josiah) were fathered by her husband. Susan did not notice her husband slipping a rope around her neck. Her evening took a turn for the worse as she experienced terror, then pain, then death when he strangled her. Her husband then strangled Josiah and set the house on fire with the expectation that this would kill Jonathan and David. He threw Josiah's corpse into a nearby wood and proceeded to a friend's house in order to play the role of the grieving husband and father when the news of his family's death was delivered to him. As it turned out, he was not completely successful in wiping out his family. Neighbours braved the flames to rescue Jonathan. David was scooped from his crib by firefighters but later died of smoke inhalation.

On May 6, 1978, Monica Jack was riding her bicycle. The twelve-year-old was headed to her home on the Quilchena reserve, located northeast of Merritt, British Columbia. It was a beautiful spring evening. As Monica pedalled her bike alongside Nicola Lake, she had no idea that the man urinating in the bushes beside a parked camper truck had been convicted of rape in the past. When Monica attempted to pass by, the man pulled her off the bike. The girl was thrown into the camper and her bike was thrown into the lake. The man drove to an isolated clearing in the forest. He raped Monica, then strangled her. He burned her body and clothing to destroy the evidence. After stuffing her charred remains under a log, the man departed. What was left of Monica's body was not discovered for seventeen years.

On June 8, 1994, Timothy Langmead was at work — a marijuana grow op in Port Coquitlam. An old friend from high school showed up with two colleagues. It was not a social call. The trio tied Timothy to a chair while they stole 170 marijuana plants, a guitar, and a VCR. Either because they did not want to leave behind any witnesses or because they were incompetent drunks, the robbers wrapped Timothy's head with twenty-four feet of duct tape. Timothy died. It is, after all, difficult to breathe through multiple layers of duct tape. Two of the robbers put Timothy's body in his van. They threw Timothy into the Fraser River and pushed his van over the edge of a cliff.

July 16, 1996, was a beautiful summer day in Williams Lake, British Columbia. Jo Anne Feddema told her husband and children that she wanted to go for a bike ride. She set out for the Williams Lake dump — taking this road because it had little traffic. Unfortunately, one of the few people going to the dump that day was a distracted driver. He was changing stations on his pickup truck radio and did not see Jo Anne until the last second. He braked, but not in time. Jo Anne's bike was knocked over. She was unhurt but unhappy. As she expressed her displeasure at the man's driving, he decided the best way to shut her up was to hit her over the head with a pipe wrench. This caved in Jo Anne's skull. The man threw the bike into the ditch and Jo Anne's body into his truck. He drove a mile further down the road and then took her a short distance into the forest. He pulled off her clothes and mutilated her genitalia so that the police would look for sexual predators. He hurried home. His wife and children believed he had been home all morning.

In the spring of 2004, Daleen Bosse had just finished her third year of the education program at the University of Saskatchewan. On May 16, she went for supper with friends from her home on the Onion Lake First Nation reserve and then to a meeting of a First Nations organization in Saskatoon. After the meeting, she decided to stop by a nightclub. There she got tipsy, met a guy, danced with him, and eventually agreed to go for a ride in the country. The man's hopes for an exciting sexual encounter did not work out as he had anticipated, so he strangled Daleen. He burned her body and put her charred remains in a small depression in the ground. He spotted an old abandoned refrigerator lying nearby, so he threw it on top of her.

On January 12, 2012, Fribjon Bjornson was a happy young man. The twenty-eight-year-old father of two had just cashed his paycheque from his work with a log-processing company. He decided to stop by the house of local drug dealers in Fort St. James, British Columbia, in order to buy a little illicit pleasure for the weekend. The three drug dealers robbed Fribjon and beat him mercilessly. They turned assault into murder by strangling Fribjon with an electrical cord and beheading him. Fribjon's body was hidden under a logjam on a river island while his head was stored in the basement. The murderers used Fribjon's $2,500 to buy a new snowmobile.

In the spring of 1994, Jodi Franz's life was hard. She was broke and separating from her husband. Her husband was harassing her and filing unfounded sexual abuse allegations against Jodi's new boyfriend. April 8 was to be a big day. She had an appointment with her lawyer to sign a petition for divorce and a meeting with the police to provide a written synopsis of her husband's harassment. Late in the evening of April 7, Jodi's husband called her to plead for a meeting. She reluctantly agreed. Her husband strangled Jodi and dismembered her into six pieces. He threw Jodi's head into the mouth of the Harrison River. From there, it entered the Fraser River and was never seen again. Her husband threw the rest of Jodi's body into the manure treatment pond of a dairy farm where he had once worked. The chemical and aeration action dissolved her. About four months later, the molecules that had once been a person were spread, along with cow manure, over a farmer's field.

In November 2011, Meika Jordan was a happy and friendly six-year-old. Her parents were divorced, but Meika appeared happy staying with her father during the week and her mother on weekends. This changed on Thursday, November 10. Her father's girlfriend "disciplined" Meika by holding the girl's hand over the flame of a cigarette lighter. Meika's father did not want her mother to find out about the resulting third-degree burn. He told Meika's mother that his girlfriend had dumped him and asked if Meika could stay for the weekend. Meika's mother consented. She never saw her daughter alive again. Meika's father and his girlfriend launched a bizarre spiral of abuse when Meika complained that her hand hurt. She was ordered to run up and down the stairs as "discipline" for complaining. When Meika ran out of breath, her father punched her in the stomach for slowing down. When this blow caused Meika to run even slower, he took to banging her head against the wall. By Sunday afternoon, Meika was dying. Her father called 911 and claimed his daughter had fallen down the stairs.

The Etibako family had fled from strife and disorder in central Africa to refuge in Vancouver. On May 15, 2006, the family was awakened by an explosion followed by a rush of flames. Adela Etibako was burned alive. So were her daughters Edita (12), Benedicta (9), and Stephane (8). Adela's son, Bolingo (19), was severely burned but survived by jumping out of a window. Bolingo's girlfriend, seventeen-year-old Ashley Singh, was also sleeping in the house and was also burned alive. The explosion and fire were deliberately created by a man seeking revenge because Bolingo had told police he'd seen the man stab someone. The man broke a window, poured five cans of gasoline into the house, and tossed a lit propane torch inside.

September 26, 1981, was a Friday. In Dawson Creek, British Columbia, Earl Jones took his wife to the bar for a few drinks. A stranger crudely propositioned Jones's wife. Earl objected by slapping the man across the face. The stranger left. All in all, a typical barroom kerfuffle, but this time it was different. The stranger waited outside in his pickup truck. When Earl and his wife started home, they noticed the truck following them. When they came to a stop sign, the back window of their car shattered. Earl was hit in the head with a bullet from a .303 rifle. He died instantly.

In August 1995, Clara Loski was ninety-five. She lived alone and was proud of her independence. One Friday afternoon, two men forced their way into her home. Clara's hands were tied behind her back with wire. Her feet were bound. Her hands and feet were tied together. Clothing was wrapped around Clara's head. She was thrown onto her bed while the two men ransacked the house looking for money. Then they left. Clara was alone, tied up, in the dark. Clara was gutsy. She struggled in an attempt to get free. The wire cut into her wrists and ankles. She continued to struggle for at least twenty-four hours. Eventually, her false teeth came loose and lodged in her throat. Clara died.

MR. BIG APPEARS

These examples show the value of an investigative technique known as "Mr. Big." These were very different crimes. The nature of the victims, the cause of death, and the motivations of the killers were profoundly different. Some victims were young; some were old. Some were men; some were women. Some were disreputable characters engaged in criminal activity, while some were innocent of any bad behaviour. Some were shot, some were strangled, and some were burned alive. Some of these killings were motivated by greed, some by anger, and some by sheer stupidity. There were similarities. None of these people deserved to die. All left loved ones behind who mourned their loss and longed for some semblance of justice. In all these cases, the police were frustrated by the harsh reality that their investigations were only partially successful. Police had identified the murderer but could not prove it in a way that would satisfy a judge or jury. Mr. Big was created in order to gather evidence and, where appropriate and possible, get a conviction.

Mr. Big was not born. He was invented. The five Ws of journalism are who, where, when, what, and why. The only group that might know the answer to the first three questions regarding Mr. Big is the Royal Canadian Mounted Police (RCMP), but if this information is recorded in their files, the RCMP is not sharing. But we can make some inferences with informed speculation. Mr. Big was created by an RCMP officer, but we don't know which one. He was first created in British Columbia. The earliest Mr. Big cases were conducted in that province, but we don't know where. We know that Mr. Big was created in the late 1980s or early 1990s, but we don't know the day, month, or year.

We can answer the "what" question. Mr. Big is an undercover operation in which police attempt to trick a suspect to disclose a serious crime by convincing him that he is joining a criminal gang.

This brings us to "why." Almost always when Mr. Big was used, the police were confronted with a brutal murder, a suspect, and a lack of proof on which to convict the suspect. Often the suspect had been interrogated but either denied committing the crime or followed the standard lawyer's advice of "just shut the fuck up." In many cases, the police wanted to file charges, but a prosecutor said there was not enough evidence to get a conviction. In one of these tense and frustrating cases, some RCMP officer had a bizarre idea. Why not have an undercover police officer befriend the suspect by pretending to be a criminal? Why not pretend to recruit the suspect into an imaginary criminal gang? Why not introduce the suspect to the imaginary leader of this imaginary criminal gang? Why not call this imaginary crime leader "Mr. Big"? Maybe the suspect could be persuaded to tell Mr. Big about committing the crime. Maybe they could get the suspect to convict himself with his own words.

My guess is that the initial reaction to this suggestion was amusement and incredulity. There were likely jokes from other police officers that the imaginative officer had been smoking British Columbia's largest illicit cash crop. The other police officers probably mocked the suggestion. No criminal, no matter how dumb, would be dumb enough to fall for that one. But desperate situations lead to desperate measures. Everyone involved was likely amazed that it worked. But because it worked, it was used again. And again. And again.

We don't know how many times Mr. Big has been used. The RCMP has made the general statement that it has used Mr. Big about 350 times. That's probably reasonably accurate, but it's impossible to verify. Other police forces in Canada have gotten into the act. The technique has been copied in countries such as Australia and New Zealand.

In researching this book, I've located 127 times that Mr. Big was created to investigate someone suspected of homicide, and 8 times he was created to investigate people suspected of crimes other than homicide. These included crimes such as launching violent home invasions and dynamiting a house in which three people were sleeping. In addition, I located one case in which the police made the very unwise decision to create Mr. Big in order to get an eyewitness identification from a witness who was either unable or unwilling to tell police who had killed his friend.

Neither I nor other researchers have been able to find a record of all Mr. Big cases. If a suspect is smart enough to understand that his new curious friends are likely police officers, the operation will end with no public record. If the suspect is convinced that Mr. Big is really a powerful leader of a criminal gang, but the suspect is innocent and smart enough not to make up a story, the operation will usually (but not always) remain invisible. The suspect may never know that his criminal friends who so mysteriously appeared and disappeared were actually undercover police officers. Even those cases where the suspect confessed, got convicted, and went to jail may remain invisible to researchers. The durable artifacts created by the justice system are reported judicial decisions and media reports of trials. If an accused pleads guilty, and there is agreement between the prosecution and defence about the recommended sentence, there is no reason for the judge to write a decision. If a defence lawyer does not object to the prosecution using the evidence generated by Mr. Big to the jury, and if the accused is convicted of first-degree murder, the trial itself will produce no written decisions by the trial judge. If the convicted murderer accepts his fate, there will be no appeal court decision. If the person who was killed was powerless, poor, or disreputable, there will usually be little or no media interest. If the trial takes place in a smaller town, media coverage will be local and difficult to locate.

Of the 127 homicide cases I located in which Mr. Big was called in, only six suspects told Mr. Big that they had not killed the victim. A few of these suspects were charged even without this disclosure, while others were convicted of lesser offences such as committing an indignity to a dead body. There are certainly other cases where a suspect denied being a killer. If no charges emerge from the investigation, it remains invisible.

In 121 of the homicide cases I examined while researching this book, the suspect told Mr. Big they killed or helped kill the victim. Of these, 51 were convicted of first-degree murder; 39 of second-degree murder; 10 of manslaughter; and 1 of conspiracy to commit murder. Five more were convicted of murder but had their convictions overturned on appeal. Five were charged but had the charges withdrawn or stayed after the courts ruled their disclosures to Mr. Big inadmissible as evidence. Nine were charged but acquitted, and one received an immunity agreement in exchange for testimony against his colleagues.

Those telling Mr. Big about their crimes often implicated others. The Mr. Big cases I've examined resulted in another forty-six people being charged with various offences. Of these, sixteen were convicted of first-degree murder, two of second-degree murder, seven of manslaughter, and one of attempted murder. Ten were convicted of offences such as conspiracy to commit murder, accessory after the fact, or committing an indignity to a dead body. Seven were acquitted of charges. Two were convicted of first-degree murder but had their conviction overturned on an appeal centring on the instructions the jury received on how to deal with hearsay evidence. They are waiting for their second trial.

The bottom line is that if a person tells Mr. Big they have killed someone, they and their associates have a very good chance of going to jail for a very long time. Even those eventually acquitted can end up being locked up for years (or even over a decade) while their cases wind their way through the courts.

Of the 121 suspects who told Mr. Big they killed someone, 115 were men and 6 were women. Because of this overwhelming male composition of suspects in Mr. Big cases, I will be using the generic pronoun "he." This gendered identification is not infallible, but it is substantively true. Killers caught by Mr. Big are almost always men.

A lot of homicides have been solved by Mr. Big. Counting only cases where the accused was convicted and the conviction was ultimately upheld after the appeal process, I've identified 129 homicide victims for whom Mr. Big has been responsible for gaining justice. Again, this is an incomplete tally. Of the identified victims, sixty-seven (52 percent) were women. Given that about 30 percent of homicide victims in Canada are female, Mr. Big is particularly effective in bringing to justice people guilty of the ultimate violent crime against women.

Over a third of these murdered women in Mr. Big cases were killed by an intimate partner, compared to just under a fifth of all cleared Canadian homicides over the past two decades. Several of the Mr. Big intimate partner homicides were carefully planned or were contract killings. Both planned and contract murders are more difficult crimes for the police to solve using traditional methods of detection than are the impulsive, unplanned, and semi-accidental killings that make up the majority of intimate partner killings. Iqbal Gill hired a man to run over his wife in a hit-and-run "accident" in order to collect a $3-million insurance policy. David Knight hired a man to strangle his wife in a staged home break-in in order to free himself to marry his mistress in Florida. Both these men were "respectable" businesspeople and leaders in the community. Both had impeccable alibis. Both got away with murder until Mr. Big struck up a conversation.

While the female victims of murderers caught by Mr. Big were disproportionately victims of intimate partner violence, the male victims were disproportionately murdered as a by-product of involvement in the illegal drug trade. Just over 40 percent of the male victims were killed either as a result of turf struggles in the drug trade or as an accompaniment to a drug-trade-related robbery — or both. This victim profile also makes detection more difficult using traditional means. There is often a surplus of potential suspects, and potential witnesses often have compelling reasons to be uncooperative with police. Some male victims don't need to be involved in the illicit drug trade in order for police to be confounded with a plethora of motivated suspects. In 1979, a Winnipeg man was found floating in the Red River with his head bashed in. He was such an objectionable character that police quickly compiled a list of eleven people with a strong motive for the killing. The investigation stalled because the finger of suspicion pointed in too many directions. Eighteen years later, Thomas Griffin told Mr. Big he had committed the crime because the man had tried to stab him in an unprovoked attack in a bar earlier that evening. This attack initially caused Griffin to be ranked eleventh on the suspect list.

The means of killing in Mr. Big cases are different by gender. The most common method of killing someone in Canada is stabbing. The second most common is shooting and the third is beating someone to death, usually with the assistance of an object. Both stabbing and beating are messy. Blood, hair, and pieces of bone from the victim are strewn about. If a person is killed by stabbing or beating, the crime scene is almost impossible to clean adequately enough to avoid detection, and the killer is usually covered with gore. DNA from the blood of the victim found on the killer's shoes or clothing is enough to make a compelling argument for conviction. Many victims in Mr. Big cases were murdered in ways that made forensic-based detection more difficult.

The male victims in Mr. Big cases were shot in over 42 percent of cases compared to the usual Canadian rate of 30 percent of homicides. Shooting kills at a distance and does not allow the victim to directly engage with the killer. As a result, the killer's DNA or fingerprints are often missing from the crime scene when someone has been shot.

Female victims were strangled in 36 percent of cases resolved using Mr. Big, compared to under 9 percent for all Canadian homicides over the past two decades. Strangling is up close and personal. It's not easy to strangle someone, so women are strangled more often than men because of differentials in size and strength. For a killer, strangling has the great advantage of cleanliness. Strangling does not leave behind blood that provides a rich field of forensic evidence to be harvested by today's highly skilled crime scene forensics experts.

These gendered peculiarities in both the killer–victim relationship and the means of causing death create gendered difficulties for police detection, but, regardless of the gender of the victim, most Mr. Big cases present a common problem for police. The killers work really hard to avoid detection. They often show a remarkable, if chilling, level of cunning. This book examines how Mr. Big obtained justice for 129 homicide victims. Their killers' attempts to avoid detection included:

Transportation and concealment. The bodies of twenty-one victims were transported from the crime scene and hidden elsewhere. Discovery of the remains sometimes came weeks or years later. This transportation and concealment of corpses delayed the start of the homicide investigation and made it more difficult for the police to obtain meaningful testimony from someone who might have seen or heard something relevant. The movement of the body can make the location of the killing impossible to find, thereby eliminating the source of most forensic evidence. Finally, transportation and concealment can destroy any possibility of police getting useful results from medical examinations. For example, in one case, the victim was found only when someone saw their dog chewing on a skull. The victim's body had been pulled apart, partially eaten, and spread around by animals. This made establishing the cause of death impossible.

Transportation and really good concealment. In another nineteen cases, the body was concealed so well that it was not discovered until the killer told or showed Mr. Big where the remains were hidden. In three cases, the killer could not even recover the body. As described above, Jodi Franz's body was converted into fertilizer and spread over a field. In another case, the body was completely burned. In a third, the body was thrown into a major river and never recovered. Homicides with no body not only present challenges inherent in transportation and concealment, but also make it very difficult to even prove that the victim has been killed. After Allan Shyback strangled his wife and buried her in his basement (pouring new concrete as part of the concealment), he used her cellphone, email, and voice mail to create an elaborate electronic record to suggest that she was alive for several weeks after going missing. Until he told Mr. Big where her remains were hidden, the police could not prove she was dead, let alone prove that he had killed her.

Burning the body. The bodies of 11 of the 124 homicide victims were burned. The effect of this on forensic evidence is self-evident. This count of bodies being burned does not include the five who were murdered by being burned alive.

Decapitation and dismemberment. Six of the victims were decapitated. Their heads were hidden in a different location than their bodies. Keith Black's head was not only cut off — it was blasted with a shotgun to make identification by dental records impossible. Another fourteen victims were dismembered in a more comprehensive fashion in order to make it easier to conceal their bodies in pieces rather than intact.

Staged sexual assault. Eleven of the female victims of homicides solved by Mr. Big had their corpses desecrated with staged sexual assaults designed to mislead the police about motive. At the low end, this staging involved pulling off the victim's clothing to have them found nude. Other killers went further, with genital mutilation. This approach to misdirecting police violates more than the bodily integrity of the victim. It can also cause the police to inadvertently tarnish the victim's reputation as they sift through her life looking for sexual motives for the killing. Friends, relatives, and lovers sometimes get treated as potential sex killers.

These efforts at concealment and misdirection have effects that go beyond making the job of police more difficult. They lend a special horror to the killings.

In a third of the cases solved by Mr. Big, the family and friends of the victim spent days, weeks, months, years, and sometimes decades before finding out the fate of their loved one. Parents did not know whether their children were alive or dead. Children did not know whether a parent had abandoned them or had been killed. In nineteen cases, the question of a loved one's continued existence was answered only by a visit from a police officer after the killer had disclosed the location of the corpse to Mr. Big. For these people, the news was desperately wanted and horribly feared.

There is more. Think of the story of Achilles, Hector, and King Priam as told by Homer thousands of years ago. The Greeks were besieging Troy. Hector, hero and son of the Trojan king, killed Achilles's friend in battle. Achilles demanded that Hector face him in single combat. The two battled as ancient heroes were supposed to battle. Achilles killed Hector. Up to this point, the story unfolded as a narration of heroic acts being performed by heroic people. Then Achilles did the unthinkable. He tied Hector's body to his chariot and dragged it around the ground between the two armies. He refused to allow the Trojans to recover Hector's body in order to provide a proper funeral. This behaviour shocked and horrified both the Greeks and the Trojans. In the night, King Priam disguised himself and crept into the Greek camp. He begged Achilles for mercy and justice. Priam could accept his son being killed. This was the fate of warriors and heroes. What could not be accepted was the desecration of Hector's body. That was intolerable. With this story, Homer was speaking to a universal human belief. The body is special. In death, it should be treated with respect. The respectful disposal of a body according to cultural traditions is an essential part of a completed human life. It is essential both for the soul of the deceased and the proper grieving process for those who are still living. Many of the killers caught by Mr. Big violated this universal cultural imperative. Whether from a desire to avoid being caught or out of bizarre, gratuitous cruelty, they treated those they killed in a way that lends a special horror to the murders. They become the stuff of nightmares rather than of Agatha Christie novels.

This leads to the core premise of this book. Mr. Big was created by Canadian police to bring resolution and some modicum of justice to horrific criminal cases. When Mr. Big arrives on the scene, it almost always means that an act of unspeakable cruelty has occurred. It means that the usual methods of policing have been only partially successful. They have allowed the police to identify a suspect. Usually, but not always, the police are correct in their suspicion. Mr. Big is designed to convert suspicion into either conviction or exculpation.

THE PARADOX OF MR. BIG

Mr. Big seeks the truth. He does so by lying. In Chapter 6, we will look closely at the power and danger of seeking truth from confession and disclosure. The most compelling evidence of guilt is provided when someone admits to a crime. We almost always lack a confession of reprehensible or criminal behaviour, particularly when the person has powerful incentives not to make the admission. If someone admits to an act when the admission runs counter to their interest — when saying "I did it" means going to jail for years or decades — we almost instinctively believe that the admission is true. Why would an innocent person admit to committing a murder? But people sometimes do confess to committing terrible crimes when they are innocent. Sometimes they are confused or mistaken. For example, impairment from drugs or alcohol, or mental illness, can create a situation where the suspect does not know what happened. He can reach a mistaken conclusion about guilt. Sometimes a person will confess because of torture. Sometimes they will confess for a reason as trivial as wanting to go to the bathroom. Sometimes they will brag about crimes they did not commit in order to impress or intimidate. As we will see in this book, confessions and disclosures of murder cannot always be taken at face value.

The term confession implies guilt: a willingness, at least temporarily, to accept punishment. A suspect talking to Mr. Big is in a different situation than someone talking to an identified police officer during an interrogation. While a statement to Mr. Big is treated in court as a confession, it is actually something a little different. It is a disclosure. The suspect is not talking about his acts with the knowledge that there are powerful incentives to stay silent or lie. The deceit inherent in a Mr. Big operation creates a situation wherein the suspect believes he has a powerful incentive to share. As the sociologist W.I. Thomas once noted, "If men define situations as real, they are real in their consequences." Suspects talking to Mr. Big believe that they are talking to a powerful crime boss who will make them rich and allow them to avoid arrest. As a result, they tell Mr. Big all about their crime. Sometimes this definition of the situation causes them to make things up. When they are arrested, the definition of the situation immediately changes. Reality intervenes in the form of handcuffs, strip searches and locked doors. If the suspect was factually guilty, the incentives that Mr. Big offered to tell the truth are now transformed into even more powerful incentives to lie. If the suspect was factually innocent, the incentives Mr. Big offered to lie are now transformed into even more incentives to tell the truth. Of the 121 cases I've examined in which the suspect told Mr. Big he was the killer, only 18 pleaded guilty. The other 103 claimed, either personally or through the mouth of their lawyer, that they had lied to Mr. Big. Of the 18 who pleaded guilty, several did so only when it became very clear that a judge or jury was not going to accept their denials.

The paradox created by different definitions of the situation and the resulting different incentives is not new. We'll take a brief break from dealing with murder in Canada in order to explore the complexities of the resulting paradox by going back eight hundred years to look at a case of adultery that may or may not have happened.

In the thirteenth century, a French poet told a story of confession and confusion. The wife of a knight had her husband's love and was the object of widespread admiration for her virtue. She became very ill and began to prepare for death by giving confession and making the requisite donations to the church. But she was still troubled. She asked her husband to summon a monk who had a reputation for saintliness. Before dying, she needed to make an additional confession to make her soul whole. The husband hurried off in search of the monk . . . but he was perplexed about her need. Instead of returning with the monk, the husband borrowed the monk's boots, habit, and horse. He waited until dark before returning to his wife's deathbed. Altering his voice to impersonate the monk, he told his wife she needed to confess to any hidden sins to save her soul.

To his distress, he heard that his wife believed her husband-to-be "too dense, too harsh and too vindictive" to satisfy her lust. She confessed that, despite a reputation for being without fault, she had obtained sexual satisfaction from the household servants. Her husband was surprised and appalled. He asked if she had anything else to confess. It turns out she did. His wife also confessed to a five-year-long affair with his nephew. The knight left, "trembling with bitterness and rage." When he returned, he discovered that his wife had not died. Confession may or may not have been good for the soul, but it appeared to have been good for her body. Her health had miraculously returned. Less healthy was the state of her marriage. Her husband's devotion turned to hostility. She realized what must have happened and recanted her confession, saying she had realized her husband was deceiving her. Her new story was that she had lied to punish her husband for his distrust.

The knight now faced a dilemma. What should he believe? Was she lying when she thought she was dying or was she lying after recovery? In the story, the knight chose to return to his original belief in his wife's innocence and virtue. He accepted her assertion that he had provided her with sufficient reasons to provide a false confession. Observers were not as convinced. The poem concludes by telling us that his credulity became a joke to his neighbours.

The story of the knight and his possibly errant wife shows that the practice of obtaining confessions under false pretences has a long history. It seems like a powerful investigative technique. If the investigator can trick a person into believing they have an incentive to truthfully confess, the truth will be told. Sinful and evil acts will stand revealed by the guilty person themselves. But there is a catch. Once the deception is revealed, the person who has confessed now has equal incentive to recant. The deception used to obtain the confession is denounced as the cause of a false confession. The investigator using deception in order to learn the truth is almost invariably placed in a quandary. Regardless of whether the person is innocent or guilty, the deception itself creates a reason to confess; revealing the deception creates a reason to recant.

Using deception to obtain a confession almost inevitably generates the necessity to choose between the confession or the recantation. One follows from the other. Sometimes the choice is clear. The confession can be externally verified. It can point the investigator towards other empirical evidence that can support or refute the veracity of the confession. In other cases, the choice is more difficult. In the case of the knight and his possibly errant wife, confirmation of her confession was probably impossible. If confronted, the servants and the nephew would have every incentive to deny making the knight — who was, after all, an armed specialist in violence in a violent age — a cuckold. As long as discretion had been practised, no verification of the confession was possible. In the end, the knight had to accept either the confession or the recantation on faith. He had to make a choice about what he believed. Like many people, the knight made his decision based on what he believed prior to setting out to obtain the confession by means of deception. He had long believed his wife to be virtuous. As a result, when presented with a somewhat plausible reason for dismissing the confession, he did so. It is almost inevitable that if he had entered the exercise with a belief that his wife was unfaithful, he would have chosen to accept the confession as truthful and valid.

Despite being over eight hundred years old, the story of the tricky knight and his maybe/maybe not unfaithful wife has a direct relevance to Canada's criminal justice system. There are over a hundred people locked up in our penitentiaries as a result of confessing to a major crime such as homicide to someone using deception in order to obtain the confession. In almost every case, those deceived subsequently recanted their confession. Like the knight's wife, they argued that their confession was false and that it had been obtained because the deception by the investigator had incentivized deceit by the investigated. For some, other evidence definitively confirmed the veracity of the confession. In other cases, the assessment of guilt or innocence came down to a choice on which of the person's statements to believe. Unfortunately for most of those people caught in this situation, they entered the process of deceptive interrogation as suspects. The knight began the process certain of his wife's virtue. In the end, he opted to continue believing what he believed before. Those people currently residing in Canada's prisons as a result of this round of confession and recantation did not get the benefit of doubt. Their deceptive interrogators began the process convinced of the person's guilt. For them, the confession rather than the recantation confirmed their beliefs.

For the balance of this book, the confounding difference in the incentives for truth between talking to Mr. Big and talking to a police officer during an interrogtation will be underlined with a terminological distinction. A person telling police that he committed a crime with full knowledge that the admission will be used against him in court will be called a confession. It is made with an acceptance, however transitory, that punishment will follow. When the suspect tells Mr. Big that he committed the crime, it will be called a disclosure. It is made on the premise that good things will follow.

THE STRUCTURE OF THIS BOOK

This book is primarily based on the tracks Mr. Big has left in court proceedings. It is an imperfect record. Sometimes deliberately, usually inadvertently, Mr. Big has sometimes covered his tracks.

We'll begin with detailed looks at three Mr. Big cases. These can be viewed as being the good, the bad, and the murky of Mr. Big.

In the good Mr. Big case, we can say with absolute certainty that Michael Bridges killed Erin Chorney. The proof provided by Mr. Big is incontrovertible. In court, his lawyer attempted to have the disclosures made to Mr. Big ruled inadmissible. When that failed, Bridges's lawyer argued about degrees of criminal culpability.

The conviction of Kyle Unger was a clear example of a bad Mr. Big disclosure. Kyle lied to Mr. Big. This caused him to be convicted of murdering Brigitte Grenier. He spent thirteen years in a penitentiary. Manitoba Justice subsequently definitively declared him to be innocent.

Nelson Hart was suspected of killing his two daughters, Karen and Krista. The circumstances were extraordinarily murky. Nelson told Mr. Big that he had murdered the two girls. He told the court that he had not. Both stories were equally believable or unbelievable. No other evidence points in one direction or the other. Nelson was convicted by a jury and acquitted by the Supreme Court of Canada. In the end, we simply do not know what really happened. Mr. Big was used in a murky case and made it even murkier.

Chapter 5 will build on these case studies by breaking Mr. Big operations into the component parts: case selection, making contact, establishing a relationship, the nudge towards disclosure, the ultimate interview with Mr. Big, and the follow-up. Every Mr. Big case is unique, but there are common patterns and issues.

These descriptive chapters will be followed by a reflection on disclosure and confession. Why are the self-implicating words of a suspect so sought after by the police and so definitive in a courtroom? Why do some people lie about committing terrible crimes? How can we distinguish between a lie and a true story in instances where truth is sometimes stranger than fiction?

Mr. Big operations require a substantial investment in police resources. They can take months and cost hundreds of thousands of dollars. In recent years, officers conducting a Mr. Big operation can expect to spend days or weeks in court justifying every aspect of the operation and act they have personally undertaken. This investment and anticipated scrutiny create a requirement that police be "pretty sure" the suspect is guilty before sending in Mr. Big. Dogged determination by the police is an essential part of every Mr. Big case. This can create a danger as determination can become transformed into "tunnel vision" or "the disease of certainty." These benefits and dangers of determination will be explored in Chapter 7.

We tend to think of criminal guilt in binary terms. The accused is either guilty or innocent. We give a thumbs up or a thumbs down. The person leaves the courthouse to go to prison or to go home. The reality is more complex. There are degrees of culpability even in killing someone, with important legal distinctions between first- and second-degree murder, manslaughter, criminal negligence causing death, justifiable homicide, and accidental death. Dead is dead, but blame is a matter of degree. In Chapter 8, we'll look at the black, white, and shades of grey in Mr. Big cases.

Mr. Big is a true-blue Canadian. He was born and raised in the Great White North. Like many Canadians, he's gone travelling. In Chapter 9, we'll look at how Mr. Big has been received in other countries with criminal justice systems that are like Canada's. He's been enthusiastically welcomed in Australia and cautiously greeted in New Zealand. In the United States and UK, Mr. Big disclosures have been admitted into evidence by courts, but police forces in these countries have not adopted the technique.

In a democratic society, we want horrible crimes to be solved. We want people who do unspeakable things to others to be punished. We want to be kept safe from criminals. To achieve this, we put tremendous powers into the hands of the police. We don't want them to abuse this power. We don't want them to use tactics that are excessively oppressive or harsh. In centuries past, torturing someone to obtain a confession was perfectly acceptable. A century ago, polite society averted its eyes as police used bright lights and blackjacks to obtain confessions. As a society, we've prohibited these methods. In practice, it is hard to know where precisely to draw the line between acceptable and unacceptable police tactics. Canadian courts often use the question of whether a police tactic would "shock the conscience of the community" to determine whether it should be allowed or prohibited. Chapter 10 explores how criticism from defence lawyers and academics, combined with publicity about the technique, has forced Mr. Big to change over the years.

In Chapter 11, we'll examine the results achieved by Mr. Big and speculate about his future.

A NOTE OF EXPLANATION ON IDENTIFICATION

This book talks about a lot of crimes and a lot of investigations. This means there are a lot of people mentioned: victims, killers, bystanders, accomplices, police, judges, and more. To keep the cases real, I've used real names of victims and perpetrators. The first time a person is mentioned in a section, I use their full name, except for those who were under the age of 18 when the offence was committed. In accordance with the provisions of the *Youth Criminal Justice Act* and standard court protocols, these people are identified with their initials. After that, first names are used for victims of the crime and last names are used for the perpetrators. I believe that victims deserve a much more empathetic treatment than do those who killed them. The differential use of names is one way of symbolically showing this. First names are also used for those who have been charged but ultimately acquitted by the courts. These people have been found innocent by our legal system and have every right to be treated that way in every respect.

Other people in the book are usually identified with generic, relational terminology. There are two reasons for this. The first is legal. For reasons that will be discussed in Chapter 10, the courts almost always impose a ban on publishing the names or identities of undercover officers. I agree with the reasons for these bans and have no desire to go to jail, so any publication ban has been scrupulously honoured. The second reason why people remain unidentified is to minimize the damage that resurrecting old pain from their lives can cause. In the biblical story from the book of Genesis, Cain murdered his brother Abel. As part of the punishment, God put a mark on Cain so he could be forever identified as a murderer. In our society, we tend to transfer this mark to other people. We stigmatize those who have been touched by violent death. The people who are not identified by name in this book have done nothing wrong. In some cases, their role is embarrassing or painful. That's why I am not telling you who they are. In a few cases, I've also extended this veil of anonymity to people who were investigated but not charged or charged but not convicted.

ORIGINS OF THIS BOOK

I wish that I had never heard of Mr. Big.

I first heard his name in 2001. I was meeting with my lawyer about a year after my wife, Beverly Rowbotham, was murdered in the backyard of our acreage north of Winnipeg. The RCMP had conducted an intensive investigation focusing almost entirely on me. It appeared to be winding down. My lawyer and I discussed next steps. My lawyer told me that in the next year or so, someone would enter my life in what appeared to be a random meeting. This person would suddenly become my new best friend. I would be offered opportunities to make some quick money in murky, shady ways. I would be introduced to a mysterious, powerful crime boss called Mr. Big. He would have some compelling-sounding reason for me to tell him any secrets about Bev's death. If I told Mr. Big that I had any involvement, I would go to jail for the rest of my life. I filed the information away in my mind.

In retrospect, I now understand that I met many of the selection criteria for a Mr. Big operation.

Most importantly, I was the husband of a murdered woman. The famous American lawyer F. Lee Bailey wrote a book called *When the Husband Is the Suspect*. He begins the book by stating that "when a wife is killed by what might be criminal means, the husband (unless he has an ironclad alibi) is the first to be scrutinized. If no other suspect appears on the horizon, police will pursue the husband relentlessly to 'solve' the crime." That was certainly my experience. My alibi made it unlikely that I'd committed the crime, but it was not ironclad. I could not be ruled out. Relentless is a very strong word, but the RCMP certainly became very close to relentless in attempting to build a case against me.

In addition to the suspicions arising simply from my being the husband of the victim, the murder itself was intrinsically suspicious. Bev had left the house to go grocery shopping. She was murdered in the backyard — while I was inside, oblivious to what was happening. Her body was transported in one of our cars to the outskirts of Selkirk — about 18 km away. Both she and the car were abandoned in a parking lot. Quite frankly, even though I knew I was innocent, I could not condemn the police for being suspicious of me.

While the police had reasons to be suspicious, my innocence made it impossible for them to build a provable case. There was no motive. Bev and I got along well. Neither of us had any substance, financial, or infidelity issues. There was no history of domestic violence or abuse. The police could find none of the traditional reasons why husbands kill their wives. They found absolutely no forensic evidence tying me to the crime. There was a lot of blood in the backyard, garage, and car — but it stopped outside the back door to our home. There were no bloody clothes, footprints, or signs of a cleanup inside our house. Trust me on this one. The RCMP looked very hard. There was also the issue of travel. If I were the killer, how had I managed to drive to Selkirk and get home without a car in a narrow temporal window — without being seen?

In many ways, it was a case tailor-made for Mr. Big. Despite this, I never met him. Years later, I discovered that the idea had been debated, but the officers leading the investigation believed that I was not a good target. In their opinion, I was a bit too smart to fall for the trick and a bit too successful to have a burning desire to join a criminal gang. As a result, I never got to meet Mr. Big. Seven years after I first heard about Mr. Big, the police managed to convince a prosecutor to authorize a murder charge.

I was arrested, charged, tried, and acquitted. Bev's case remains unsolved; my sons and I may never know who ended her life. There is some DNA evidence that might eventually identify a suspect. If it does, Mr. Big represents one of the best available means of completing a prosecutable case. After my acquittal, I returned to university and got a PhD in sociology and criminology. My experience made me much more interested in issues of crime, punishment, and justice.

Police, prosecutors, and most members of the general public view Mr. Big as a good guy who puts bad guys in jail after they've committed terrible, otherwise-unsolvable crimes. Defence lawyers and most of my fellow academics view Mr. Big as malignant and evil. They correctly note that Mr. Big has the potential to generate disclosures from the innocent. They then commit the logical fallacy of assuming this means that most of the disclosures are false and that most of those convicted as a result of Mr. Big operations are innocent. Based on the many judgments I've read, I believe that most judges take a more nuanced and careful approach than either of the binary alternatives of "good" and "bad." Most judges believe that Mr. Big is a very powerful tool that can bring the guilty to justice, but that without due care and attention, it is capable of causing the innocent to be convicted as well.

My own opinion on Mr. Big comes closest to the judicial view, although I reach it from a more personal and experiential basis. My perspective comes from two moments in my life. I once sat up waiting for dawn. I was trying to figure out how to tell our two sons, aged three and five, that they would never see their mother again. Almost eight years later, I felt the handcuffs go on my wrists and listened as a police officer told me I was being charged with murder. I was wondering if I would ever be allowed to see our sons again. From this first horrible experience, an intellectual commitment to justice was transformed into a special kind of desire to see murderers caught and punished. From the second, an intellectual commitment to due process in the legal system became transformed into a special kind of fear of the innocent being wrongfully accused and convicted. I believe that by the time you finish reading this book, you will understand that properly conducted Mr. Big operations can help achieve my desire to punish the guilty and protect against my fear of convicting the innocent.

CHAPTER 2

The Good: R v. Bridges

At 8:30 p.m. on Sunday, April 21, 2002, Erin Chorney received a phone call while spending the evening at her mother's place. Erin told her mother that she would be back in an hour, kissed her younger sister goodbye, and got into a car that had just pulled up outside. Only two people ever saw Erin alive after she entered that car. One of them murdered her.

Erin was eighteen years old. Her parents were separated. She lived with her father and sixteen-year-old brother while working at a dry-cleaning business that her father managed in Brandon, Manitoba. Erin was good-looking, friendly, vivacious, and fun-loving. Indeed, perhaps Erin was a bit too fun-loving for her own good. She loved to party hard. Erin had received treatment in the past for drug and alcohol abuse; this had not been completely successful in curtailing consumption. Erin had a much bigger problem — her boyfriend. She had been dating twenty-one-year-old Mike Bridges for about four months. He was jealous, domineering, and verbally abusive. He had become violent. Three weeks earlier, Bridges assaulted Erin by choking her. Erin might have died during the assault but for the intervention of a friend and Bridges's mother. Erin and her friend had filed a complaint with the Brandon police. Bridges was arrested, charged, and released pending his court date. The conditions of his release included prohibitions on having any contact with Erin or consuming alcohol. Like many people in an abusive relationship, Erin was torn. Family and friends told her that she should leave Bridges forever. She knew this was good advice, but love, even unwise love, can be a powerful thing.

Erin's mother did not know Erin was meeting Bridges that Sunday evening. Bridges recruited a friend to place the call so he could get Erin on the line. The friend was in the car when Erin was picked up. He believed that the three of them would watch a movie together at Bridges's home. To the friend's surprise, the agreed-upon plan suddenly changed. Bridges wanted to be alone with Erin. The friend was dropped off. Bridges took Erin to his home. Bridges mother and younger brother were out of town.

Later in the night, Erin called her brother to ask for a ride home. He objected. It was late. School was the next day. Erin seemed unconcerned and withdrew her request. The next morning, Erin had not returned home. This did not cause concern. It was not unusual for her to crash on a friend's couch. Her family expected her to return home slightly dishevelled and a bit hungover, but cheerful and . . . alive. Another day passed. And another. Erin's parents and siblings got worried. They started phoning her friends. Nobody had seen or heard from Erin since she left her mother's apartment. The worries escalated. Erin's mother filed a missing person report with the Brandon Police Service. The police joined the search. The searchers could find nobody who had seen or heard from Erin.

Quite naturally, the police wanted to talk to Erin's boyfriend. They discovered that two days after Erin had disappeared, Bridges pleaded guilty to his outstanding assault charges. He paid a fine and was placed on probation. When questioned by police about Erin's disappearance, Bridges appeared co-operative. He readily admitted that he had violated the terms of his conditional release by contacting and being with Erin. He described using his friend to deceive Erin's mother. Bridges's story was that he had taken Erin to his home. They had talked for a few hours and decided to be friends but not lovers. Bridges claimed Erin left his house to buy cocaine. He reported that he had offered to walk with her to her destination but she refused his chivalry. Bridges told police he would be happy to take a lie detector test. Bridges's story about the early part of the evening was confirmed by his friend.

Bridges's story left him as the last known person to see Erin alive. She had either left his house and disappeared elsewhere or she had never left his home. The implications of the second option were obvious. Bridges, after all, was legally prohibited from being in contact with Erin because he had, by his own admission and guilty plea, choked her less than a month earlier. Numerous friends confirmed that Bridges was the kind of potential son-in-law every parent dreads. Bridges's statement had subtle but disturbing features consistent with guilt. For example, when talking about Erin, Bridges always referred to her in the past tense. The police interpreted this as a sign he knew she was dead. The Brandon Police Service's investigation into Erin's disappearance took two completely different tracks. The first was based on the possibility Bridges's statement was true — that Erin had, in fact, left his house healthy and happy. The second assumed that Bridges lied during his police interview. The logical conclusion was that he had killed her.

To pursue the possibility that Erin had left Bridges's house, the police sought public assistance. They held press conferences asking for anyone with knowledge of Erin's whereabouts to come forward. Erin's parents participated in these appeals. They begged Erin to come home if she was able to hear their pleas. An organization called Child Find Manitoba became involved. Erin's picture and description became familiar sights in western Canada as thousands of posters were put up. Manitoba Crime Stoppers produced a television ad asking for leads. The massive publicity effort yielded over 160 reports of Erin "sightings." Each one was investigated. Each one was shown to be false or unverifiable. Erin sightings were about as common as sightings of Elvis Presley. The difference was that the Erin sightings were taken seriously and investigated.

Meanwhile, the police also investigated the possibility that Bridges had murdered Erin. They obtained search warrants to conduct intensive forensic searches of Bridges's home, his mother's car, and his father's nearby acreage. No evidence was found. Bridges's phone was tapped. Police conducted highly visible searches near his home in the hope that he might be provoked into incriminating action. Bridges's movements were watched. Bridges was asked to submit to a lie detector test. He reneged on his earlier commitment.

As time went on, the police became more convinced of Bridges's guilt. After all, if Erin went somewhere after leaving his house, some sign of her whereabouts would have surfaced. The police were not alone in their suspicions. Most people in Brandon believed that Erin was dead and Bridges was responsible. The rumour mill worked overtime. One popular theory arose from the fact that Bridges's father worked at a local funeral home. Based on this, many people "knew" that Bridges's father had helped his son dispose of Erin's body by secretly cremating her. Another theory arose from the fact that Bridges was employed at a local pork processing plant. Based on this, other people "knew" that Bridges had secretly turned Erin into wieners. The police investigated and ruled out these theories.

By the fall of 2003 — over a year after Erin's disappearance — the investigation was at an impasse. The Brandon Police Service asked for the assistance of the RCMP. They asked for Mr. Big.

THE MR. BIG OPERATION

The Mr. Big operation directed at Bridges has been intensively documented by *Winnipeg Free Press* reporter Mike McIntyre in the book *To the Grave: Inside a Spectacular RCMP Sting*. This book is the best publicly available description of a Mr. Big operation ever written. Much of this chapter is based on McIntyre's research.

In designing the operation directed at Bridges, the RCMP faced two challenges. The first was that it had not been proven that Erin was dead. It was possible that she might surface at any time. Even if she did not, it was possible that Bridges was telling the truth. The operation could have had the result of allowing Bridges to effectively clear himself. As a result, care was taken to minimize the operation's disruption in Bridges's life if he was innocent. The second challenge was Bridges's lifestyle following Erin's disappearance. Bridges was not spending a lot of time in public places such as bars, both because he was on probation and because of the consensus of community opinion that he had killed Erin. Bridges had become a recluse. This made establishing initial contact difficult.

To engage with Bridges, the Mr. Big operation staged a survey of people's radio listening habits. A good-looking female plain-clothes officer went door-to-door asking questions about listening patterns. The reward for participation was a chance to win a paid trip to Calgary to see a Flames NHL hockey game. Bridges was a winner. The female officer drove Bridges to the Winnipeg airport for the trip. He was introduced to a male undercover officer posing as another winner. The two had adjoining seats. By the time they arrived in Calgary, they were well acquainted. At least that's what Bridges thought. When they arrived in Calgary, the pair met another dozen "contest winners" for a reception. It was a clever bit of psychological manipulation. When he became part of the bigger group of strangers, Bridges naturally gravitated towards the one person he already knew. In this way, it seemed as if he had taken the lead in creating a relationship. The next day, the two met again for the flight back to Winnipeg. The undercover officer explained his boss had summoned him to Saskatoon. Given that Brandon was between the two cities, would Bridges like a ride home from the airport? Bridges did. The officer looked up Bridges again a few days later to report that his boss asked him to undertake unspecified duties in a small city in Manitoba. The undercover officer said he was thinking of locating in Portage la Prairie or Thompson. Bridges suggested Brandon. His new friend agreed this was a fine idea and recruited Bridges for apartment hunting. The Mr. Big operation was off and running.

From this opening, the operation proceeded with many standard features of a Mr. Big operation. Bridges was recruited to perform mysterious tasks such as delivering packages in exchange for payments of one or two hundred dollars. Because Bridges had lost his driver's licence as a result of driving while impaired, he had to use the Greyhound bus for these tasks. The undercover officer turned this into a positive by explaining that someone on a bus was less likely to be stopped by the police than someone driving. Bridges's tasks increased in responsibility and payment. He was introduced to other members of the mysterious gang. He overheard telephone conversations the officer was having with "the boss." Bridges got to handle and count large sums of money. He was told that some of this wealth could stick to his fingers if he was accepted by the boss as a full member of the gang. Bridges was repeatedly told that the boss did not care what a person had done in the past, but that absolute honesty within the group was a condition of membership. He was told that the boss was "like Santa Claus" in his ability to know who had been good (telling the truth) and bad (lying to the boss). Bridges wanted in.

Most of the contact between Bridges and the undercover officer was designed to establish trust and build a relationship. Three scenarios had more specific purposes.

In order to test Bridges's reaction to violence against women, a female undercover officer was accused of stealing a package. Bridges was recruited to help track her down and recover the package. He and the undercover officer spent a day roaming around Winnipeg before "finding" her in a motel room. The undercover officer instructed Bridges to watch from the vehicle and honk if police approached. Bridges watched through the open motel-room door as the woman appeared to be savagely beaten. She appeared to be reduced to a bloody mess. The undercover cop emerged from the room with his hands covered in what appeared to be blood. Bridges congratulated him on a job well done.

In order to stress the consequences of lying to the boss, Bridges was introduced to an undercover officer posing as another wannabe gang member. This person was described as having a bit more seniority than Bridges. He was about to have the interview with the boss necessary to be approved for full membership. Bridges was excited and more than a little jealous. A few days later, the cell phone of the undercover officer who had been cultivating Bridges "happened" to ring while he and Bridges were having lunch. It was the boss. The wannabe member had failed the honesty test and been told to leave the gang. The undercover officer later explained that the person had been a suspect in a home invasion in which an elderly couple had been viciously beaten. When asked about it, the prospective member denied being under police suspicion. Bridges was told that it did not matter whether the perspective member had done the crime or not. What mattered was that he had lied about having been under police suspicion. The boss didn't care about guilt or innocence. What the boss did care about was that the prospective member lied about being a suspect. That made him unreliable. The punishment was banishment from the group. This drama was played out to stress the importance of honesty and show that the consequence of lying to Mr. Big was expulsion from the group but not physical harm.

Bridges soon revealed he was a suspect in Erin's disappearance but was not ready to admit guilt.

The final step was to convince Bridges that the boss had the power to "fix" problems. Bridges witnessed an elaborate procedure ostensibly designed to retroactively create an alibi for someone in need of one. The undercover officer explained the boss could fix problems gang members had with the law. He suggested that someone already serving a life sentence would be willing to confess to a murder. This would "solve" a crime by allowing police to clear the case. This interested Bridges. A false confession from anther person would not only ensure his own long-term freedom, but also remove the unpleasant legacy of suspicion. It is unpleasant to be viewed as a murderer while living in a small city. Mr. Big's ability to have someone else confess would make a lot of problems go away. The only catch was that the fabricated confession needed to be convincing. Complete honesty and details would be vital if the plan was to succeed.

With this three-step process, the RCMP established that Bridges had no objection to violence against women. They demonstrated that honesty with the boss was the key to full membership in the gang. The penalty for dishonesty was to be told to go away. They demonstrated that Mr. Big could and would make legal problems disappear regardless of guilt. Bridges was primed to tell the truth. Bridges began to hint that he had been responsible for Erin's death.

Bridges's first disclosure was cautious. He said that he and Erin had quarrelled. He had pushed her. She had fallen and hit her head. He had disposed of her body successfully. If this version of events was accurate, Bridges could be convicted of manslaughter and committing an indignity to a dead body. If convicted, he would probably be looking at about a decade in prison.

This cautious disclosure was not enough. Since Erin's body had never been found, the key to any confession from someone already serving a life sentence would be the ability to reveal where Erin's remains were hidden. Without this, a fabricated inmate confession would not convince the police the confession was genuine. If the proof of a pudding is in the eating, in this case the proof of the confession needed to be in the digging. Having told the undercover officer that he had killed Erin, Bridges now had to tell him where he had hidden Erin's remains. If he failed to do so, the boss would not allow membership into the gang since the whole truth was not being told. Bridges's life would return to its pre-operation "normal." If Bridges told him where Erin's body was, he would pass the job interview with the boss. Perhaps encouraged by his friend's non-judgmental, problem-solving orientation to the initial disclosure, Bridges gave a full explanation of events.

In his new disclosure, Bridges answered the two key questions facing the police. He revealed where Erin's body was and he revealed how he had killed her without leaving forensic evidence for police to find.

Bridges said he first strangled Erin and then drowned her in the bathtub to finish the job. He said that the night after he had killed Erin, he had taken her body to Brandon's cemetery and buried her in a fresh grave. He had avoided leaving any trace of his work by piling the dirt on a piece of cardboard while digging. Bridges took the officer to the cemetery and showed him where the grave was located. It was now January, so everything was covered with snow. Bridges remembered the name on the grave. He helpfully spelled it out for the undercover officer.

The RCMP let a few days pass. Under the cover of night, they dug enough to confirm the presence of an extra body in the grave. They wired a Winnipeg hotel room for audio and visual recording. Bridges's long-anticipated interview with the boss was scheduled. The undercover officer drove Bridges to the appointment, stressing the need for absolute honesty. When they got to the hotel room, the officer suggested a rehearsal. Bridges agreed. He told his story.

In the videotaped disclosure, Bridges said that he and Erin had quarrelled because she was unwilling to drop the assault charges against him. In response, he had choked her until she lost consciousness. Realizing that this would result in more charges, Bridges decided to finish the job. He cut the electrical cord from his mother's hair dryer and attempted to strangle Erin with it. This effort failed. She stubbornly continued to breathe, so Bridges carried Erin into the bathroom and held her head under water for twenty minutes. None of this left any blood in the house or on his person. Bridges said he took off Erin's clothes, cut them up into small pieces and threw them into the garbage. He burned her ID. He hid her purse and shoes for eventual disposal. To eliminate the possibility of leaving hair behind while moving her body, Bridges wrapped Erin's head in Saran Wrap. He also wrapped her feet together because he wanted to keep them from flopping around during transport. After completing these preparations, Bridges caught a few hours' sleep before using the daylight hours to locate a suitable disposal site. During this time, Erin's body stayed lying in the bathtub. The next night, by the light of a full moon, Bridges wrapped her in a sheet and buried her in another person's grave.

After Bridges finished rehearsing his story in front of the hidden video camera, the police were ready to make an arrest. Mr. Big, in person, did not even need to make his appearance. Bridges had given the police all they needed.

When Bridges completed his disclosure, there was a knock on the door. The undercover officer told Bridges it was Mr. Big. Two big guys walked in. For a brief moment, it seemed to Bridges that the boss he'd been so eager to meet looked familiar. The person he thought was Mr. Big looked a lot like a member of the Brandon Police Service. Bridges quickly learned that the resemblance was not a coincidence. After being placed under arrest and informed of his rights, Bridges asked to speak to a Winnipeg lawyer. Bridges also had a question for the arresting officers. "Tell me one thing. Is [undercover officer's name] a cop?"

The final stage of the investigation was recovering Erin's body. A large tent was put over the gravesite. The ground was thawed. A team of police, medical examiners, and archeologists painstakingly uncovered Erin's naked body. She had been wrapped in a sheet. Her head and feet were wrapped in Saran Wrap. There was an electrical cord around her neck. In addition to knowing her location, Bridges had disclosed every detail about the disposal of Erin's body. There was less precision about the exact cause of death. Too much time had passed. The autopsy showed that two small bones in her neck had been broken. This was consistent with strangulation. It was impossible to determine whether the ultimate cause of death had been drowning. The only evidence of this was Bridges's disclosure.

THE LEGAL PROCESS

In his book *To the Grave*, *Winnipeg Free Press* reporter Mike McIntyre reports that Bridges's lawyer attempted to negotiate a plea bargain with an offer to have Bridges plead guilty to second-degree murder. This carries a mandatory minimum sentence of life with no parole eligibility for ten years. McIntyre reports that the lawyer proposed a joint recommendation from both the defence and prosecution of a fifteen-year parole eligibility restriction. The Crown prosecutor rejected the proposed deal. He wanted a first-degree murder conviction. Like second-degree murder, this carries a mandatory life sentence. The difference is in the parole eligibility. With a first-degree conviction, a convicted murderer does not become eligible for parole for twenty-five years. In either case, the sentence is life. There is no guarantee that someone will be granted parole at the end of this period.

The legal difference between first- and second-degree murder or manslaughter is intention and premeditation. If Bridges pushed Erin and she died by hitting her head, he committed manslaughter.

If he intentionally killed her in a single spontaneous incident, he committed second-degree murder. By proposing that Bridges plead guilty to second-degree murder, his lawyer was conceding that Erin's killing was intentional. In rejecting the proposed guilty plea, the prosecutor argued that while the initial choking might have been spontaneous, the drowning was premeditated and deliberate.

The combination of Bridges's videotaped confession and the recovery of Erin's body from someone else's grave created a narrow range of outcomes for the case. If a jury watched Bridges confessing and heard how Erin's body had been recovered, they would vote to convict Bridges of something. No other inference than guilt was logically possible from the juxtaposition of these two pieces of evidence. There was no viability in an "I did not do it" defence. A juror who bought such a story would have been about to leave the courtroom to buy the Brooklyn Bridge. It was highly unlikely that there would be one person this gullible on the jury. It would be inconceivable for there to be twelve of them.

The only hope Bridges had for an absolute acquittal would be if the disclosures were ruled inadmissible as evidence. His lawyer therefore attacked the Mr. Big operation. He asked for a voir dire to consider the admissibility of the evidence coming from the Mr. Big operation. A voir dire is a court hearing held in the absence of the jury. Witnesses are called as the defence and prosecution attempt to convince the judge to allow or refuse to allow particular evidence, witnesses, or areas of inquiry. The judge must rule on questions such as the procedural legality of how the evidence was collected, whether the evidence provides information about the crime ("probative") or would merely influence a jury's perception of the accused ("prejudicial"), or whether an "expert" witness is an expert who would have something useful for the jury to hear. The judge must do all this while continuing to respect the jury's role as "triers of fact" — the ones who must actually pronounce guilt or innocence.

In the voir dire hearing, Bridges's lawyer argued the combination of the prospect of easy money, Bridges's admiration for the undercover officer, and his belief in the power of the mysterious crime boss combined to cause Bridges to want to claim credit for Erin's murder even if he was innocent. Bridges's lawyer made this argument with skill and passion, but he had two insurmountable problems. The first was that Erin's body had been found where Bridges said it could be found in the condition that he had described. The defence lawyer's second problem was the way the Mr. Big operation had been conducted. The police had been very careful. The level of inducements had been kept fairly low. No violence had been threatened. Bridges had been repeatedly told he could walk away at any time without harm. Indeed, he believed that he had seen this happen in the case of another wannabe gang member. The importance of truth and honesty had been repeatedly stressed. Murder was an inconvenience that the boss would look after, but it did not increase stature in the gang, and it was not a condition of membership. The undercover officer had never brought up the topic of Erin's death. That always came from Bridges. The simple reality is that Bridges disclosed because he wanted to disclose, not because he had been forced to do so. That's the way the trial judge saw it. He said in his voir dire ruling:

> I note that any possible benefits of belonging to this organization were not held out to the accused conditional on him confessing to a crime. On the contrary much evidence was heard as to the emphasis placed on the necessity of telling the truth if one wanted to be a member of this organization.
>
> The accused was the target of this undercover operation to investigate the disappearance of his ex-girlfriend. The undercover officer did not mention the death of the ex-girlfriend until after the accused brought it up. Even

when the accused mentioned his ex-girlfriend, the officer repeated all the boss wanted to hear was the truth.

There is no question the accused had to talk to the boss to become a member of the organization, but, the choice was his and that was made clear to him. The accused knew he could walk away without repercussion. At no time was the accused told he had to prove himself as a criminal to become a member of the organization.

I was impressed with the scenario devised to bring the accused within the trusting fold of the criminal organization and the emphasis placed on telling the truth to be a member.

I agree with the Crown that there exist guarantees of reliability within the scenario portrayed to the accused. The accused provided great detail of how he disposed of the body, where it would be found and the condition it would be found in. During the course of the confessions the accused was made aware that the organization would be retrieving the body to dispose of the evidence. It was therefore apparent to the accused that all the information he related would be verified. If he did not tell the truth the organization would know and he would not become a member. The motive which caused him to confess would also operate as the motive which caused him to tell the truth.

Having found the statements to the undercover police officer meet the threshold tests of necessity and reliability, the statements will be admitted as evidence before the jury.

With this ruling, it became almost inevitable that Bridges would be convicted of causing Erin's death and go to prison for a long time. The only questions remaining were "convicted of what?" and "for how long?" Bridges's lawyer argued that the last, most detailed disclosure was exaggerated because Bridges was a small puppy "trying to bark like a big dog." During Bridges's original disclosure, he said death was accidental. He had shoved Erin. She had fallen and hit her head. She had died. Bridges's lawyer argued this was the truth. There was a problem. While the medical examination could not determine the precise cause of death, Erin had broken bones in her neck rather than in her skull. This is more consistent with strangulation than hitting one's head. Bridges's story of attempting to finish the job of strangulation with the electrical cord from his mother's hair dryer had confirmation from the cord recovered with Erin's body. The disclosure of drowning to complete the murder could not be independently confirmed. The broken neck bones and the electrical cord suggest that Bridges's last story was much closer to the truth than his first one.

Bridges's lawyer made the argument that Bridges's detailed confession was partially false. In doing so, he conceded the accuracy of the essential fact. Bridges had killed Erin. The lawyer's argument was that Bridges's degree of purposeful planning and premeditation was exaggerated. The alleged falsity was a matter of degree.

Bridges himself did not tell the jury his disclosure was either false or exaggerated. He did not testify on his own behalf, but relied on his lawyer to speak for him. The onus is on the Crown to prove that the accused committed the crime, not on the accused to prove they did not. That being said, the videotaped disclosure meant that the jury needed to be convinced that the story was exaggerated. Bridges's reliance on a surrogate to make this argument made the task more difficult. There are only two people who know why Bridges did not testify on his own behalf. Bridges is not talking about it and his lawyer is legally prohibited from doing so. There are a number of potential reasons. If the defence lawyer knew that Bridges's detailed confession was accurate, he would be committing a serious ethical violation by knowingly leading perjured testimony. Another possibility is that Bridges, his lawyer, or both knew that Bridges was incapable of standing up to a cross-examination. This is not necessarily an indication of guilt. Whether a person is guilty or innocent, being cross-examined by a highly skilled, competent, and experienced prosecutor is not a walk in the park eating an ice cream cone. It's entirely plausible the defence lawyer concluded that the prosecution would turn Bridges into witness stand roadkill. McIntyre suggests yet another alternative. The jury had watched several hours of video recordings of Bridges talking to police — both officially and undercover. McIntyre observes that perhaps the lawyer decided "the jury had already seen and heard enough of his client."

The jury did not take long to reach a verdict of first-degree murder. As Bridges was being led away, someone in the courtroom called out, "Too bad this isn't Texas."

Bridges's lawyer appealed the conviction. Although he huffed and puffed to the media that the appeal would challenge the legality of the Mr. Big operation as a mechanism to generate false disclosures in general, the actual appeal argument presented in court implicitly accepted the fact that Bridges had killed Erin. The lawyer argued disclosure was exaggerated rather than wrong on the core fact of culpable homicide. This was a bit like a child claiming he was falsely accused of eating the cookies because he ate only some of them. In any event, the Manitoba Court of Appeal had no sympathy for the argument. The appeal of the first-degree murder conviction was dismissed. Bridges has been in prison ever since. At the time this book was written, he was seeking early parole release under the terms of the "Faint Hope Clause" in the *Criminal Code*. The results of his efforts are, at this point, indeterminate.

THE GOOD: MICHAEL BRIDGES GOES TO PRISON

It is a simple, indisputable fact that Bridges killed Erin. In admitting to this evil act, he provided verifiable details that could not have been known by anybody other than Erin's killer. His defence conceded this central point at his trial. The Correctional Service of Canada recently told a court that Bridges has accepted responsibility for the killing and shows remorse. We can be sure that Bridges killed Erin with as much certainty as we know the sun always rises in the east and sets in the west. There is no doubt of his guilt.

Until meeting Mr. Big, Bridges had avoided any legal consequences of killing Erin. The Brandon community had reached a verdict and had imposed a social penalty, but in our system of justice, partial ostracism is not an adequate penalty for homicide. The police had been stymied. Despite the highly suspicious circumstances of Erin's disappearance, without Erin's body they could not establish beyond a reasonable doubt that she was even dead. Either by planning or by dumb luck, Bridges killed Erin without shedding blood. Forensic techniques are primarily "blood-based," so the crime scene was devoid of clues. There were no witnesses. Bridges's explanation to police was consistent enough to trump its inherent lack of credibility. Both the police and the public could — and did — suspect, but they could not prove.

The only way this impasse could be broken would be for Bridges to disclose what he had done. A general drunken statement to a friend would not suffice. For Bridges to be charged and convicted, he needed to lead investigators to Erin's body. Only this would show beyond a reasonable doubt that she was dead and he had killed her. Mr. Big made this possible. Without this investigative technique and its highly skilled application by the RCMP, Bridges would have gotten on with his life. He would have avoided legal punishment. Over time, the impact of the community sanctions would have diminished. Bridges would have gotten away with murder. Erin's parents, her brother, her sister, and her friends would have always wondered what had become of her. Losing a loved one to murder creates a terrible pain in those left behind.

But in the absence of knowledge, the imagination is left to provide explanations. Horrible as reality can be, the imagined can be worse.

In this case, Mr. Big did what he was invented to do. To Michael Bridges, he delivered legal sanctions for an evil act. To those who loved Erin Chorney, he delivered the horror of certain knowledge to replace the greater horror of the imagined.

CHAPTER 3

The Bad: R v. Unger

Saturday, June 23, 1990, was a big day for young people living near the Manitoba town of Roseisle. There was an all-day, outdoor rock music festival at a nearby ski resort. Sunshine. Music, both good and bad. Lots of alcohol and drugs. Friends, both old and those about to be made. School ending in a week. This was rural Manitoba's version of teenage heaven.

Brigitte Grenier was a popular Grade 11 student from the nearby town of Miami. That June for Brigitte, a year from graduation, life was good. She was class president and a member of the organizing committee for the upcoming graduation at Miami Collegiate. Brigitte was also graduating from the sheltered protection of childhood. This was the first year her parents had permitted attendance at the music festival. Brigitte left her home with two friends. She never returned. The next day her naked body would be found in a creek near the festival site. Death had been caused by strangulation. Brigitte's corpse had been beaten so badly that, had she still been alive, her head wounds would have killed her. It was as if the killer wanted to kill more than once. Brigitte's body had been further desecrated with sharp sticks shoved into her vagina and anus. There were bite marks on her breasts and on one arm. None of the wounds was of the type normally associated with defensive struggle. Brigitte had not been able to resist her attacker. Her death came from a sudden, unrelenting assault that continued after she was dead. When her body was found, it presented a sight that the members of the rural detachment of the RCMP had never seen before and which they would never forget. The savagery of the killing gave the police a special motivation to bring the killer or killers to justice.

Local teens Tim Houlahan and Kyle Unger were seventeen and nineteen, respectively, that June. There were differences between the two. Houlahan was socially popular; Kyle was not. Houlahan had never met Brigitte before; Kyle had attended the same small-town school. Legally, Houlahan was a minor. Kyle was not. When the police wanted to interview Houlahan, they had to ensure his parents were present. Kyle was on his own.

There were also similarities between the two. Both went to the music festival with hopes of sex and the certainty of drugs and rock and roll. Both drank alcohol and consumed less legal chemical pleasures. Both were interested in Brigitte. In this, Houlahan quickly won out. He was a witty stranger her own age, while Kyle was two years older with a somewhat disreputable reputation based on some petty theft convictions and an impaired driving charge. Kyle was also known as a chronic, fantastic liar. Houlahan spent much of the evening dancing with Brigitte while Kyle was relegated to the group of frustrated males who gather on the fringes of these kinds of events.

About 1:30 a.m., Houlahan went into the woods with Brigitte. He emerged three and a half hours later. Brigitte never did.

When Houlahan emerged from the woods, he joined his friends sitting around a bonfire. His clothes were wet, muddy, and dishevelled. His face was dirty and scratched. He was bloodied. He was silent and withdrawn. After his friends asked for an explanation about his appearance, Houlahan said he'd gone for a walk in the woods with a girl. He said someone had jumped him and beat him up. His friends were amused. Some suggested it had been the girl's father. Houlahan joined the laughter. He drank more beer, ate a hot dog, and eventually slept over at a friend's house.

Kyle also went into the woods that night. He went twice. His first visit was around 1:30 a.m. and was brief. When he returned to his friends, he reported seeing Brigitte "going at it with some guy over there." An hour later, Kyle told a friend he was off "to go look for some tail." He returned about half an hour later claiming success. His friends dismissed this as typical Kyle "bullshit." Unlike Houlahan, Kyle's appearance did not draw any attention. His clothes were not muddy. He had no scratches or blood on him. His behaviour was normal. As dawn approached, Kyle left the music festival. Like Houlahan, he slept at a friend's house.

When Brigitte's body was discovered the next afternoon, the police quickly turned their suspicious eyes towards Houlahan. After all, he was the last person seen with her. They had gone into the woods together. He had returned; she had not. Both his physical appearance and behaviour had caught his friends' attention. Houlahan was an obvious suspect. He was formally interviewed twice by the RCMP.

In his first interview, Houlahan told police that he and Brigitte had consensual sexual intercourse. He claimed that when they were finished, he was attacked by an unidentified male and knocked out. Upon regaining consciousness, he returned to the festival and told his friends. The RCMP were dissatisfied with this version of events. They had questions. Why, for example, had he not looked for Brigitte after regaining consciousness? Why had he simply resumed partying? There were other issues. The blood on Houlahan's shoes matched Brigitte's type rather than his own.

In addition to interviewing Houlahan, the police tried to talk to everyone who had seen Brigitte. Kyle was among those questioned. He reported talking to Brigitte a few times early in the evening and seeing her in an embrace with someone in the woods. In response to the standard questions, Kyle told police that he did not have any knowledge of the murder and had not been involved in her death. He was treated as a potential witness rather than as a suspect.

After his interview with police, Kyle jokingly told a friend that he was going to be arrested for murder. It soon stopped being funny. A few days later, Houlahan changed his implausible story. In his second version of events, Houlahan repeated his claim of consensual sex followed by an attack. This time he identified Kyle. He said Kyle viciously attacked Brigitte. Houlahan said that after Kyle killed and desecrated Brigitte, he ordered Houlahan to punch her a few times and assist with disposal into the creek. In this version, Houlahan admitted to post-attack complicity but denied involvement in the murder itself. He claimed his complicity was the result of fear and intimidation. After Houlahan told this story to the RCMP, Kyle was arrested.

There were a lot of questions the police could have asked Houlahan. How come he waited passively while Kyle was attacking Brigitte? How come he didn't tell anyone about the attack when he returned from the woods? How had Kyle been able to intimidate him into compliance? And why did he initially lie to police? The police did not dwell on these questions. The reason was simple. The police believed it would have taken two people to transport Brigitte's body and throw it into the creek. As a result, they believed this two-person scenario no matter what the inherent difficulties with plausibility were.

After the police arrested Kyle, evidence problems quickly emerged. They were ignored. Kyle had been out of sight of his friends for about half an hour. When he emerged from the woods, his clothes were clean. If Houlahan's story was true, Kyle's clothes would have been as dirty and dishevelled as Houlahan's were. The police speculated that Kyle "could have" gone to the nearby house of a friend and changed. The resulting problems with the time window were ignored, as were witness reports stating he was wearing the same clothes at dawn as at dusk. Brigitte had been left with bite marks on her breasts and arm. Kyle immediately agreed to provide an imprint of his bite marks. The medical examiner said Kyle was not the biter. Houlahan refused to allow police to compare his bite with the marks found on Brigitte's body.

Other than Houlahan's story, the only thing connecting Kyle to the murder was a hair. Three were found on Brigitte's clothing. A scalp hair was found on her pants. A male pubic hair was found on her sock. A forensic expert said these were consistent with samples from Houlahan. A third hair was found on Brigitte's sweater. The forensic expert said it was consistent with Kyle's scalp hair.

Kyle spent five months in remand custody because of the nature of the charge, his slightly disreputable reputation, Houlahan's story, and a hair. At the preliminary hearing, it became apparent to the prosecutor this was not enough. The judge was not buying. The prosecutor made the strategic decision to stay the charges. The charges disappeared, but only conditionally and temporarily. The prosecution retained the right to reintroduce the charges during the next twelve months. For the police, convinced of Kyle's guilt, it meant the clock was ticking. They had twelve months to build a case sufficient to sustain a prosecution. It was time for Mr. Big.

SUMMONING MR. BIG

The RCMP had a problem to resolve before summoning Mr. Big. The ultimate result of a Mr. Big operation is the recorded disclosure. Under Canadian law, surreptitious recordings are similar to wiretaps of telephone conversations. A judicial warrant must be obtained to authorize the recording. The police must convince a judge that there are solid grounds for suspicion but that other investigative tools are insufficient to get at the truth. In Kyle's case, this was a problem. The prosecutor had just stayed the charges because of insufficient evidence. The police and prosecutor had painted themselves into a corner.

To escape from their self-imposed trap, the police turned to an old friend — the jailhouse informant. Kyle had spent five months in remand custody. This placed him at significant legal risk. Inmates in remand are waiting for their day in court. Their future is uncertain and their fate is subject to decisions made by prosecutors. Charges can be dropped or modified. Sentencing recommendations can become milder. The inmates understand that the police and prosecutors care more about getting convictions in some cases more than in others. This means deals can be made. Any prosecutor will go soft on an assault or burglary case to get a conviction on a case involving a high-profile, extremely violent, sexually motivated murder of a photogenic teenage girl. For a prisoner facing charges for a serious but not heinous crime, getting placed in the same cell as someone like Kyle Unger was like drawing the Get Out of Jail Free card in a Monopoly game.

Canadian courts used to accept the testimony of jailhouse snitches on a regular basis. Many people have gone to prison for long periods of time at least partly on the basis of the testimony of cellmates. The problem is that, as a group, people awaiting trial for criminal offences are not the most trustworthy witnesses. They have a lot of incentive to lie. Ask yourself the following questions: "If you could get out of spending two years in jail by making up a little lie about what someone might have whispered to you in the night, would you be tempted? If you could soothe your conscience by telling yourself that you were helping convict a rapist and murderer, would that make you even more likely to tell police what they wanted to hear?"

In 2001, a retired Supreme Court of Canada judge conducted an inquiry into a wrongful conviction in Manitoba. Looking at the case of Thomas Sophonow, the judge said:

> Jailhouse informants comprise the most deceitful and deceptive group of witnesses known to frequent the courts. The more notorious the case, the greater the number of prospective informants. They rush to testify like vultures to rotting flesh or sharks to blood. They are smooth and convincing liars. Whether they seek favours from the authorities, attention or notoriety they are in every instance completely unreliable. It will be seen how frequently they have been a major factor in the conviction of innocent people and how much they tend to corrupt the administration of justice. Usually, their presence as witnesses signals the end of any hope of providing a fair trial. . . . Jailhouse informants are a uniquely evil group.

It was in this pond that the RCMP went fishing for grounds for the warrants needed to use Mr. Big. They found three remand centre inmates who were willing to say that Kyle made incriminating statements.

Two reports were vague and ambiguous. There are two possible explanations for these reports. The first, and most likely, is that the informants were lying. The second is that Kyle fell victim to a peculiar feature of remand centre culture. Fame is fame. Like most people, those being held in remand respect fame. Notoriety arising from high-profile or very serious charges brings a certain kind of quasi-respectful attention. It's possible that an immature young man known for his chronic bullshitting said more than was either accurate or wise.

The statement reported by the third jailhouse informant left no room for ambiguous interpretation. An inmate told police he had been in a remand centre cell with Kyle following the court appearance at which the charges were stayed. This inmate said as Kyle was waiting for the paperwork to be completed for his release, Kyle said, "I killed her and I got away with it." If true, this would be a damning statement, but as evidence it was very vague. It provided no details that could be used for verification or falsification. There was a bigger problem, though. It was impossible for Kyle to have made this statement to the inmate in the time and place reported by the inmate. Kyle had been released from custody directly from the courthouse and was never returned to a cell with an inmate possessing both big ears and a big mouth. Just as the police explained away the anomaly of Kyle's clean clothes on the night of the murder by saying he "could have" gone to a friend's house to change, they theorized that Kyle "could have" made this statement the day before his court appearance after being told by his lawyer what the next day would bring.

In any event, the assistance from the jailhouse informants did the trick. The necessary judicial authorizations were obtained for audio, but not video, recordings. The Mr. Big operation was off and running.

After his charges were stayed, Kyle was still in a lonely and ugly place. The public had been told that two people had been responsible for Brigitte's murder. Because Houlahan was a minor, his identity was kept secret. Kyle's name and face, however, had been widely publicized. Now charges had been stayed, but the police and prosecution had not declared Kyle innocent. As far as the public could see, Kyle had been the beneficiary of a smart lawyer and some legal technicality. Before being charged with Brigitte's murder, Kyle had been a socially inept, vaguely disreputable although largely unknown person without a lot of friends. His social isolation intensified when most people believed he was a rapist and murderer.

The Mr. Big team made contact with Kyle by staging a vehicle breakdown at the end of the driveway at the farm where he was staying. Kyle wandered down to be helpful. The two undercover officers said they were stranded while awaiting parts. Kyle hung around and chatted. He told the undercover officers he had just gotten out of jail after being accused of murder. The undercover officers pretended to be impressed. Kyle was invited to join them in Winnipeg. It was the first time he'd ever stayed in a hotel room. It was a nice one — a penthouse suite with a stocked mini-bar. The undercover officers hinted that they were part of a powerful criminal organization. Kyle talked about his recent legal difficulties. The officers responded by interpreting his statements as meaning he had "whacked" someone and gotten away with it. Kyle denied being the killer, but his protestations were ignored.

Nine days after meeting the undercover officers, Kyle met Mr. Big, who said, "[One of the undercover officers] tells me you whacked somebody. That's fine with me. That's, that's fuckin' excellent. It's the kind of thing that, uh, know that I'm dealing with somebody that's on my fuckin'— somebody that I can trust . . . That's the kind of person I'm looking for." Up till then Kyle maintained he had not killed Brigitte. In the presence of Mr. Big, he did not deny this misportrayal of his story. Soon he was making an active disclosure. Kyle even took the undercover officers to the site of Brigitte's murder to explain what happened.

But there were problems with Kyle's disclosure. Years later, a Manitoba Court of Queen's Bench judge noted that Kyle told Mr. Big that he committed the murder acting alone, that he disposed of the sticks used in the murder by throwing them into the river, and that he killed Brigitte near a bridge. He even took Mr. Big to see the bridge. The judge said, "The difficulty with these details is that they were not true." The original accusation against Kyle was that Houlahan and Kyle acted together. The sticks had been shoved into Brigitte, not thrown into the creek. The bridge had not been built when Brigitte was killed.

There was another problem with the reliability of Kyle's

disclosure. In addition to telling Mr. Big that he had murdered Brigitte, Kyle said he had gone to Rio de Janeiro for a rock concert; owned a "souped-up" snowmobile used in races; had taken a demolitions course and worked in Alberta doing demolitions; and had broken his neck in a motorcycle accident necessitating three months in traction and eighteen months in a wheelchair. These claims were demonstrably untrue, if not outright ludicrous. Kyle was nineteen. If he had done everything he told Mr. Big he had done, he'd be pushing thirty. The *Diagnostic and Statistical Manual of Mental Disorders* (DSM), published by the American Psychiatric Association, diagnoses this kind of behaviour as a treatable mental disorder known as "grandiose delusion." The condition is also called mythomania and pseudologia fantastica or, more simply, pathological lying. Whatever the name, the lies told have no benefit to the person telling them; the stories are long, complex, and make the teller either a hero or a victim. The teller of the lies often appears to believe them. Kyle possessed all the diagnostic symptoms of this condition.

Kyle's disclosure to Mr. Big was profoundly unreliable. It was made by someone who exhibited all the symptoms of a pathological liar. Its details were demonstrably false. It contradicted both the other piece of evidence against him (Houlahan's story) and the police theory of the crime. The police and prosecutor agreed that it was "good enough."

After making his disclosures to Mr. Big, Kyle was happy. He phoned a friend to say he was about to be admitted into a powerful criminal gang because he had convinced them that he had committed a murder. He had convinced Mr. Big, all right. The day after this phone call, Kyle was re-arrested and re-charged with murder.

THE COURT PROCESS

After Kyle's arrest, the prosecution proceeded with a first-degree murder charge with a direct indictment. This allowed the case to go directly to trial without having a preliminary hearing. The first time Kyle had been charged, the prosecutor had run into trouble at the preliminary hearing. For the second attempt, he skipped this step.

Kyle was tried jointly with Houlahan. Joint trials make sense when several defendants are charged with the same crime. It allows for a more coherent and comprehensive presentation of evidence, saves time, and eliminates the need for repeated court appearances by witnesses. In this case, a joint trial created problems for Kyle's defence. Houlahan's videotaped confession to police that implicated Kyle was admissible in court *against Houlahan*. For Kyle, this meant Houlahan's accusatory confession was presented to the jury without having the right to cross-examine Houlahan to expose shortcomings and inconsistencies. The trial judge legally resolved this issue by telling the jury (seven times) that they should consider Houlahan's confession only when deciding Houlahan's guilt or innocence but to ignore the confession when making decisions about Kyle. Maybe the jury did just that. We'll never know. In Canada, it is against the law for a jury member to talk about what happened in the jury room. It seems reasonable to assume that the judicial instructions were less effective than the Memory Charm that was the mainstay of Professor Gilderoy Lockhart in the Harry Potter books and movies. Without a magical wand, the effectiveness of a judge saying "obliviate!" is questionable.

Kyle's lawyer attempted to have the Mr. Big disclosures excluded as evidence on the grounds that the operation was unfair and violated Kyle's constitutional right to avoid self-incrimination. The voir dire hearing focused on the process more than the reliability of the resulting disclosure. The trial judge was unsympathetic, saying:

> I am not suggesting for a moment that they should resort
> to means that are contrary to the law, or so unscrupulous

and abhorrent, as to offend the standards of the community. But neither should they be compelled or obliged to play by the antiseptic standards or the gentlemanly rules of cricket. There is, after all, a real world out there, with real crime and criminals, as well as victims, and the police should be able to employ such investigative techniques within the limits prescribed by the law as the facts of the particular case and their investigative experiences indicate . . .

I find it difficult to accept that a reasonable dispassionate person, aware of the difficulties in the investigation of the case, would consider the undercover operation and use of tricks by the officers, as being unfair, or so unacceptable, indecent, and outrageous, that the evidence that was derived from that operation, if admitted as evidence in the trial of the accused, could bring the administration of justice into disrepute.

At the preliminary hearing, the evidence against Kyle was Houlahan's statement to police and the hair. This had not been enough. At the trial, the hair was joined by the testimony of the jailhouse informants and Kyle's own disclosure to Mr. Big. As discussed above, when deliberating about Kyle, the jury was told to ignore Houlahan's videotaped accusation.

Kyle took the witness stand to tell the jury he had lied to Mr. Big. He said that he made up the story to impress the undercover officers and gain admission into the putative criminal gang. Although we do not know the way jury members view any individual piece of evidence, the bottom-line result suggests that they believed his disclosure to Mr. Big rather than his witness-stand denial. Kyle was convicted of first-degree murder. This is not an inexplicable decision. The jury was asked to believe that Kyle was telling the truth as he was admitting being a liar.

While Kyle testified in his own defence, Houlahan did not. As we saw in the Michael Bridges case, there are many reasons why an accused and his lawyer might make this decision. They might feel that the prosecutor failed to prove guilt beyond a reasonable doubt. In that case, testifying presents an unnecessary risk. Calling any defence witnesses, including the accused, changes the order of the closing statements. If the presentation of evidence ends when the prosecution rests its case, the defence gets the last word when making closing arguments. If any defence witnesses are called, the prosecutor gets the right to make the final summation. The accused and his lawyer might feel that — guilty or innocent — the accused would not stand up well under cross-examination. Getting caught in a lie or even being ambiguous can damage the credibility of the accused. Losing your temper while being goaded by the prosecutor is almost always fatal to chances of acquittal.

Canadians have the constitutional right to avoid self-incrimination, so prosecutors cannot argue that a decision to refuse to testify is a sign of guilt. In this case, Kyle's defence lawyer argued that Houlahan's refusal to testify and to provide bite marks for comparison with the marks on Brigitte's body were indications of Houlahan's sole guilt.

Both Houlahan and Kyle were convicted of first-degree murder. Both appealed.

The primary basis for Kyle's appeal was the argument that his disclosure to Mr. Big should have been excluded as evidence. It was the same argument made to the trial judge. It had the same result before the appeal court judges. Kyle's lawyer also argued that the trial judge should have been more explicit in warning the jury about the reliability dangers of this kind of disclosure. The appeal court said that the trial judge had adequately addressed this issue. The jury, after all, were the triers of fact. They had done what they had been asked to do: evaluate the evidence, assess credibility, and make a decision. Kyle's lawyer also argued that the trial judge's refusal to separate the trials had been improper. The appeal court judges were unsympathetic to this argument as well.

Houlahan's appeal was based on different grounds and had a different result. His lawyer argued that the closing argument made by Kyle's lawyer resulted in a violation of Houlahan's constitutional rights by arguing that silence was an indication of guilt. Houlahan's lawyer argued that the trial judge should have stopped this line of argument or, at the very least, done a better job of explaining the law in his ruling. The appeal court agreed. Houlahan's conviction was overturned and a new trial ordered.

After the decision of the appeal court, Kyle Unger was dispatched to prison with a life sentence. Tim Houlahan faced a new trial. Before going through this process, Houlahan committed suicide.

Houlahan's sudden and self-inflicted demise created an ambiguous situation. His conviction had been overturned, so he had not been legally convicted of the crime and is therefore legally presumed to be innocent. The reality is that Houlahan would almost certainly have been convicted. The case against him was exceptionally strong. He was the last person seen with Brigitte. He had a good window of opportunity to kill her. Many witnesses were available to attest to his scratched, muddy, and dishevelled appearance. His semen was inside her and her blood was on his shoes. He had confessed his involvement to police. Even if his story was fully believed and his diminished culpability was accepted, he would still be looking at significant prison time for his role after Brigitte's death. The first jury had shown no indication that it thought his claim to have been an intimidated bystander to the killing was credible. It is difficult to see how a different jury would reach a different conclusion. Houlahan was, and is still, legally innocent. This status would almost inevitably have changed if he had not committed suicide.

KYLE'S EXONERATION

After Kyle's appeal, he continued to insist that he was innocent, but these claims were ignored by most people. There's an old joke that if you visit a prison you'll find only "innocent" people to talk to. It's not true, but it is true enough that Kyle blended in as just another inmate claiming an injustice had been done. As he slowly approached parole eligibility, his claims of innocence began to work against him. One consideration for parole is a demonstration of remorse. The first step towards demonstrating remorse is an acceptance of responsibility. This is irreconcilable with a claim of innocence. It is a dilemma eventually faced by all who have been wrongfully convicted. Refusing to confess and accept responsibility usually eliminates the possibility of parole. Mr. Big had given Kyle an incentive to make a false disclosure. This disclosure had landed him in prison. It began to appear that his only way out of prison would be to make a false confession as well.

As far as almost everybody was concerned, Kyle became a bad memory slowly being forgotten — a vicious rapist and murderer getting his just deserts. In his corner were his parents and the members of the excellent Winnipeg law firm that had represented him. He also began to receive support from the Association in Defence of the Wrongfully Convicted (AIDWYC).

Things began to change after Kyle had been in prison for a decade. Lawyers working with the AIDWYC had taken up the case of James Driskell. Like Kyle, James was a Manitoba man convicted of first-degree murder in the early 1990s. Unlike Kyle, James had not met Mr. Big or made a disclosure. Instead, the prosecution had relied on damning testimony from two unsavoury former colleagues. Like Kyle, the only forensic evidence connecting James to the crime scene was human hair. In James's case, three hairs were found in his van that were identified as being "consistent" with those of the victim.

Kyle was convicted on the basis of a hair, three jailhouse informants, and his own disclosure to Mr. Big. A confession/accusation by the original primary suspect may have also played a role but was legally irrelevant. James was convicted on the basis of three hairs and the testimony of two former colleagues.

When the lawyers from the AIDWYC took up James's case, the evidence against him came undone. The hair was sent to a lab in the United Kingdom that was pioneering the use of DNA testing in criminal forensics cases. The lab reported back that the hair in James's van did not match the murder victim's hair. What's more, all three hairs found in the van came from different people. So much for the "consistent" matching. More news followed. The two key witnesses against James testified that they were on the witness stand only because they wanted to see justice done. This was perjury. They had been amply rewarded for their testimony. One received a secret immunity deal on arson charges in Saskatchewan and payments totalling $83,000. The prosecution failed to disclose these benefits to James's defence lawyer and did not correct the record when their star witnesses committed perjury. In 2003, James was released on bail as the AIDWYC applied to the federal justice minister for a review of the case. In 2005, the minister overturned James's conviction and ordered a new trial. Manitoba Justice prosecutors called no evidence and James was acquitted. Finger-pointing, a Commission of Inquiry, and a $4-million compensation settlement followed.

In the fallout from the James Driskell case, Manitoba Justice reviewed cases in which the prosecutors had relied on microscopic hair analysis, for which the accused was convicted after pleading not guilty and had lost an appeal based on an assertion of factual innocence. Kyle fit these criteria. The hair found on Brigitte's sweater was sent to the lab in the United Kingdom for DNA analysis. The lab reported that the hair was not from Kyle's head. His lawyers joined with the AIDWYC to request a review of his case by the federal justice minister. In 2009, the conviction was overturned.

It's most accurate to describe the response of Manitoba Justice to this turn of events as inconsistent. Sometimes it behaved in a way that was principled and respectful of Kyle's restored status as legally innocent. Other times, it was petty and vindictive.

It started with petty and vindictive. Kyle applied for bail so that he could get out of jail pending a new trial. Manitoba Justice opposed the application. It claimed that the falsity of the hair evidence did not undermine its case and there were problems with the release plan contained in the bail application because he would be living outside of Manitoba's jurisdiction. He planned to stay in British Columbia with his parents (they had moved to that province in order to be able to visit him in prison on a regular basis). The prosecutor also said that available supervision would be inadequate — because the government had just cut funds for the program.

The judge hearing the bail application was unimpressed with the prosecutor's objections. The judge noted that the jailhouse disclosures were no longer admissible and the hair evidence had been proven to be false. All that remained was Houlahan's statement to police and Kyle's disclosure to Mr. Big. The judge noted that these two pieces of evidence contradicted each other and that key parts of the Mr. Big disclosure were false. In any event, Houlahan's confession/accusation would be inadmissible since he was not available for cross-examination. The jury had convicted because the Mr. Big disclosure was supported by the hair and jailhouse informant evidence. Both of these were gone. The judge concluded that "the defence has established, on a balance of probabilities, that there is new, reliable evidence that is sufficiently material to raise very serious concerns as to the reliability of the original conviction." The judge pointed out that Kyle had been involuntarily transported from Manitoba to British Columbia and it was not his decision to cut the funding for the supervision program. To use either as a justification to keep him locked up pending a new trial would be "very unfair." Bail was granted.

With this, Manitoba Justice threw in the towel. In accordance with the protocol established with James Driskell, the case was brought to court. The prosecution presented no evidence. Kyle was acquitted. He was now permanently legally innocent. Manitoba Justice conceded that he had been wrongfully convicted — that he was factually innocent.

After briefly taking the high road by exonerating Kyle, Manitoba Justice returned to being petty and vindictive. The province had just completed two inquiries into high-profile wrongful conviction cases. Manitoba Justice decided a third inquiry would be unhelpful or unnecessary. Perhaps the department had had enough of a spotlight on their misadventures.

There also remained the issue of compensation for the wrongful conviction. The other two recently exonerated Manitobans received multi-million-dollar compensation packages based on the recommendations of the inquiry judges. By the time Kyle was exonerated, the Manitoba government was tired of paying for its mistakes. In the press release announcing Kyle's exoneration, the government said, "Compensation in this case was deemed to be inappropriate as it was Unger's confession to undercover officers that caused the charges to proceed to trial and conviction." Manitoba Minister of Justice David Chomiak followed up by telling CBC that "without his confession, he would not have been charged. Without the confession, he would not have been convicted. Twelve men and women in a jury convicted him." In a sense, Chomiak was correct. Without his Mr. Big disclosure, Kyle would not have been charged or convicted. There was no meaningful evidence against him. Still, stressing the jury conviction as support for a flawed process while admitting that a person was innocent seems extraordinarily churlish. There is no doubt that Kyle made a serious mistake in 1991 when he told Mr. Big he killed Brigitte. At the same time, the police and Manitoba Justice prosecutors made some serious mistakes as well. Even while exonerating Kyle, Chomiak glossed over that part of the story.

In 2009, it appeared as if Kyle would be the only one to pay for his mistakes. Upon hearing that Chomiak had ruled out compensation, Kyle's lawyer told CBC news, "I don't know whether to laugh or cry. To be turned down before we asked — it's remarkable. . . . We'll deal with that. . . . They make so many mistakes. . . . They just compounded it, if that's the decision." Kyle sued for compensation for his wrongful conviction and his long years in prison. The Manitoba government fought the case for a decade. In 2019, on the eve of the trial, they settled out of court. The terms of the settlement were kept secret, so Manitoba taxpayers don't know the financial cost of the wrongful conviction that arose from a flawed investigation and a bad Mr. Big disclosure. As for Kyle, money cannot replace the lost years of his life.

CHAPTER 4

The Murky: R v. Hart

Karen and Krista Hart woke up on the morning of August 4, 2002, in Gander, Newfoundland. It promised to be a fun and eventful day. The twin three-year-old girls were going to a Demolition Derby, part of the community's week-long Festival of Flight. Given their age, the girls would likely not have followed the "four rounds of metal-grinding, heart-pounding action," but they would have been an attraction in their own right. Cute twins always draw attention. Karen and Krista were cute. Their mother carefully dressed them for the big day. They could anticipate a lively day being the centre of attention.

By the end of the day, both Karen and Krista were dead. Krista had been pulled from a local lake. Emergency medical technicians, staff at both the emergency room at the Gander hospital and the intensive care unit in the hospital in St. John's, desperately tried to keep the child alive. In the end, there was no measurable brain activity. The medical team conceded defeat. Karen was pulled from the lake a few hours after Krista. There were no desperate and vain attempts to maintain life since she was pronounced dead upon arrival at the hospital.

At one level, there was no mystery about how Krista and Karen died. They drowned. Two three-year-old children ended up in a lake. They had not learned how to swim. Their lungs filled with water, their breathing stopped, and they died. Help did not arrive in time. This simple explanation is unsatisfying. Being immersed in the water caused their deaths, but the obvious question was, How did they end up in the water? There were two possibilities. They fell in or they were pushed in. They were either the victims of a tragic accident or of a cruel homicide. The members of the Gander detachment of the RCMP quickly opted for the second alternative. In the circumstances, their conclusion was not unreasonable. Indeed, it was the consensus opinion of the residents of Gander.

Krista and Karen were born into a home environment that social workers describe as high risk. Both parents were poorly educated, rarely employed, and usually on social assistance. When the babies left the hospital, their first diapers, cribs, and formula were provided through the kindness of strangers, friends, and relatives. Child protection workers were regular visitors.

The babies' father was Nelson Hart. He was big in physical stature but poorly endowed in the attributes required for success in modern Canadian society. He had left school after education officials decided a fourth attempt to complete Grade 5 would be futile. He suffered from epilepsy and had frequent seizures. The combination of low intelligence and his medical condition made Nelson undesirable in the labour market, so Nelson was reliant on Newfoundland's social assistance system for his income. The long-term effects of idleness and dependency further eroded his ability to be productive and self-sufficient.

The babies' mother was Jennifer Hicks (the couple were married a year after Krista and Karen were born, after which she became

Jennifer Hart). Jennifer left school after Grade 9, but of her own volition. Before meeting Nelson, she worked as a waitress.

Jennifer had a strong nurturing instinct, which she believes contributed to her being attracted to Nelson. She regularly referred to her husband as "my son." Pity and a desire to help have been the initial basis of more than one relationship but are rarely the foundation for a healthy and stable marriage. By the time Jennifer discovered she was pregnant, she had joined Nelson in depending on social assistance for subsistence and had discovered that living with him was less than optimal. She described her partner as demanding, morose, uncommunicative, and obsessed with video lottery terminal (VLT) gambling at the local bar.

After the twins were born, things continued to deteriorate. Nelson received an insurance settlement from a motor vehicle accident but did not report the money to social services as required by law. Unpleasantness followed. The family shuttled between Gander, St. John's, and Prince Edward Island, thereby creating more dislocation. Jennifer and the girls had stays in transition houses and periodically took shelter with relatives. Nelson's obsession with VLT gambling worsened and became more expensive. Social workers were involved; it appears their concerns were more about the capacity of the parents to provide the necessities of life than the danger of physical harm.

While Jennifer was giving Krista and Karen the full benefit of her strong nurturing instincts, Nelson was, by most accounts, a disengaged father. He had little to do with the children and was almost never alone with them. Two explanations for this have been presented. The story told to social workers was that he did not want to be alone with the girls because he feared being incapacitated by an epileptic seizure. This presented his detachment from his daughters as arising from concern for their safety. However, in a book called *Mr. Big: The Investigation into the Deaths of Karen and Krista Hart,* co-authored by Colleen Lewis and Jennifer Hart a dozen years after the girls' deaths, a more sinister explanation was presented. In this account, Jennifer reported she was afraid to leave the girls alone with their father because she feared for their safety. In her book, Jennifer reported Nelson was jealous of any attention paid to the children. She reports she caught him pinching the children and sabotaging their baby carriage.

Both explanations are rooted in a concern for the children's safety but have very different implications. With one, the decision was primarily Nelson's based on a factually grounded concern about his capacity to ensure their safety. With the other, the decision was Jennifer's based on concern that Nelson posed a danger to his own children. The explanations are not completely mutually exclusive. People and relationships are complicated. This is illustrated by two contrasting decisions by Jennifer. Four months after the birth of her daughters, Jennifer had a tubal ligation. In her co-authored book, Jennifer reports that she "had already figured out she did not want any more children with Nelson." Eight months later, she married him.

On the morning of August 4, Krista and Karen could look forward to a good day in a life that had been less than idyllic. Their mother prepared them for the day but needed to get ready herself. Nelson offered to take them outside to play. Jennifer agreed. Placing the girls under the sole care of Nelson was an unusual event. What actually was agreed to or understood is significant. Again, two explanations exist. In the version presented to the police and courts, Jennifer understood Nelson was taking the children to the lake. There was a playground with a swing set near the water that the girls had enjoyed playing on the previous evening. In the version presented in her co-authored book, Jennifer said her understanding was that Nelson would take the girls to a small park adjacent to their apartment building.

After they had been gone for about forty-five minutes, an agitated Nelson burst into the apartment. He reported that Krista was in the water. Jennifer asked about Karen. Nelson replied that he forgot her. They raced to the lake. Krista was floating face down near a dock, but there was no sign of Karen. Jennifer attempted to find a pole to pull Krista from the water. Nelson drove away to seek help. Emergency personnel arrived, pulled Krista from the lake, and attempted to resuscitate her. Jennifer accompanied Krista to the local hospital and subsequently to the hospital in St. John's. Eventually the medical staff took Krista off life-support. Meanwhile, back at the lake, Karen's body was discovered.

The RCMP posed questions. How did the girls end up in the lake? Was it an accident or homicide? If it was an accident, was there criminal negligence involved? When tragedy strikes, police begin the process of assigning blame.

The police were immediately struck by the difference in the demeanour of the two parents. Jennifer was hysterical in her grief. Nelson was quiet and withdrawn. He appeared indifferent. To the police mind, this was suspicious. In reality, there is no single way people express grief. Some externalize; others internalize. Some exhibit; some suppress. But the contrast was there. Nelson's response did not seem quite normal to the police and was interpreted as a sign of possible guilt.

If Nelson's demeanour seemed suspicious, his explanation of the events convinced the police of his guilt. Nelson told the RCMP he had taken the girls onto the dock. They were kneeling down to look at some fish when Krista fell in. Nelson said he panicked and raced home to get help from Jennifer. Nelson said he forgot about Karen and left her standing on the dock. The police doubted the veracity of this story. More simply, they believed Nelson was lying. What normal person would act in such a way? Nelson doggedly stuck to this implausible story through a hard eight-hour interrogation conducted a month after the girls' deaths. Then the story changed. A few days after his interrogation, Nelson admitted he lied. His new explanation was that he had an epileptic seizure and was not aware of the girls going towards the water. When he came out of the seizure, Krista was in the water already. Nelson said that his unusual response to the situation was caused by disorientation created by the seizure.

Nelson's second version of events was more plausible than the first. It accounted for the girls getting to the water and for his unusual response. If Nelson had presented this explanation immediately, there is a reasonable chance the police would have believed him. Nelson's problem was how to account for the change in his narrative. In a homicide investigation, the police have an absolutist view about the veracity of testimony. They assume that the reason people lie is to cover up guilt. Nelson claimed he lied because he was afraid of losing his driver's licence if he admitted to having a seizure. The police viewed this explanation for his lie with the same skepticism as they viewed the lie itself. What kind of father, having just lost two children, would be primarily worried about his driver's licence? Despite the explanatory power of Nelson's second story, it was rejected precisely because it was his second story.

In police terminology, the case went cold. It would be more accurate to say that it reached an impasse. The police were confronted with a disreputable parent who had a history of deceit to officialdom and involvement with child protection services. The children had died in suspicious circumstances. There were no witnesses. The medical evidence was equally consistent with homicide and an accidental drowning. Nelson presented an explanation that was plausible, but belated. He had taken six weeks to present his story, so there was ample time to have constructed a lie. It was time for Mr. Big.

NELSON HART MEETS MR. BIG

Things did not go well for the Harts after the death of their daughters. Nelson was already an outcast in the small, tightly knit community of Gander. He had been viewed as a lazy, deadbeat welfare cheat who behaved oddly. Now he was viewed as a lazy, deadbeat welfare cheat who had murdered his children. The doors of polite society — and even impolite society — were closed. About the only people who did not ostracize Nelson were his wife and his mother. Even with them, relations were strained. The Harts' living conditions worsened as a result of erratic behaviour, gambling, and impulsive geographic relocations. Nelson was becoming increasingly paranoid that people were watching him and talking about him. As the old saying goes, just because you are paranoid does not mean they are not out to get you. Nelson's paranoia was justified.

On the surface, the police had abandoned their efforts to prove Nelson's guilt. Below the surface, the shark was approaching. Officers were being recruited, scripts were being prepared, and funding was being authorized for a Mr. Big operation. The police were certain that Nelson was guilty of murdering Krista and Karen. They were determined to get a disclosure of his guilt.

Mr. Big appeared when Nelson and Jennifer had reached bottom. A series of precipitate moves left them with no furniture, no money, and no prospects. They were sleeping on the floor of an apartment at the bottom of the low-end rental market. The sounds of rats moving about kept Jennifer awake at night. One day Nelson was approached by a stranger seeking — and willing to pay for — help. The stranger explained he owned a trucking company and that his sister had brought a truck to Newfoundland but had developed a taste for alcohol and VLT gambling. The stranger asked Nelson to show him the likely places to look for her. They eventually located the imaginary sister. By this time, Nelson thought he had found a friend.

Nelson was hired for a number of driving and delivery tasks. These became progressively more mysterious and lucrative. As the operation progressed, it outgrew Newfoundland. Nelson was introduced to a second undercover officer. The geographical range of tasks was extended to Halifax, Montreal, and Vancouver. Nelson's life was transformed. Fresh from sleeping on the floor in a rat-infested apartment, Nelson was sleeping on 200-thread-count sheets on soft beds in swank hotels. After living on a meagre diet of boiled potatoes and bologna, he was eating in high-end steak houses. After destitution, he had an income. It was task-specific and hence erratic. But for Nelson, it was wealth beyond imagination: $15,720 over four months. Cash. Fifty- and hundred-dollar bills. Best of all, the amounts were increasing. There were hints of a really big operation coming up with an equally big payday. The figure of $25,000 was raised. There was a catch. Access to this bonanza was conditional. Nelson had to be approved by the mysterious boss of the crime organization, Mr. Big.

The tasks increased in responsibility. Nelson was told a member of the organization had been arrested for impaired driving. It was imperative that something be recovered from the person's car. Nelson helped break into the police compound, locate the car, and retrieve a package. Later, he learned the package contained $30,000. Nelson was asked to count the money to verify that it was all there. Counting large sums of money became a regular task. It conveyed a sense of an incredibly rich organization. Nelson was shown the organization was capable of violence. When meeting with a member of another imaginary crime organization, the undercover officer slapped the person's face simply for saying his name. The officers talked about controlling prostitution in Montreal and suggested that violence was often required to keep the prostitutes in line. Nelson was asked if he had it in him to engage in such acts. He assured the officers that he did.

It was not smooth sailing for the RCMP. Despite his eagerness to join the gang, Nelson was a tough nut to crack. His reluctance to make a disclosure was a sign of either caution or innocence. The operation deadline and funding requirements kept getting extended. Ultimately, police spent $416,268 on transportation, hotel rooms, room service, trips to casinos, and restaurant meals.

There were other problems. On one occasion, Nelson was told to carry a locked suitcase from Halifax to Montreal. At the Halifax train station, security officials with a sniffer dog demanded to see the contents. Nelson was as surprised as the security personnel to learn the suitcase contained unopened packages of photocopier paper. In order to explain why he was carrying so much paper, he said it had been on sale. The search threatened to derail the operation. Even Nelson Hart could wonder why he was being paid to hand-deliver photocopier paper from Halifax to Montreal. His handlers were up to the challenge. When Nelson reached Montreal, he was praised for his cool handling of the situation and was taken to a casino. Officers entered his hotel room and substituted the handle of the suitcase with one containing fake diamonds. Later, Nelson was allowed to see the "diamonds" being taken from the handle. The task, the security stop, and the inability of the security personnel to find any contraband were all implicitly explained. The unexpected vigilance of security in the Halifax train station had threatened to blow the entire operation, but the quick and imaginative response of the RCMP turned the potential catastrophe into a positive. It was also illegal. The trial judge later ruled entry into the hotel room constituted an illegal search, since no warrant had been obtained.

Nelson became emotionally attached to the undercover officers. He believed them to be the first friends he had ever had. Further, they were friends who had transformed his life from abject poverty and social isolation to one of affluence and excitement. He openly and repeatedly professed his love for the two undercover officers. They, in turn, continually stressed the importance of trust and absolute honesty between friends and criminal colleagues.

As the fourth month of the operation drew to a close, Nelson was deemed ready to meet Mr. Big. In preparation, he accompanied one officer on a trip to the Canada–United States border. They took pictures of the terrain and GPS readings of border locations. The undercover officer hinted this was preparation for the big, lucrative upcoming operation. Participation would be limited to those who had been fully vetted and approved members of the gang. Those with outstanding undisclosed secrets would not be eligible for the big payday. The undercover officer later testified that Nelson confessed to killing his daughters at this point, while Nelson denied he gave this confession. Because of the circumstances in which the disputed confession occurred (or not), there was no audio recording of the conversation.

A short time later, Nelson was introduced to Mr. Big. He was told that a problem had emerged. Mr. Big said his sources in the RCMP had reported that a witness to the deaths of Krista and Karen had come forward. Mr. Big said the witness could be "taken care of" but he needed to know exactly what happened. Nelson repeated his epileptic seizure story. Mr. Big told him to stop lying. Nelson then provided his third version of the events on August 4, 2002. Nelson said he decided to kill the girls to prevent his brother from obtaining custody. He said he used his shoulder to push the girls into the water as they stood on the dock. There were two problems with this explanation. The first was that Nelson's brother had never applied for custody of the girls or indicated he wanted to. The second problem was with the description of the killing. Nelson was a big man. Krista and Karen were small three-year-old girls. It was difficult to see how a standing Nelson could have used his shoulder to push the girls into the lake.

Nelson was sent back to Newfoundland. A few days after his disclosure to Mr. Big, an undercover officer took him to the lake where the girls had drowned to re-enact the crime, ostensibly so that the officer could see where, or if, the witness had been hiding. Nelson was told this was in preparation for "taking care" of the witness. At the lake, Nelson gave a revised version of his "pushing the girls in" story. He said he tricked the girls into leaning down to peer in the water in the hopes of seeing some fish. All it took was a small nudge. With this revision to his story, Nelson repeated the pattern of his explanation to the police immediately following the girls' deaths. He initially provided a story that contained elements that were implausible and later made revisions that addressed the worst points of implausibility.

Nelson was told to take Jennifer to the local Walmart and get recorded by a security camera at a precisely specified time. The purpose of this exercise was said to be the creation of an alibi for Nelson while the witness was being "taken care of." Nelson eagerly complied. In doing so, he signified he was happy to be part of an implied murder conspiracy. With that, a warrant was obtained for Nelson's arrest.

THE COURT PROCESS

When Nelson was arrested, his first request was that he be allowed to call one of the undercover officers. Even at this point, he believed that the officers were both his friends and members of a powerful criminal organization. He was informed the undercover officer was "one of us." The transcripts of the exchange do not convey tone of voice, but it is not unreasonable to assume that the arresting officers were both amused and pleased by the effectiveness of the deception.

On June 13, 2005 — almost three years after the deaths of his daughters — he was charged with two counts of first-degree murder. He applied for, and was denied, bail.

As a consumer of legal services, Nelson was an exceptionally difficult client. He passionately believed he was entitled to the best in legal representation. At the same time, he possessed very limited knowledge in how to judge the quality of legal representation and did not possess any money. Further, Nelson was paranoid before the Mr. Big operation. This paranoia was heightened after the first two friends he had ever made turned out to be undercover police officers intent on sending him to jail for the rest of his life. It made Nelson a difficult person for lawyers to defend.

Newfoundland's legal aid system quickly agreed that Nelson qualified for legal aid and appointed a staff lawyer to his case. Nelson decided that this lawyer was not adequately serving his interests and demanded a different lawyer. Legal Aid appointed another staff lawyer. Nelson insisted that no Legal Aid staff lawyer was good enough and demanded the right to choose his own lawyer at Legal Aid expense. As the legal process worked its way through the courts, Nelson's demands got increasingly difficult to accommodate. The demand that Legal Aid pay for a private lawyer of his choice evolved into a demand that he be provided the services of a lawyer of his choice, but that this lawyer not be paid by Legal Aid. When the courts eventually agreed to appoint legal counsel with the bills to be paid by the Office of the Attorney General rather than by Legal Aid, Nelson refused to accept a lawyer appointed by the court even though the court appointment was the mechanism needed to provide him with the lawyer he demanded. Things got stranger. At one point, Nelson insisted the only acceptable lawyer was the province's Attorney General.

After Nelson was convicted and it appeared he would be representing himself at the appeal hearing, an amicus curiae ("friend of the court") was appointed to protect Nelson from himself. Nelson refused to meet with him. At another point, Nelson's wife applied for legal guardianship of her husband so that she could ensure he had legal representation. The court rejected this application. After all, Nelson was convicted of killing her children. If she became convinced of his guilt, it would not be in his best interests to have her directing his legal team. It was an astute decision. Jennifer concludes her co-authored book with a personal statement that "Nelson needs to pay for what he did to my girls and me. I won't stop until I get justice."

One reason for Nelson's difficult relationship with legal counsel appears to have been an abiding belief that anyone trying to help him was part of another conspiracy to betray him. In reality, Newfoundland's Legal Aid system, Office of the Attorney General, courts, and members of the private bar demonstrated a sincere commitment to protecting Nelson's interests. In doing so, they exhibited remarkable patience. Nelson's conviction was eventually overturned in spite of his own efforts rather than because of them. Nelson's difficulties in working with legal counsel help explain the length of time it took for his case to work its way through the courts.

Nelson's trial began on February 27, 2007. He was convicted by a jury one month and one day later. In a very real way, the trial hinged on the voir dire over the admissibility of his disclosures to Mr. Big. Everyone agreed that Nelson had taken his daughters to the lake. Everyone agreed that they had drowned. The issue came down to whether they fell or were pushed into the water.

It was also clear that if a jury watched a video of Nelson admitting to the murders to gain acceptance into a criminal gang, if they saw him re-enact the crime, if they knew that he was willing to conspire in the killing of a potential witness . . . the jury would almost certainly find him guilty. If they heard or saw none of this, there was no evidence to contradict the accident story. The voir dire lasted a week. Nelson and ten RCMP officers involved in the Mr. Big operation testified. Relying on precedents set by earlier Mr. Big cases, the trial judge ruled the disclosures were admissible.

Nelson's last faint hope was to convince the jury he had been lying when he confessed to Mr. Big. Nelson said he would testify, but when the moment came, he told the judge that the stress of testifying in front of a packed spectator gallery would trigger an epileptic seizure. The exchange between Nelson and the judge was confusing. It appears there was a misunderstanding between Nelson and the judge. Nelson appeared to be objecting to the physical presence of the spectators but not to his testimony being public. The judge appeared to believe that Nelson was requesting that the testimony be "in camera." Citing past court rulings about the importance of transparency of criminal trials, the judge refused to empty the spectator stands. The needs of both Nelson and the court process could have been met by providing a video link to spectators in another room, but this was not done. Nelson refused to testify and forfeited his last, slim chance for acquittal. The jury knew that Nelson told Mr. Big he had killed his daughters, and now he refused to take the stand in his own defence. In these circumstances, an acquittal was inconceivable. Nelson was convicted and sentenced to life imprisonment with no possibility of parole for at least twenty-five years.

The case went to the Court of Appeal of Newfoundland and Labrador. There were two primary grounds for the appeal. The first was the argument that the Mr. Big confessions should have been rejected. The second was that the refusal of Nelson's request that the spectators be cleared from the room effectively blocked him from any chance of acquittal. Predictably, Nelson's actions and relationships with his lawyers delayed and almost scuttled the appeal process. Newfoundland's criminal justice system, as a collective entity, went the extra mile to ensure his arguments were properly made and heard. All three appeal court judges hearing the appeal agreed that the conviction should be overturned because of the denial of the request to clear the spectators. Two of the three ruled the disclosures to Mr. Big should have been disallowed. The inducements offered, the financial and emotional dependency of Nelson on the undercover officers, and his generally pathetic circumstances made the confession unreliable. They also pointed to the inconsistencies in the disclosures and the lack of any corroborating evidence.

The case went to the Supreme Court of Canada. By this time, Nelson's case had become a vehicle for a challenge to Mr. Big operations. As will be discussed in Chapter 10, defence lawyers, civil rights organizations, and legal academics were united in a desire to have Mr. Big retired. As a result, the case was imbued with much more significance than the fate of a person convicted of murdering his daughters. The justice departments of Canada, British Columbia, Quebec, and Ontario were given intervenor status to defend Mr. Big. Lined up to oppose him were lawyers from the Association for the Defence of the Wrongfully Convicted, the Criminal Lawyers' Association of Ontario, the Canadian Civil Liberties Association, the Association des avocats de la défense de Montréal, and the British Columbia Civil Liberties Association. Fourteen lawyers presented verbal arguments to the Supreme Court and another six presented written arguments. Nelson Hart's future had become a cottage industry in the legal profession.

The Supreme Court unanimously agreed with the Court of Appeal of Newfoundland and Labrador that the conviction should be struck down as a result of the spectator issue. Overturning Nelson's conviction simply on this basis would not change much.

The big question, the one that attracted all the additional legal firepower, was how Mr. Big, in general, should be treated by courts in Canada. In the past, the Supreme Court had described the Mr. Big technique as "skillful police work." Now it was being asked to declare the technique illegal. For the police, a ruling that Mr. Big was no longer permissible would mean that a technique that had solved more than two hundred murder cases would no longer be available. For the legal system as a whole, a ruling that the Mr. Big procedure violated constitutional legal principles would create a legal quagmire. Canada's prisons had a lot of prisoners who had been convicted because Mr. Big had been condoned — and encouraged — by the Supreme Court. A ruling that the process was unconstitutional and illegal would keep a lot of lawyers busy for a long time. Omelettes are hard to turn back into eggs.

The Supreme Court tried to strike a balance. The legal issues will be discussed in more detail later in the book, but the essence of its ruling was that Mr. Big was legally permissible, but it was a tool that had to be used with care. The possibility of generating a false disclosure was real. It was like a table saw: great for cutting wood but easy for a carpenter to lose a finger. Protective safeguards were deemed essential and the courts were instructed to maintain vigilance in making sure these protections were in place in every Mr. Big case. The Supreme Court set out guidelines for Mr. Big operations.

This left the question of what to do with Nelson. The Supreme Court acknowledged the new standards did not exist at the time of his trial. He had been convicted and his conviction overturned. In normal circumstances, a new trial judge would determine whether the process used to obtain Nelson's confessions was permissible under the new criteria. This would take the whole process back to "square one" after nine years. The majority of the Supreme Court justices had no appetite for this. They opted to effectively end the affair by ruling that Nelson's disclosures violated the new standards. A few days later, a Newfoundland prosecutor announced there was no chance of a conviction in the absence of the disclosures. The charges were withdrawn. Nelson Hart was let out of prison. With the exception of outstanding assault charges arising from his time behind bars, his legal journey was over.

CONSIDERING THE MURKY: SUMMING UP R V. HART

Perhaps the best summary of the case comes from a judge with the Court of Appeal of Newfoundland and Labrador. In overturning Nelson's conviction, he concluded by writing:

> Did Mr. Hart confess falsely — or truthfully? We will never know with any degree of certainty or even assurance on the basis of the trial that occurred. In fact, without a truthful confession from Mr. Hart, we will not know whether a crime was committed at all.

If Nelson Hart was guilty, he had ample reason to lie to police. If he was innocent, he had reason to lie to Mr. Big. If he was guilty and telling the truth to Mr. Big, he had an even more compelling reason to lie about lying. In the absence of any corroborating or refuting evidence, trying to find the truth becomes like making one's way through a carnival funhouse maze featuring distorting mirrors. Reality, when one sees it, is impossible to recognize.

It gets worse. Nelson Hart was proven to have a tendency to lie persistently. No matter what the truth, he lied about something and stuck to these lies. At the same time, he was pathetically easy to manipulate. Even after arrest, he had trouble understanding that the undercover officers were not his friends.

If Nelson Hart was innocent — if he had an epileptic seizure that resulted in his daughters drowning — the police would have been skeptical of his seizure story but would have likely accepted it. But he lied. He lied with a story that was profoundly implausible. He stuck with this lie for six weeks and through an eight-hour interrogation. In doing so, he was much more consistent than convincing. Then he changed his story. His second version of events was more plausible, but he had to explain why he had lied. The police believed that no normal father would lie about the circum-stances of an accidental death of his daughters unless he had a very compelling reason — such as the possibility he was covering up an even more sinister truth. Nelson's explanation was that he lied to avoid risking losing his driver's licence. The police believed that no normal father would be scheming to keep his driver's licence the day his two daughters tragically died. The police were right. No normal person would do such a thing. It's a question of priori-ties. The police therefore reached the conclusion that Nelson Hart murdered his daughters. This was a logical and reasonable conclu-sion, but it rested on the assumption that Nelson would behave as a normal person. In reality, there is nothing in Nelson's biography to suggest he regularly operated within two standard deviations of functional normalcy. A functionally normal person would not have behaved the way Nelson says he did for the reasons he gave. It is not inconceivable, however, that Nelson did so.

In this murky situation, Mr. Big did what he was invented to do. He got a disclosure. Was it a truthful or a fabricated disclosure? The only person who might know is Nelson Hart himself. But not necessarily. Memory is malleable; by this point, even Nelson may not know what really happened. The RCMP made a valiant and determined effort to seek the truth. They were not trying to frame Nelson Hart for a crime they knew he did not commit: they were acting on the belief — far from an irrational belief — that he had killed his twin three-year-old daughters. If Krista's and Karen's deaths were murder, it was indeed a crime that would shock the conscience of the community.

But we are left forced to acknowledge that Mr. Big made a murky situation even murkier. A coin flip would have as much chance of finding out the truth as would any further investigation. Under our system of law, the probabilistic chances of a coin flip cannot be the basis of establishing guilt beyond a reasonable doubt.

CHAPTER 5

The Anatomy of Mr. Big

The investigations of Michael Bridges, Kyle Unger, and Nelson Hart — the good, the bad, and the murky — show us the essential character of Mr. Big. A horrible crime has been committed or is believed to have been committed. The police believe they know who is responsible but cannot provide evidence that will allow a prosecutor to prove a case beyond a reasonable doubt. The investigation has reached an impasse. Mr. Big is summoned to help.

Mr. Big has an individual and a collective identity. On the one hand, Mr. Big is the putative leader of an imaginary criminal gang. In this role, an undercover police officer collects the disclosure that sends the suspect to jail. On the other hand, Mr. Big also refers to the entire undercover operation. People who have committed a murder don't seek out Mr. Big by wandering into a hotel room to give a videotaped disclosure. Just as a steer grazing in a pasture is delivered to the butcher by a complex series of planned actions, the suspect is delivered to Mr. Big by an efficient delivery system. The objective of the beef transportation operation is to deliver the steer fat and tender. The objective of the Mr. Big operation is to deliver the suspect to the butcher — the person called "Mr. Big" — ready to make a disclosure. When viewed as the entire undercover operation, Mr. Big usually consists of six components.

The first step is *case selection*. About 30 percent of homicides remain uncleared by police. For one of the unsolved homicides to become a Mr. Big case, there must be a suspect who could prove susceptible to the seductive charms of Mr. Big.

The second step is called the "bump." An undercover agent creates a pretext to *establish contact* with the suspect. Insurance salespeople say "cold calls" present the most difficult challenge to making a sale. The challenge facing the Mr. Big team is to make contact with a paranoid suspect in a way that quickly establishes a relationship with an undercover officer.

The third step comes after the suspect is bumped. "Scenarios" are created. They are acts in a play that are partly scripted and partly improvisational. The first scenarios *build a relationship*. An element of criminality is then introduced. The suspect is groomed to trust the undercover officer and become susceptible to the idea of disclosure.

Step four is the "nudge." The suspect is given a positive *reason to disclose*. A sense of urgency is created. This is based on the same psychology as a time-limited super-special sale from a car dealership or department store.

In step five, the person of Mr. Big enters. His job is to *harvest the disclosure* before a hidden video camera.

If Mr. Big is successful in getting a disclosure, one step remains before arrest. The *disclosure is evaluated* to determine whether it fits known facts or whether new lines of investigation must open.

When a disclosure has been obtained and verified, the suspect is arrested and transformed into the accused. Mr. Big presents his evidence in court and the accused is usually transformed into the convicted. The prison doors slam shut. Justice is served — except in the odd case where it is not.

While most Mr. Big operations follow the same basic plot, there is almost infinite variation within this common structure. Each case, each suspect, each scenario is different. People are often unpredictable. This makes the complex series of human interactions in every case unpredictable. Mr. Big operations have changed over the years. A Mr. Big operation in 1990 was very different than one in 2015. The police have learned. Some learning was caused by discovering what techniques worked the best in generating a disclosure, while some was caused by the challenges of defence lawyers at trials. Mr. Big operations have tended to become longer, more complicated, and less crude.

Let's now consider each of the six steps of a Mr. Big operation in detail.

CHOOSING APPROPRIATE TARGETS

It is tempting to say Mr. Big is summoned when the police want to investigate a crime. This is usually true, but not always. Erin Chorney had disappeared. The police believed she had been murdered but did not know whether she was even dead. Similarly, the police knew Karen and Krista Hart had drowned but did not know whether this was from a criminal act perpetrated by their father. In both these cases, the first essential part of Mr. Big's task was to find evidence that a crime had been committed. These cases are not unique.

Sometimes the medical cause of death does not assist in determining whether a homicide happened. Two-year-old Noah Cownden, for example, died of a head injury while in the care of his stepfather, who told police the child slipped while hopping out of the bathtub. The medical examiners said the injury was probably caused by an intentional blow, but the bathtub explanation was possible. The issue was whether the death was an accident or a homicide. If a homicide, there was no doubt as to who the killer was. Mr. Big was summoned.

When someone disappears, murder may be suspected but can be hard to prove. People sometimes intentionally leave their normal life behind. They can make themselves very difficult to find. Others die by causes other than murder, but their bodies cannot be located.

In February 2008, Dennis Cornish suddenly disappeared without a trace. Dennis was a marijuana grower in British Columbia. Police believed he was murdered by his friend and business associate, Darin Randle, who said that he was also mystified by Dennis's disappearance. Police did not believe him, in part because Randle normally phoned and texted his partner several times a day — up until the evening Dennis disappeared. Police speculated that this abrupt termination of communication was because Randle knew there was no point in trying without a Ouija board. Mr. Big was summoned.

In both these cases, nobody was convicted of homicide since the deaths were eventually deemed to be probably accidental.

In most cases where Mr. Big is summoned, it is clear a crime has been committed. When someone has been shot several times or their head caved in with a baseball bat, foul play can be assumed rather than suspected. The case is a "Who done it?" rather than a "Was it done?"

Sometimes the prime suspect is obvious. In Chapter 2, we saw how police used deduction to reach a conclusion about the obvious suspect. Michael Bridges had a history of violence directed at Erin Chorney *and* was the last person known to have seen her alive. If she was dead, he was the obvious suspect.

In cases where the victim was involved in the drug trade or other criminal activity, the police will often hear rumours "on the street" about who was responsible. In 2008, two men decided to rob marijuana dealer Kevin Bowser in a home invasion. The robbery went badly. Kevin was repeatedly stabbed with a machete. The robbers fled without stolen drugs, without stolen money, and without their machete. Police eventually heard rumours that Alexander Vouzzo was one of the murderous but incompetent robbers. Mr. Big was summoned.

Accusations are often made anonymously, but sometimes a person will put their name behind it. In 2002, Fort McMurray, Alberta, was booming. Dax Mack took advantage of the housing shortage to rent a room to Robert Levoir. It was a mistake. Robert was a petty thief who stole the piggy bank belonging to Mack's son. Rather than evict the undesirable tenant, Mack shot him five times and burned the body. Robert was listed as "missing." He might have stayed that way except Mack told a friend about the murder. They were overheard. The police were notified. Mr. Big was summoned.

In other cases, a more tortuous route is taken in reaching Mr. Big. On December 4, 1976, Michel Laflamme came out of a Shoppers Drug Mart to discover his wife strangled in their car. He said she was alive when he went into the store. Police were skeptical but could not find any evidence to the contrary or shake Michel from his story. The investigation reached an impasse and was slowly forgotten. Almost. Nearly two decades later, Michel was charged and convicted of conspiring to kill his third wife. This caused the police to remember their suspicions about the death of his first wife. When Michel got out of jail, Mr. Big struck up an acquaintance.

There are also cases in which the police know, and can prove, who was directly responsible for a crime but want to know more. On the morning of October 8, 1997, Robert Holtham left his house to drive to work. A few minutes later, a neighbour became concerned because Holtham's wife, Leonora, was not answering the phone. The neighbour looked in the window of the Holthams' home. Leonora was lying on the floor with her head bashed in. When an ambulance and the police arrived, the Holthams' two children were also found. Six-year-old Jenny was dead and eight-year-old

Cody badly injured. When police approached Holtham at his workplace, there was blood on his clothing. Holtham was arrested, questioned, and released pending the results of DNA testing on the blood. Immediately after the funerals, Holtham left town to take up residence with a girlfriend. The police did not need Mr. Big to make a case against Holtham, but they wanted to know if the girlfriend was involved. Mr. Big was summoned to run an operation directed at the couple.

The genesis of other Mr. Big operations was even more unusual. On two occasions, a murderer initiated contact with police to confess to unsolved killings. In both cases, they pointed the finger at accomplices, who were then introduced to Mr. Big. We'll look at these cases in more detail later in this chapter.

Once a suspect has been identified for a known or potential serious crime, the police assess the subject's potential as a target for Mr. Big. Some, like the author, are deemed to be poor targets who are unlikely to be tricked by the Mr. Big technique. Others are rejected as potential Mr. Big targets because it would be too dangerous or legally compromising for the undercover officers. It is difficult to recruit a person into an imaginary criminal gang if they are already a member of a real one. Trying to recruit an actual member of organized crime into an imaginary Mr. Big gang would be like trying to convince a real Rotarian to join an imaginary Kiwanis group — except it is much more dangerous. Mr. Big works on crime gang wannabes, not on actual crime gang members.

The final consideration is how long ago the crime occurred. Mr. Big has had success in solving cases that are very cold, but it can be difficult to verify the accuracy of the disclosure. Evidence decays with time. Physical evidence is lost, destroyed, or disintegrates. Witnesses forget or die. Memory becomes imprecise. Who can remember exactly where they were at a particular hour on a particular day twenty-six years ago?

In the introduction, we learned of the rape and murder of

twelve-year-old Monica Jack. Monica was killed in 1978. Her killer, Garry Handlen, became a Mr. Big target in 2013. He disclosed details of Monica's murder that could be verified against evidence collected thirty-five years after her death. Handlen also told Mr. Big he killed another girl in 1975. Like Monica, she was a twelve-year-old Indigenous girl riding her bike when she was abducted, raped, and killed. In both cases, there was evidence that Handlen was in the neighbourhood. In the case of the 1975 killing, evidence had either decayed or been so publicized that it was impossible to verify the accuracy of Handlen's disclosure. Handlen told Mr. Big that he had raped and murdered two young girls. He was charged with two counts of murder. One resulted in a conviction and a life sentence. The other charge was stayed after that aspect of the disclosure was ruled inadmissible by the judge. The passage of time creates problems. Sometimes these can be overcome; sometimes they cannot be.

While a case can be too old to be suitable for Mr. Big, it can also be too fresh. In the infancy of Mr. Big, police sometimes used him as a shortcut for other investigative techniques. In 1990, Sister Florine Brun was murdered in church after a choir practice. Marven McIntyre was seen lurking outside. He was arrested and interrogated. McIntyre denied being the killer. He was released. His cellmate during this brief period of arrest was an undercover RCMP officer. After McIntyre was released from jail, he had an "accidental" meeting with his former cellmate in a convenience store. They bonded. McIntyre was introduced to Mr. Big, disclosed guilt, and went to jail to serve a life sentence. Mr. Big quickly solved the crime and got a conviction. But there is a problem with this approach. The ultimate moment of a Mr. Big operation is getting a videotaped disclosure. To make the surreptitious recording, the police need a warrant. These warrants should be issued only when other investigative techniques are inadequate to solve the crime. When Mr. Big has been activated too soon, defence lawyers have argued that other means had not been tried. These challenges have generally been unsuccessful, but they forced officers to spend more time on the witness stand justifying their decision to use Mr. Big as a first, rather than as a last, resort. There is a risk that the resulting disclosure would be ruled inadmissible as evidence. Over time, police have become slower to use Mr. Big.

Calling on Mr. Big has become a bit like Goldilocks's porridge tasting. Just as Goldilocks didn't like her porridge too hot or too cold, a homicide case can be too new or too old for Mr. Big's taste. The "just right" time for a Mr. Big case is after the investigation has reached an impasse but before other evidence has decayed. This "just right" period is usually between six months and five years after the crime was committed.

Sometimes timing is out of the hands of the police. In the introduction, we looked at the case of Earl Jones, who was shot in the head after a barroom dispute. His killer was an Irish citizen living in the United States named Thomas McDonald. He was in Canada working on a construction project. After the shooting, police put up roadblocks as part of an organized search. An officer was told to look for a truck with only one functioning headlight. McDonald, planning on a long drive through the night, had taken the time to change the broken headlight. Safety first. This allowed him to slip by the roadblock and get to the United States. Canadian authorities did not have enough evidence for an extradition order. Two decades later, McDonald wore out his welcome in the United States and was deported. He ended up in Britain, where he was soon convicted for manslaughter after hitting a roommate over the head with a sledgehammer. When released from prison on parole, he slipped back into Canada. It was a mistake. Twenty-nine years after killing Earl, McDonald became the target of a Mr. Big operation.

Once a case and suspect have been identified, an operational plan is developed and vetted.

The RCMP pioneered Mr. Big and conduct most of the Mr. Big operations in Canada, since smaller police departments lack the resources and expertise. In the early days of the technique, the RCMP classified Mr. Big as a minor undercover homicide technique. The approval process was quick and informal. As Mr. Big operations have become longer, more expensive, and subjected to increased levels of scrutiny, the approval processes have become formalized and rigorous. A Mr. Big operation will consume hundreds of hours of police officer time and the expenditures of tens (sometimes hundreds) of thousands of dollars. Some operations have the potential to create significant public controversy. RCMP leaders are bureaucrats, so Mr. Big is now approached with bureaucratic caution. The grounds for suspicion must be laid out. A social and psychological profile of the suspect must be provided. The mental health and capacity of the suspect is considered. The suspect must "be of operating mind" when engaging with people before being targeted. Finally, the impact of a possible disclosure on the overall case is evaluated. At one time, this does not appear to have been given much attention, since a videotaped disclosure of the suspect proclaiming guilt was "good enough" for conviction. Today, a disclosure that cannot be verified by other evidence is not likely to be admissible in court, thereby making the whole exercise pointless. Before the RCMP dispatch Mr. Big, a detailed operational plan must be developed. This includes the general plan for the operation, budget, and staffing requirements. The proposal goes up the chain of command. Prior to 2012, Mr. Big operations were approved at a divisional level. Since that time, approval from national headquarters must be secured as well.

From time to time a local police force will undertake a Mr. Big without the involvement of the RCMP. Some, like the Calgary Police Service, appear to select cases appropriately and conduct well-planned operations. Other police forces function a bit more like Inspector Clouseau and have run into difficulties.

"THE BUMP": MAKING CONTACT

Once the police know or believe a serious crime has been committed, have identified a suspect, have determined that the suspect might be susceptible to Mr. Big, and have exhausted other investigative methods, they can call on Mr. Big. They immediately face a major problem. How can they engage with the suspect in a way that builds ongoing interaction? It is not easy. Most people are suspicious of and reserved towards strangers. People who have been the focus of a police homicide investigation tend to be even more suspicious and reserved than most. It is an experience that creates paranoia regardless of guilt or innocence.

The police term making contact with the suspect for a Mr. Big operation "the bump." They begin with surveillance of the suspect. From the information obtained, a script is written and officers are recruited as actors. When all is ready, the suspect is bumped.

In the chapters describing the good, the bad, and the murky of Mr. Big cases, we've seen three of the most common bump techniques. Michael Bridges was snared with the contest winner bump. The suspect wins a contest to go to an event. This being Canada, NHL hockey games are the favourite. He meets another friendly winner — who just happens to be an undercover officer. Kyle Unger was hooked by our human desire to be helpful. He fell for the "my vehicle broke down, could you help me" bump. The case of Gordon Hathway, who murdered his landlord in Saskatoon, illustrates a variation on the broken vehicle bump. The undercover officer asking for help was good-looking and female. This increased the odds of the target being inclined to help. Hathway then met this officer's "boyfriend," who completed the bump. Nelson Hart was tricked by the common "help me find my sister" bump. It's amazing what a combination of a request for a favour and a promise of some money can do.

We've already seen a fourth common bump technique. Marven

McIntyre, accused of killing Sister Florine Brun, fell for the jail cellmate bump. In his case, he met the undercover officer while under arrest for the case being investigated. In a variation, the police take advantage of the disorderly lives of many Mr. Big targets. For example, Christina Asp was arrested for an unrelated parole violation so that she could meet an undercover officer.

While variations on the contest winner, lost sister, broken vehicle, and jail cellmate bumps are the most popular with police, bumps can be more elaborate.

In the introduction, we learned about the beating death of six-year-old Meika Jordan. After her death, her father and his girlfriend were not going out much; people suspected of beating a child to death find their social life becomes restricted. This presents bumping challenges. Surveillance revealed that Spencer Jordan and Marie Magoon were looking for a house to rent. They saw an ad for a great deal on the perfect house. It was owned by the police and happened to be still unrented. It was too good a deal to pass up, even though the landlord kept the garage for storage. The landlord spent quite a bit of time doing mysterious things in the garage. Jordan and Magoon were curious. A successful bump was made.

The bump can also arise from the legitimate economic activity of the suspect. Decades after caving in a man's head with a baseball bat and throwing him in the river, Thomas Griffin was making his living as a house painter. An undercover officer hired him to paint her house. In another case, David Lowe worked as a car salesperson after murdering his business partner. The undercover officer posed as a chatty but mysterious car buyer. In two cases, real estate was the key to the bump. Jason Klaus inherited his parents' farm after they were shot and incinerated in their home. An undercover officer happened to be looking for a farmyard just like his to use for storage. Alan Steele was a realtor whose cocaine addiction almost completely destroyed his practice and caused him to kill a friend. The undercover officer posed as a mysterious client wanting to buy houses.

Sometimes the bump can be indirect. The police believed that Penny Boudreau strangled her twelve-year-old daughter, fabricated a sexual assault, and dumped her body in a ditch. The undercover officer became friends with Boudreau's boyfriend and was, in due course, introduced to his target. Sometimes the bump is repeated over and over. In 2003, the RCMP were trying to investigate a man named Clarence Smith for a homicide committed eleven years earlier. Clarence did not lead the most sedentary life. The undercover officer would make contact and start developing the relationship. Clarence would move; contact would be broken; a new bump would be organized. The undercover officer became like Bill Murray's character in the movie *Groundhog Day*: trapped in an endless cycle of "accidental" meetings with Clarence.

Two bumps stand out for their audacity.

In 2000, Robert Noyes was in jail. He decided to change his ways and offered to provide information on seven homicides. He confessed and pleaded guilty to second-degree murder for all seven. Noyes told police that he had partners and became an RCMP informant. He was temporarily released from prison to bump his former partners.

The bump on David Langlet was similar. In 2000, Langlet and a friend shot a drug dealer after disputes about turf and reliability. Nine years later, Langlet's friend found himself owing a lot of money to some very tough drug dealers. As a judge noted, he was "very motivated to look for a way out of his criminal lifestyle." The friend walked into a police station to negotiate a deal. He confessed to a long list of criminal offences, including the murder. He agreed to assist police in their investigations of the homicide. In exchange, the friend was allowed to plead guilty to all his crimes and accept a cumulative sentence of two years less a day. He also negotiated a payment of $100,000 and a salary of $4,000 per month while working as an informant. Langlet's friend had a serious motivation to do a good job. If the police caught him in a lie or if he failed to do what the police asked, the deal was off. After this deal was negotiated, Langlet's old friend travelled back to Vancouver. He tracked Langlet down through an ex-girlfriend. Langlet was overjoyed to hear from his old buddy and catch up on all the news. They met at a restaurant for supper. The old friend told Langlet about his activities over the past decade. He left out a few bits. The bump was made.

"SCENARIOS": GETTING READY TO MEET MR. BIG

Once a suspect has been successfully bumped, the Mr. Big operation begins in earnest. As was noted earlier, it is useful to think of Mr. Big in two ways. "Mr. Big" can refer to the entire operation or an individual. If a movie was made about a Mr. Big operation, both the movie and the starring role would have the same name, but there would be many others in the cast.

An RCMP Mr. Big operation has a lot of people involved. There is a "control" officer who remains invisible to the suspect and serves as the scriptwriter, director, and producer of the drama being created. Contacts with the suspect are called "scenarios." Each is planned in advance and reviewed after completion. The lead actors are one or two officers who maintain primary contact with the suspect. Their job is to build a relationship and groom the suspect for a disclosure. They are joined by other undercover officers in "cameo" roles. These roles range from toughs pretending to be mob enforcers to stunt people getting beat up in staged violence. Mr. Big, the person, appears at the end of the drama. He is always a highly skilled and experienced interrogator who obtains the detailed videotaped disclosure that will be watched by the judge and jury. Mr. Big is the equivalent of the big-name star playing a major but limited role in a movie. He gets the glory and is featured in the trailer, but the heavy lifting is done by the officer-actors who have prepared the suspect for the ultimate scene.

The first scenarios following the bump allow an undercover officer to build a relationship with the suspect. Predator and prey become friends. It is generally an unequal friendship. There's no way to put this politely: most Mr. Big suspects have an element of "loser" about them. There have been exceptions, but most of them are not materially or socially successful people. But, like everyone else, they have aspirations. They want to advance in the world. The undercover officer becomes a role model for the suspect's aspirational goals. The officer drives a nicer car. He eats in nicer restaurants. He appears to travel a lot and stays in hotels. He always has a big wad of cash. The officer usually picks up the tab when taking the suspect to a restaurant or strip club. The undercover officer is friendly and complimentary to the suspect, but the relationship is one of superior to lesser, leader to follower, guru to acolyte. The bonding exercise creates a relationship in which the suspect wants to be just like (he thinks) the undercover officer is.

As the relationship develops, the officer remains mysterious about the source of his prosperity. Just as curiosity kills the cat, it also traps the suspect, who begins to fill in answers himself as the officer asks the suspect to perform small errands. These activities, at first, usually appear legal but are too high-paying. The pay becomes higher as the activities became more suspicious. When someone is paid a hundred dollars to transport a sealed package and abandon it in a specified location at a specified time, it must mean there is something fishy and illegal going on.

The psychological key to transitioning from setting up an admiring friendship to creating a desire to join a criminal gang is allowing potential suspects to reach their own conclusions. We've seen how Spencer Jordan and Marie Magoon rented a house and became sociable with the landlord, who was spending a lot of time in the garage. Other people visited the garage. They were all mysterious. Jordan and Magoon watched the comings and goings. They speculated. Just over a century ago, the German sociologist Georg Simmel explained that possession of a secret gives the possessor power. The content of the secret is irrelevant. Being denied access to the secret creates a desire to know and gives the secret-holder power over the secret-seeker. This insight was employed by the undercover officer/landlord. Spencer and Magoon started asking about what was happening in the garage. The officer remained secretive and mysterious. Spencer and Magoon concluded something illegal was going on. The undercover officer told them that they were as smart as Sherlock Holmes. Any suspicions Spencer and Magoon might have had about their landlord being a police officer were neutralized, since they were not asked to believe anything except in their own brilliance.

The transition from friendship to criminal relationship is a key moment in a Mr. Big operation. About a quarter of suspects walk away from the relationship at this point, either because they don't want to become involved with criminal activity or because they suspect their new friend is an undercover police officer.

As the operation creates an aura of criminality, the undercover officers face a problem. To convince the suspect they are criminals, they have to act, well, like criminals. They drink. They swear. They respond to misogynist or racist comments with ones that are even more misogynist or racist. They take the suspect to strip clubs instead of to church. When a suspect forgets his package of cocaine in the officer's car, it is returned. Defence lawyers argue that providing a jury with details of the accused's participation in a Mr. Big operation is inherently prejudicial because it documents them doing unsavoury acts. The undercover officers bear the same burden. For example, because they make misogynist or racist comments in order to establish trust with a suspect, under cross-examination they are often accused of being misogynist or racist. The actor who shot John Wayne in a movie destroyed his acting career because moviegoers saw him as the man who killed their hero. Undercover officers playing a role face a similar hazard to their reputation.

Public safety can be a concern. The officer has to have a drink with the suspect but can't drive while impaired or knowingly allow the suspect to do so. The extent of these tricky ethical questions is highlighted by two controversial Mr. Big operations.

One of the most ethically controversial Mr. Big operations involved two suspects under the age of eighteen. If there is an underage suspect, the usual practice is to wait until the youth becomes an adult before starting the Mr. Big operation. In this case the Mr. Big operation was run while the youths were still underage. Complicating matters even more from a legal and ethical perspective was the fact that these youths were permanent wards of the Alberta Minister of Community and Social Services. Legally, the government was their parent, with a legal obligation to protect them from harm. At the same time, another arm of government — the RCMP — was launching an undercover operation aimed at throwing them in jail. These two Mr. Big operations stemmed from the same case. The two youths, then aged fourteen, escaped from a juvenile detention facility near Edmonton. They embarked on a spree of theft, vandalism, and mayhem culminating with their arrest after driving a stolen pickup truck a hundred kilometres an hour down Whyte Avenue in Edmonton while shooting pedestrians with a pellet gun. At the acreage from which the truck was stolen, two people were found dead. The two teens denied killing the people or seeing the bodies. There was no blood or other forensic material on their clothes or in the truck. It could not be established that they had a gun. After much internal debate, the RCMP launched Mr. Big operations against the two teenagers. This ethically complicated situation got worse. It was normal for undercover officers to have a drink with suspects. These two were underage. Buying them a beer was against the law. It got worse. The undercover officers learned one of the youths was having a sexual affair with a female staff member from a youth detention centre. She was a person in a position of authority. This made the youth the victim of a serious *Criminal Code* sexual offence, but stopping the sexual exploitation would blow the Mr. Big operation. It got even worse. The youth announced that he was going to murder the woman's husband. The undercover officers had to keep the Mr. Big operation going without allowing this man to be murdered. It was an ethical, legal, and moral quagmire.

Another case involving serious legal and ethical challenges came in the operation directed at David Langlet. As we saw earlier, he was bumped by his old friend and criminal partner. The friend not only bumped Langlet but also was employed by the RCMP as one of the two primary undercover operatives building a relationship with Langlet. This had potential to blow up in the faces of the RCMP. One night it almost did. Langlet and the undercover operative were dispatched in an RCMP-owned van to pick up a crate. They both believed it contained firearms being smuggled into Canada. While running this errand, the pair bought a case of beer and reminisced about the good old days. They were having a good time. Too good. The undercover operative began driving erratically at high speeds. He inadvertently shook off the appalled RCMP officers who were following in a surveillance vehicle. He eventually hit a roundabout at high speed and caused extensive damage to the van. The case manager was, according to the judge who later reviewed the operation, "very concerned about the night's events, including that [the undercover officer] was driving while his ability was impaired and had damaged the van. At that point his continued involvement in the investigation was in jeopardy." The concern was understandable. If another vehicle had been hit instead of a traffic roundabout, the consequences for everyone involved would have been unpleasant.

Once the suspect makes the transition into activities believed to be criminal, scenarios are created to achieve specific goals. The intent of these are to build trust, to psychologically prepare the suspect for disclosure, and to address anticipated objections from defence lawyers. When the activities are described in media reports of a trial, some seem odd, if not outright bizarre, but these strange-sounding scenarios have specific objectives.

We'll begin by looking at an example of a scenario designed to forestall a defence lawyer's attacks on the Mr. Big disclosure. The RCMP believed Robert Balbar had smashed his girlfriend's head in with a blunt instrument, transported her body to the nearest river, and thrown her in. Her battered, bloated, and decomposed body was found about a week after her disappearance. Balbar had received a brain injury in the past. He was living on a disability pension supplemented by low-level drug dealing. Because of the brain injury, scenarios were designed as tests of Balbar's cognitive and reasoning capacity. The undercover officer created "follow the clues" treasure hunts in which Balbar had to read and follow directions, make decisions, and engage in sequential logic. At the trial, the defence lawyer produced two psychologists who testified that Balbar's IQ was so low that he was not capable of exercising his own judgment when talking to Mr. Big. The prosecutor successfully countered by pointing to the practical, in-the-field tests of intelligence and cognition. Nobody was claiming that Balbar was the sharpest knife in the drawer, but if he was as intellectually challenged as the psychologists claimed, it would have been impossible for him to successfully complete the assigned tasks.

Some scenarios involve staged violence. The suspect watches the undercover officers intimidate and slap around other police officers playing the role of people who have committed some transgression. Theatrical props such as blood-coloured dye capsules make the violence seem real. Sometimes the staged violence goes further.

Gordon Hathway was asked to participate in the collection of money owed as a result of a drug deal. While Hathway served as a lookout, a female RCMP officer playing the role of the debtor's girlfriend was threatened, bound with duct tape, gagged, and locked in a horse trailer until her boyfriend arrived with the money. When the officer playing the part of the debtor showed up to buy back his girlfriend with the money owing, he was pistol-whipped.

Jason Dix thought he saw and participated in a homicide. He had been recruited to serve as a lookout while the undercover officer entered a mobile home in the tiny British Columbia hamlet of Yahk. The officer was carrying a shotgun. In what a judge later described as the "Whack at Yahk," Jason heard shots. He saw the undercover officer emerge from the trailer, turn around, and fire more shots inside. The officer threw the shotgun into the bush and jumped into the car with a suggestion they leave quickly. Jason was told that the person owing money had shot at the officer. The recalcitrant debtor, Jason was assured, was now dead.

When these cases come to court, the accused almost always argue this staged violence caused them to make their disclosure to Mr. Big out of fear. The prosecution counters with testimony or video about the behaviour of the accused. Most often, they seem eager rather than fearful. For example, Jean Ann James was seventy when she participated in a staged-violence scenario. She responded by assuring the undercover officer that she was an "A to Z girl." Hathway's response to the staged kidnapping and pistol-whipping was to complain that he had not been given a gun. Others go further. When Balbar was asked to serve as a lookout at a potentially violent debt-collection scenario, he showed up with a replica handgun and a can of bear spray. The undercover officers had to disarm him in order to proceed with the scenario safely. This demonstration of initiative and enthusiasm by a suspect is not unusual. When Thomas McDonald participated in a debt-collection scenario, he made helpful suggestions to the undercover officers, including cutting off the debtor's fingers, hanging a castrating tool on his testicles, turning a pit bull loose on the debtor, and leaving him hog-tied to a chair for three days. The next day, he joked about the incident in a wiretapped telephone conversation to his brother. In court, McDonald claimed his disclosure to Mr. Big came because he was terrified by the undercover officers.

The violent scenarios are not designed to intimidate the suspect into making a disclosure. They are designed to achieve two very different goals.

The first is to test the suspect's views about violence. If the suspect expresses horror about the violence and severs his relationship with the undercover officer, he's less likely to be a murderer. Much time and effort can be saved.

The second reason is psychological. Mr. Big suspects understand that other people might recoil from a disclosure of murder. The scenarios involving staged violence give the suspect moral permission to disclose. Mr. Big case managers believe people respond best to empirical evidence. If the suspect is to be convinced that the fictional crime organization will not pass moral judgment on their homicidal acts, they must be shown rather than told.

The violent scenarios are not the only ones in which the suspect is shown rather than told. The wealth of the criminal organization is tangibly demonstrated. In almost every Mr. Big operation, the suspect sees large amounts of cash changing hands. He doesn't just see the money. He is asked to count it. The implied promise of future wealth becomes real during the act of caressing hundred-dollar bills. The exercise also serves as a cognitive test and an opportunity to praise the suspect for his abilities. The undercover officer admires the suspect's ability to count.

Because defence lawyers argued disclosures were the result of fear inspired by the violent scenarios, Mr. Big case officers ensured the staged violence was always directed at people who were not members of the fictional criminal gang. Outsiders had reason to be fearful, insiders did not. By the time of the Mr. Big operation on Michael Bridges, this distinction was explicit. Bridges got to know an officer posing as another prospective gang member. This officer was portrayed as having been caught lying to Mr. Big. His only penalty was to be kicked out of the gang and told to go away. Not beaten. Not murdered. Just exiled.

Over time, scenarios to demonstrate the lack of violent consequences because of a failure to disclose have become more elaborate. Jaycee Mildenberger was invited to a convivial "going-away" party for a gang member who had been asked to leave. In a Mr. Big operation run by the Ontario Provincial Police, Roy Niemi was actually kicked out of the fictional crime gang. A year later, he "accidentally" ran into the undercover officer who had posed as his earlier sponsor. This officer told Niemi that he too had been kicked out, for unrelated reasons. Together they contacted Mr. Big and begged for a return to his good graces. Niemi got a life sentence after telling Mr. Big that he'd strangled a young woman and slashed her naked body to make police believe it was a sexual assault. His claim to have disclosed because of fear was countered by the empirical evidence that he'd once suffered no violence after he'd kept his mouth shut.

Embedded into the scenarios are lectures, lessons, and demonstrations about telling the truth and the need for honesty within the gang. Suspects are told repeatedly that Mr. Big does not care what a gang member did in the past. Mistakes and problems are forgiven and can be fixed. The one thing Mr. Big cannot tolerate is dishonesty. Before the suspect meets Mr. Big, he is told repeatedly that the price of lying to the boss is expulsion from the group. Mr. Big's ability to detect lies and his sources of information are portrayed as uncanny. Lie and you will be caught and expelled. Tell the truth and you will be accepted and protected. This mantra is constantly invoked. It generates detailed, accurate disclosures and serves as protection from defence lawyer challenges in court after the suspect, as he almost always does, recants the disclosure once he realizes whom he made it to.

When the suspect is judged ready to make a disclosure (or when the operation has simply gone on "long enough"), another type of scenario becomes key. The suspect is shown that Mr. Big has the power to "fix" people's problems. This starts with the primary undercover officer making general comments about how much he owes Mr. Big for getting him out of serious legal trouble in the past. He is then shown that Mr. Big can solve legal problems and has access to police records and inside information. Examples of concrete problem-solving are demonstrated.

In Chapter 2, we saw how Michael Bridges was shown what appeared to be the retroactive creation of an ironclad alibi for someone who needed it. Sometimes the opportunities to demonstrate Mr. Big's problem-solving abilities arise spontaneously. For example, Gordon Hathway was told to drive a car carrying an undisclosed, but presumably illegal, cargo from the Tsawwassen ferry terminal near Vancouver to Kelowna. The undercover officer told Hathway to stay straight and sober. Hathway agreed. He promptly interrupted his journey to buy a bottle of vodka. Just outside of Kelowna, he rear-ended a truck. He attempted to flee the scene but was apprehended. The attending police officer called an ambulance. Hathway (falsely) told the officer that he had hepatitis, so she did not go close enough to smell the alcohol on his breath. When the ambulance reached the hospital, Hathway fled. He called the undercover officer to break the bad news. Hathway was chastised mildly for his incompetence but praised for his honesty. The Mr. Big case officer scraped the omelette back into the eggshell. The RCMP reimbursed British Columbia's publicly owned insurance company, ICBC, the $20,000 cost of the accident. Hathway was told that Mr. Big had fixed the problem because Hathway had been honest. He was convinced Mr. Big could fix other problems . . . such as homicide.

THE NUDGE: MOVING TOWARDS DISCLOSURE

When the Mr. Big operation has gained the trust of the suspect and made him eager to join the criminal gang, he is nudged towards disclosure. This is a key transitional moment. We've seen how the undercover officers have to overcome the suspect's natural suspicion and paranoia to begin the operation. This paranoia is even more intense when it comes to disclosure. If the Mr. Big suspect is guilty — and most are — they have a secret that can put them into prison for a very long time. For many, revelation means dying in prison.

Secrets are hard to keep. They build up inside, but sharing some secrets has very painful consequences. The ancient Greeks had a myth about a barber with a secret. The barber had the honour of cutting the king's hair. This blessing turned into a burden after Apollo declared the king to be an ass and gave him donkey ears. The king, who was vain as most kings are, covered his shameful ears with a turban. The only person who knew the truth was the barber, who was promised a painful death if the secret got out. He resolved his need to speak about the secret by digging a hole in the bank of a river. He whispered his secret — "the king has the ears of an ass" — into the hole. He filled in the hole. The roots of the reeds heard the secret. They told the rest of the plant. The reeds told other plants. The birds and insects heard the plants gossiping. Pretty soon everybody knew that the king had donkey's ears, and the barber's life came to a premature and painful end.

Most Mr. Big suspects have probably never heard the story of the unfortunate barber, but they understand that disclosure is intrinsically dangerous. They have been very good at keeping their mouth shut. This was why Mr. Big has become necessary. Murdering blabbermouths have a more direct pathway to prison, but these suspects still felt pressure to tell someone. Some of the killers felt remorse. Some felt pride. Some just wanted the respect of the undercover officer. The elaborate scenarios create both a desire and a willingness to share their secret, but they often need a nudge to disclose.

In some cases, a nudge is not needed. The suspect raises the issue spontaneously. This usually happens sequentially, with the first step being mentioning they knew someone who had been murdered. The next step is telling the undercover officer that they were a suspect, followed by hints of culpability. Then come more direct statements that they have killed someone. Sometimes the suspect makes a general disclosure of guilt about the case Mr. Big was investigating. Some suspects are cagier. It's not uncommon for Mr. Big suspects to first disclose that they have killed someone who is in fact still alive, was murdered by someone else, or who never existed in the first place. This false disclosure is a test. If the officer reacts in a police-like fashion, or even expresses displeasure, the suspect has not put himself at risk. When this happens, the undercover officers respond to these disclosures while the case officers contact the relevant police forces for follow-up. Sometimes these unexpected disclosures are true. Brian Casement was a suspect in the death of a street person in Vernon, British Columbia. Casement casually mentioned that he had once killed someone — in Saskatoon, Saskatchewan. Casement described how he raped and strangled a young Indigenous woman in Saskatoon. He said he hid her body so successfully that it had never been found. Saskatoon police confirmed that a woman matching Casement's description had disappeared at the right time. The Mr. Big operation branched out. Casement eventually showed Mr. Big where he had hidden the woman's body and was convicted of first-degree murder. Ironically, he never disclosed responsibility for the death that he was originally being investigated for and was cleared of suspicion for that death.

Usually, however, a nudge towards disclosure is needed. Sometimes this is a soft nudge. Najib Amin was nudged into talking about killing a woman when the undercover officer "happened to" drive by the apartment building where he suffocated his victim. Cleophas Decoine-Zuniga began his disclosure after police put up posters describing the stabbing he was suspected of committing and asking for information.

Sometimes the nudges are less subtle.

We've already met Spencer Jordan and Marie Magoon, who "disciplined" Jordan's six-year-old daughter to death. Spencer was in Vancouver with the undercover officer when Magoon telephoned in a panic. The police had just come by their house looking for Jordan, claiming to have an arrest warrant for murdering his daughter. This was a lie — or at least premature. The nudge was successful in causing Jordan and Magoon to disclose their respective roles.

Fellow Calgarian Allan Shyback was in Winnipeg with the undercover officer. He received a call from the Calgary Police Service telling him that a search warrant for his home was about to be served. Since Shyback's wife was buried in the basement, he became distraught and explained his dilemma to the sympathetic undercover officer.

Sometimes a nudge by police does not seem so official. While his wife was away visiting family, Andrew Keene invited a female friend to his apartment for some drinks. The visit didn't go well. Keene strangled his friend, dismembered her, and buried pieces of her body in different places. Once Keene had been successfully bumped and prepared for disclosure, he was nudged while attending a hockey game with the undercover officer. Another police officer who conducted the initial investigation "accidentally" ran into the pair. The officer pretended to be drunk. He confronted Keene and said, "I know you killed Alexandra Flanagan." After this encounter, the undercover officer demanded to know what the exchange had been about. Keene disclosed that he was a suspect in a murder investigation and eventually showed Mr. Big where he had hidden Alexandra's torso. He was convicted of second-degree murder.

Jaycee Mildenberger also fell for a nudge by a known police officer pretending to be impaired. In this case, the nudge was made in a restaurant. The "off-duty" RCMP officer who had initially questioned Mildenberger "drunkenly" promised imminent arrest.

The "drunken investigating officer" nudge has been effective but works best when the suspect has a stable residence in a small town or city. If he has moved or is living in a big city, a "chance" encounter with a known and feared investigating officer lacks plausibility. Mr. Big teams have developed a versatile variation of this kind of nudge. It can be called the "traffic stop" nudge. It happens when the suspect and the undercover officer are driving somewhere. They are pulled over for a traffic violation. The traffic enforcement officer does a "routine" identification check and tells the suspect the police computer database shows him as the target in an active murder investigation. After the traffic cop leaves, the undercover officer demands an explanation. The suspect has been successfully nudged towards disclosure and prison.

Sometimes the nudge can appeal to emotions other than fear of getting caught. Michael Kelly shot his common-law wife in the head and dumped her body in the woods. Four years later, land surveyors found her remains. Kelly was the prime suspect. Mr. Big was considered, but Kelly did not seem to be a likely prospect for membership in a criminal gang, so police got innovative. An officer posing as an insurance adjuster called to tell Kelly that his late wife had an insurance policy for $3,000. The adjuster showed up with the money and a release form. Just as Kelly was about to sign, the adjuster pretended to notice that the wording on the release applied to all policies. He told Kelly not to sign. He would investigate. A few weeks later, the adjuster reported that the insurance company was trying to stiff Kelly out of a $571,000 policy. Payment had been withheld because of Kelly's status as a suspect, but the duplicitous insurance company was trying to trick Kelly into signing a release. The undercover officer claimed he had a friend that could clear Kelly of suspicion in order to get the policy paid out. It was an effective nudge. The process of disclosure began. After Kelly was arrested, he told the police, "I thought I smelled a rat a long time ago, but I let my greed get the best of me."

An appeal to greed as a nudge is usually created as a supplement to the suspect's lingering fear of getting caught by the police.

Most people who become the subject of a Mr. Big operation are not really long-term thinkers. Immediate gratification is more powerful than long-term promise; in other words, short-term greed trumps long-term greed. We've seen how Nelson Hart was led to believe that there was the potential of a big payday in the future. This is a common component of the nudge towards disclosure. Usually the nature of the impending big job is left opaque since the suspect's imagination fills in convincing details. On other occasions, the job is explicit. David Langlet was offered $12,500 to help with a contract killing. He raised his glass and said, "Fuck, I can get a nice place now." His new residence turned out to be the Kent maximum security prison. It wasn't really that nice. Five months after his arrival, Langlet was found dead in his cell.

Most nudges have two components. They give immediacy both to the fear of getting caught for their murder and to the promise of financial gain that comes with full membership in the criminal gang. A third appeal can also be effective. Pride. The undercover officer preparing David Lowe for disclosure took him on a road trip from Vancouver to Edmonton. They went to a fancy restaurant where the undercover agent had a long, convivial meal with other undercover officers playing the role of senior gang members while Lowe was exiled to the bar to wait as his superiors enjoyed their meal. Lowe was bitter about not being allowed to join the dinner. The undercover officer mocked Lowe's presumption, saying the people at the supper were "serious" while Lowe was "just a car salesman." Lowe protested that he too was "serious" because he had once "whacked" a guy. Pride is one of the seven deadly sins. It can be effective as a nudge.

MEETING MR. BIG

Occasionally the subject of a Mr. Big operation does not need to meet Mr. Big in person. We've seen how Michael Bridges rehearsed his disclosure in front of a hidden video camera. John Ethier made an even more dramatic shortcut to the standard script. In 1981, Ethier had a drunken quarrel with his girlfriend and hit her over the head with a hammer twelve times. He left the apartment, sobered up a bit, established an alibi of sorts, returned home, and reported a horrific discovery to police. Nineteen years later, the RCMP sent in Mr. Big. The relationship with an undercover officer was established. This activated feelings of guilt, so he walked into the nearest police station and demanded to speak to an officer to confess to a murder. The police thought he was a nut and told him to go away. Ethier persisted. Eventually a detective heard his confession and started to follow up. He was startled to learn that Ethier was the target of a Mr. Big operation.

Bridges and Ethier were exceptional. Most Mr. Big operations culminate in a meeting with the person of Mr. Big. The suspect has been bumped, groomed, and nudged. Often, he has given partial disclosures to the undercover officer grooming him. Sometimes these were detailed but, given the nature of working undercover, they were not recorded on audio or video. The officer's testimony can be presented in court but is not as compelling for a jury as a video showing the suspect disclosing in detail. The unrecorded disclosure can be denied; the videotaped one cannot be. The videotaped disclosure usually provides a strong rebuttal to claims that the disclosure was coerced or was the product of intimidation. In these candid camera moments, the suspect does not look fearful or intimidated. He usually looks cheerful and happy. After all, as far as he knows, his disclosure will both gain him entry into the criminal gang and get the police off his back forever. It is enough to bring a smile to any murderer's face.

Much preparation goes into the ultimate session with Mr. Big. By this time, the undercover officer has established a trust relationship with the suspect. There have been numerous lectures and lessons about the importance of always being honest with Mr. Big.

Sometimes the suspect has met Mr. Big in person a few times, but often it is their first meeting. Either way, the suspect is like an inhabitant of the Land of Oz. Mr. Big is the Wizard: powerful, all-knowing, mysterious, and majestic. The difference is that there is a camera behind the curtain.

The session usually takes place in a hotel room. Hidden cameras and microphones have to be installed. Other rooms have been rented to hold the equipment, technical staff, and sometimes arresting officers. Legal preparations have been made. In order to clandestinely record the discussion, the police have obtained a judicial warrant. Great care and attention to legal niceties must be taken. When Peter Fliss's case went to trial, the judge ruled the video of his disclosure to Mr. Big was inadmissible because, in his opinion, the application for the warrant had not contained enough detailed information. The police had more information that they could have provided, but it had not been asked for. This ruling complicated Fliss's journey to prison. A relatively straightforward case resulted in a four-year journey through appellate courts, culminating with the Supreme Court of Canada upholding Fliss's conviction.

The RCMP has experimented with this ultimate session with Mr. Big. In the early days of the technique, threats were sometimes used. Two cases where the people were innocent point to the problems of this approach.

Clayton Mentuck had been arrested and charged for the murder of Amanda Cook. There was no real evidence. After the charges were stayed, Clayton was targeted by a Mr. Big operation. At the ultimate meeting, Mr. Big hinted Clayton would be killed if he did not disclose guilt. Clayton refused, so Mr. Big upped the ante. Not only would Clayton's own life be in danger, but the undercover officer grooming him would be in danger. Clayton began to waver. Mr. Big then promised disclosure would allow Clayton to sue the police for a million dollars. Clayton gave a very murky, hesitant disclosure.

The trial judge was unimpressed, saying that "the police must be aware that as the level of inducement increases, the risk of receiving a confession to an offence which one did not commit increases, and the reliability of the confession diminishes correspondingly. In this case, in my view, the level of inducement was overpowering."

We saw earlier how Jason Dix believed he'd witnessed the undercover officer kill someone at the "Whack at Yahk." He met Mr. Big a short time later. Mr. Big said Jason now "had something" on a member of the criminal gang. As a result, the gang needed to "have something" on him as protection from betrayal. Despite the intimidating situation, Jason refused to disclose his involvement in the murders he was suspected of. That ended the Mr. Big operation. Jason and Mr. Big went their respective ways. The "we need something to hold over you" approach was flawed. It is based on a negative appeal and provides no incentive to provide detail. Even if threats generate a disclosure, a defence lawyer can plausibly argue the disclosure was a lie generated by fear and intimidation. After all, who wouldn't be a little worried when someone you believed to be the ruthless leader of a violent criminal gang was hinting that you must talk or die?

Another flawed approach to getting a disclosure was the "impress us" approach: "Convince us that you are really cool and tough." This approach was used on Cody Bates. He was one of three people who set out to scare a drug dealer away from their turf while robbing him. The plan went wrong when the hammer on a shotgun caught on a sleeve — not Bates's sleeve. The unfortunate drug dealer lost his head, or at least most of it. Bates met Mr. Big and was encouraged to demonstrate his toughness. He lied by telling Mr. Big that he had been the actual shooter and that he shot intentionally. He portrayed himself as a cool, calculating murderer rather than the scared accomplice of a bumbling, incompetent shotgun-holding robber. If Bates's disclosure to Mr. Big had been accepted at face value, he would have been convicted of first-degree murder and sentenced to life in prison with no chance of parole for twenty-five years. As it was, his lawyer was able to convince the prosecutor the disclosure was exaggerated. Bates pleaded guilty to manslaughter and received a sentence of eight years.

These intimidating or approval-seeking approaches to generating a disclosure have almost disappeared from Mr. Big operations. They were subject to challenge by defence lawyers and were not great at getting details. These older, crude approaches could often generate a guilty ruling by a jury — if the disclosure was seen by the jury. As Mr. Big disclosures were subjected to increased scrutiny, it became clear that something better was needed if Mr. Big disclosures were not to be ruled inadmissible.

The most effective, and therefore the most common, technique now used by Mr. Big to get a detailed, accurate, and unchallengeable disclosure can be called the "dying guy" approach. The suspect is told that there is a person — sometimes dying of cancer, sometimes already in prison serving a life sentence — willing to confess to the murder. The suspect is told that this person owes Mr. Big a favour or wants money for his family. The suspect is told that this confession will completely "clear" him of the crime. Not only will he never be charged or convicted, but also the police will stop all investigating. With the "heat" from being the target of police suspicion completely removed, the "cleaned" suspect will be welcomed into the gang. Added bonuses can include the elimination of insurance company recalcitrance about payment of life insurance policies and exoneration in the court of public opinion. The suspect is told that for this scheme to work, the person making the false confession must know every detail of the crime.

In some cases, the dying man is a kind of *deus ex machina* introduced by Mr. Big at the ultimate videotaped meeting. In other cases, the ground may have been prepared during the preparatory scenarios as the suspect meets a gang member described as having cancer. In a few cases, the suspect even visited the cancer patient in the hospital and saw him hooked up to tubes and monitors. When Mr. Big proposes that this individual will confess on the suspect's behalf, it seems very real.

The dying man gambit is remarkable in the detail it generates. Suspects show Mr. Big where bodies are buried. They stage video-taped re-enactments. They recover murder weapons and present them to the undercover officers. If there are accomplices, the suspect will approach them in order to obtain confirmation. They create the defence lawyer's worst nightmare. Because of the quality of the disclosures generated, the dying man gambit has become the industry standard for Mr. Big operations. Some version has been used in almost every recent Mr. Big operation.

When a Mr. Big operation strays from the "dying guy" script and reverts to intimidation, the courts express displeasure. Earlier in this chapter, we met Michel Laflamme. The police were forced to wait till Michel got out of prison for conspiring to murder his third wife before using Mr. Big to generate a disclosure about the murder of his first wife. During the preparatory scenarios, Michel saw a member of the gang being threatened with a handgun jammed in her mouth. Mr. Big said he would be compelled to "lose" both Michel and the undercover officer serving as his sponsor into the group if there was no disclosure. Michel had every reason to believe that neither he nor his friend would survive the day unless he made a satisfactory disclosure, so he said he'd stran-gled his first wife. He was convicted of first-degree murder, but the conviction was overturned by the Quebec Court of Appeal, which also imposed a stay on further proceedings. Outcomes such as this reinforce the tested and trusted "dying guy" approach.

THE FOLLOW-UP: CONFIRMING THE DISCLOSURE

In the early days of Mr. Big, disclosure was almost immediately followed by handcuffs. The video of the suspect saying "I did it" was good enough to obtain a conviction. This is no longer the case. This is an area where criminal defence lawyers have contributed to quality improvement in Mr. Big operations.

The simple fact of the matter is that people sometimes lie when telling Mr. Big that they are guilty of murder. Sometimes the suspect discloses a homicide not on the investigators' radar. Investigation often shows that these disclosures are fictitious. The fact that some Mr. Big suspects claim they've murdered someone who is still alive is conclusive proof that not every disclosure is true. For a disclosure to stand up in court — or even to be accepted as evidence in court — it must be verified. The disclosure must be compared with the known facts about the case. If there is congruence, the disclosure is deemed reliable. If the disclosure does not align with other evidence, it is treated as suspect at best.

Verification can be a challenge. Clarence Smith told Mr. Big he murdered an elderly man named Ray Alcock. Clarence also said he committed other murders. Some were people who were still alive, while other victims he named were never born. Clarence said he had once disposed of a body by cutting it open and filling the stomach with cement. He said he threw the weighted victim into a lake. Clarence claimed to be a hit man for a group of Indigenous elders and that he worked as a diamond mine consultant and a lawyer. None of this employment could be verified. He claimed to have been convicted for smuggling machine guns into Canada, but no record of this conviction was on file within the justice system. He claimed to have murdered a man twice — once by strangling and once by a staged drug overdose — and left him in a room at a specified hotel. No corpse had ever been found at that hotel by the cleaning staff. Clarence said his son had died at a specific hospital. No record of the death existed. He claimed he had blown up a paper mill as an environmental protest. Nobody working at the paper mill was aware it had ever been blown up. Clarence also said he could turn into a wolverine and could appear and disappear at will. While most of Clarence's disclosures were dismissed as fantasy, the police knew that Ray Alcock had been murdered, so he was charged. In acquitting him, the judge said, "I can only conclude it would be unsafe to convict under such circumstances. Of the many and extraordinary lies told by Mr. Smith, was he telling the truth in whole or in part about what happened at 1346 Cotton Drive? I simply cannot say from the evidence before me."

Clarence Smith presented an extreme case of the difficulties inherent in attempts to verify the details of disclosures. A disclosure does not need to be this extreme to be impossible. In Chapter 4, we saw the nature of the case made Nelson Hart's disclosure unverifiable. There were two versions of events on the table. The evidence fit either one equally well. Neither could be proven or disproven.

Sometimes the passage of time can create the same sort of problems. A disclosure had been obtained from Michel Laflamme through intimidation. This disclosure was also unverifiable. The passage of time decayed the evidence collected in the initial investigation to the point where there was, for all practical purposes, none available.

The gold standard for verification of a disclosure is the suspect leading the undercover officers to a body well enough hidden that it has not been discovered. In Chapter 2, we saw the result of Michael Bridges's revelation that he had buried Erin Chorney in another person's grave. It was tough to argue this knowledge had been gained in an innocent way — Bridges's lawyer didn't bother to try. In another case, Ryan Kam had suddenly disappeared. Franjo Perovic told Mr. Big that Ryan was killed in a drug deal rip-off. Perovic asked his victim to sit on a couch during the transaction. He did not draw attention to his partner hiding behind the couch with a hatchet. The murder was well planned. The killers bought a cheap carpet to catch the blood and a large sports bag to transport the body. A grave had been pre-dug in an isolated part of the forest. A few days after Ryan was buried, Perovic returned to the site to plant grass seeds over the grave. Perovic showed Mr. Big where Ryan was buried. Hardware store records documented the purchase of a hatchet, shovel, carpet, sports bag, and grass seed. Perovic told Mr. Big that he'd stolen Ryan's expensive watch and sold it to a friend. The friend confirmed making the purchase. The watch was recovered and entered in evidence at the trial. At his trial, Perovic claimed he had lied while making his disclosures to Mr. Big. He was convicted of first-degree murder.

Not every disclosure can be verified as well as the one made by Franjo Perovic. Not every body is hidden and not every murder is as well planned and organized. Ironically, a lack of planning and organization can make post-disclosure verification more difficult. Bodies are usually discovered before the Mr. Big disclosure, so the killer is not the only one who knows where it was concealed. In a spontaneous homicide, people use the tools and material at hand rather than leaving a verifiable record of purchases. The police are forced to use other means of verification.

The most important method of verifying Mr. Big disclosures is a comparison of the disclosure with the known facts. If a person tells Mr. Big that he shot the victim but the medical examiner reported death due to strangulation, the disclosure will not be of much use in court. Indeed, a discrepancy this large would likely lead the police to conclude that the disclosure was bogus. Cases with discrepancies this significant don't generally get to court. More typically, the discrepancies are much smaller.

On January 19, 1975, two fourteen-year-old girls went missing from Richmond, British Columbia. Their bodies were found on February 6 in bushes near an electrical tower. They had been sexually assaulted. The two girls were about equal height and weight. One had been stabbed nine times, the other twenty-five times. Robert Bonisteel received a visit from Mr. Big in 2002. The long delay was because Bonisteel had been in prison for rapes in Saskatchewan and Manitoba committed a few weeks after the bodies of the two girls in British Columbia were found. Bonisteel was a prime suspect in the two deaths, but police needed to await developments in DNA technology and his availability to Mr. Big before proceeding. Bonisteel described the murders to Mr. Big. He said one girl was pudgy and one was thin. He said he'd stabbed one girl once and the other twice. The defence argued these discrepancies made the disclosures unreliable. The prosecution argued the passage of twenty-seven years made precise, clinical recall impossible. The jury and the appeal court judges sided with the prosecutor.

Another case of minor discrepancies between evidence and disclosure came in the case of Paul Felker. A young Indigenous woman was hitchhiking from Fort St. John, British Columbia, towards Regina, Saskatchewan. She did not get too far. Felker picked her up, had sex with her that may or may not have been coercive, slit her throat, and abandoned the young woman's body in the bush alongside the Alaska Highway. Felker became acquainted with Mr. Big in 2006. As in the case of Bonisteel's murders, developments in DNA technology made his connection with the victim more provable. Felker took Mr. Big to a spot on the highway and said he thought that he had abandoned his victim "around here." He was 1.6 km away from where the body had actually been discovered. It's 75 km from Fort St. John to Dawson Creek and most of this distance is through bush that all looks pretty much the same. Sixteen years had passed. The murder occurred in the summer, while Felker's nostalgic visit with Mr. Big came in January. The defence argued the discrepancy made the disclosure unreliable. The prosecution argued that he'd come pretty close, all things considered. There were other issues. Felker told Mr. Big that he'd strangled the woman before cutting her throat. The medical examiner had not found signs of strangulation. Felker had told Mr. Big he'd been wearing a condom and had not been able to perform sexually. His semen was found inside his victim. These were discrepancies, but the jury did not agree they were grounds for an acquittal.

Because accurate knowledge of details about the crime has become a measure of the reliability of a disclosure (or a post-arrest confession), the potential source of this knowledge becomes important.

Earlier in this chapter, we learned that one of Garry Handlen's two disclosures about similar rapes and murders was ruled as inadmissible. One reason for the rejection of the second disclosure was the passage of time had decayed evidence. There was an additional reason. The case was the subject of two television documentaries in which investigating officers revealed detailed evidence. Their motivation was doubtlessly good. They wanted to prod people with knowledge about the killing to come forward. Sometimes people possess knowledge that could be relevant, but in the absence of knowing about the case, the potential witness does not come forward. If you see a man running down the street, your observations about his appearance remain irrelevant until you learn that there was a shooting a block away a minute before you made your observation. Your new knowledge of the case causes you to pick up the phone and ask to speak to an investigator. It is impossible to predict what detail might trigger someone to come forward with information, so detail makes unsolved crime documentaries more effective at generating tips. There is a danger, though; the widespread sharing of information can undermine the reliability of a disclosure by giving the suspect details of the crime that can be repeated. Such was the case in the second Handlen disclosure. He had watched the documentaries. His lawyer was able to show that all the detailed information disclosed could have been obtained by watching television rather than from being the rapist and killer.

The justice system itself can also be the source of detailed knowledge about the crime and make verification of the reliability of a Mr. Big disclosure problematic.

Most of the people meeting Mr. Big have already been interrogated by the police. In many cases, their interrogation has been guided by an approach known as the Reid interrogation technique. This technique will be discussed in more detail later. It includes convincing the suspect the case against them is overwhelming. A guilty verdict is assured, so the suspect might as well confess. This process of convincing the suspect of the inevitability of conviction includes revealing evidence. The Reid interrogation technique is effective at generating confessions, but when the technique does not cause the suspect to confess, it can create future difficulties for Mr. Big. A suspect can provide details known to him because of what he's been told by police. If the suspect is guilty, the reliability of the disclosure is subject to challenge because this detailed information *could have* come from the interrogation. If the suspect is innocent, the detailed information *was* provided by the police during interrogation.

Similar problems arise from court proceedings. When Clayton Mentuck provided his reluctant disclosure to Mr. Big, all the details had been revealed during earlier court hearings.

The issue of what the suspect could legitimately know about the case becomes important in the verification process for Mr. Big disclosures. Paradoxically, public release of incorrect information can strengthen the reliability of a disclosure. In 1999, sixteen-year-old Darcy Drefko disappeared. Her body was discovered by hikers a month later. Darcy had been strangled. Her family wanted to create a small memorial where her body was found. The police directed them to a location four and a half kilometres from the actual site. The local newspaper published an article about the discovery of the body and the memorial. Pictures of the location were published. Everyone in the area except the hikers, the police, and the killer possessed incorrect information about where Darcy's body had been dumped. A year later, Patrick Fischer met Mr. Big and showed him the correct location. Fischer failed to convince a jury that his disclosure to Mr. Big was a lie.

When on trial, people who have disclosed details of the crime to Mr. Big will desperately attempt to establish other means by which they could have obtained their knowledge.

In the introduction, we learned about Clara Loski. The ninety-five-year-old woman suffocated when her false teeth became dislodged as she struggled to free herself after being tied up and abandoned by two robbers. Daniel Nette provided a detailed disclosure to Mr. Big. He even knew the type of knots used when Clara was tied up. In court, he claimed his disclosure was a lie. He told the jury he had arrived at Clara's house with larceny on his mind, only to discover the back door already broken open. He entered and discovered Clara already dead. This, he said, was how he knew all the details. The jury was skeptical.

Other defendants find a jury more sympathetic to their explanations. In a Toronto case, Liban Omar told Mr. Big how he'd robbed and killed a drug dealer. The crime was captured on security camera video, so police could confirm every detail. Liban's disclosure got every detail right. He even included details they did not know but verified afterwards. Liban told Mr. Big he'd disposed of his victim's ring and the murder weapon. This property disposal was confirmed. The prosecutor had every reason to believe Mr. Big had delivered a case on which to convict the suspect. He was wrong. Liban testified. He said he lied to Mr. Big, that he had been at home on the night of the killing. A friend — the actual killer, according to Liban — arrived. The friend told him about the killing and gave Liban the ring and the gun. That, said Liban, was how he knew the details of the crime and possessed the victim's property and the murder weapon. On cross-examination, the prosecutor wanted to know the identity of the friend, but Liban refused to tell, saying he did not want to be known as a snitch. The jury acquitted Liban of the murder charge. The judge convicted him of contempt of court, noting Liban had voluntarily taken the witness stand and sworn to tell the truth, the whole truth, and nothing but the truth. Liban had either lied or told less than the whole truth. One way or the other, Liban had broken his vow and either gotten away with murder or allowed someone else to do so. Liban was sentenced to four years on the contempt conviction. It was serious prison time but a lot less than life.

The need to verify Mr. Big disclosures has helped make "holdback evidence" a routine part of homicide investigations. These are unique facts about the crime that can be known only by the investigators and the killer — or, at the very least, someone who was present at the crime scene. In a properly investigated homicide investigation, the holdback evidence will be identified very early and kept a closely held secret. For example, sixteen-year-old Chelsea Acorn was murdered by Dustin Moir and his father, Jesse West. The father-and-son murder team buried Chelsea. By the time hikers stumbled across her body, the passage of time and the processes of decomposition made it very difficult to learn much from the crime scene, but the police noted that whoever had hidden Chelsea had encountered and cut many tree roots. When telling Mr. Big about the crime, Moir complained that roots made burial difficult and described exactly how they had cut them.

Holdback evidence is part of the case management in a homicide investigation. It is something that is established in advance. Mr. Big guides the discussion to allow the suspect to either show his knowledge or reveal his ignorance.

The disclosure will usually also generate leads for follow-up and confirmation. We've seen how mention of Franjo Perovic's purchase of grass seed and Liban Omar's statement that he'd sold the victim's ring were subsequently verified to confirm the reliability of the disclosure. There are four broad types of confirmatory follow-up: the location of forensic evidence; the documentation of preparations or cover-up activities; discussions with other people involved in the crime; and explanations as to why these kinds of evidence do not exist or appear anomalous. We'll examine each of these in turn.

We've already seen the most extreme kind of forensic confirmation of a Mr. Big disclosure. When Michael Bridges told Mr. Big that Erin Chorney was buried in someone else's grave, it provided a wealth of forensic follow-up. The yield is not usually that rich, but a disclosure can lead to forensic evidence compelling to a judge and jury. Dax Mack told Mr. Big he burned his former tenant in a firepit. The burning was not one hundred percent complete — and the shell casings from the cartridges used in the shooting were also found. Jaycee Mildenberger told Mr. Big that he'd burned his victim's clothing in the wood stove at the local snowmobile organization's clubhouse and hidden the murder weapon in the forest. The police found traces of clothing in the wood stove and a knife exactly where Mildenberger told them he'd hidden it. His defence lawyer was reduced to arguing that the clothing fragments could have belonged to someone else and there was no proof that the knife was the actual murder weapon.

The follow-up confirmation can also be in the form of supporting witness testimony rather than from physical objects. Robert Balbar told Mr. Big he'd hidden his girlfriend's body in a large picnic cooler and enlisted the unwitting aid of a taxi driver and a friend to transport the body in a two-step process to the river. Both these unwitting accomplices confirmed Balbar's disclosure.

Witness testimony can support disclosure of pre-murder preparations as well as post-murder cover-up. George Allgood shot his ex-wife and her new partner while they were sleeping in bed. He told Mr. Big whom he'd obtained the shotgun and the shells from. The person confirmed the story and later told the court he had been horrified when he learned he'd unwittingly supplied the murder weapon. Allgood claimed the weapon supplier was lying in order to gain revenge over a previous dispute. He had diffi-culty convincing the jury of this — perhaps because the police approached the witness in follow-up to the disclosure. If the witness was hostile to Allgood and intent on a devious revenge, it would be more likely he would have approached the police rather than the other way around.

Follow-up with witnesses is trickier for police when the disclosure identifies other people who were involved as criminal participants rather than as unwitting assistants. The people who helped Balbar transport his picnic cooler and the person who provided Allgood with the shotgun could be openly approached and asked. They had no skin in the game or reason to deceive the police. When asked what they knew, an immediate answer was supplied. There was no reason to doubt their credibility. It's more complicated when associates are involved in the crime or knowingly involved in the preparations or cover-up. Conspirators present both opportunities and challenges for the police as they verify the disclosure to Mr. Big.

In some cases, the suspect who made a disclosure to Mr. Big becomes the means to bump the other suspect. A new, very quick Mr. Big operation is run. The first suspect introduces his new friends to accomplices and convinces them to confirm his disclosure.

A teenage girl in British Columbia, for example, recruited her ex-boyfriend to help murder her current boyfriend. Another boy supplied a rifle "borrowed" from his father's gun case. After the trio became adults, police used a Mr. Big operation to get a disclosure from the girl. The undercover officers and the girl went around to each of the boys. They confirmed the girl's disclosure. In so doing, they made her conviction more certain as well as putting them-selves in prison. If the police can record a conversation between accomplices, the results can be even more useful.

The use of the initial Mr. Big target as a means to bump other people involved is particularly useful for contract killings.

David Knight was an Ontario entrepreneur having an affair in

Florida. Rather than divorce his wife, he hired a former employee, Graham MacDonald, to murder her. A Mr. Big operation was directed at MacDonald. After the disclosure to Mr. Big, the undercover officers helped MacDonald contact Knight to seek money needed to make a payment to a dying guy willing to confess to the murder. Knight agreed to contribute to the cover-up fund. It is possible the Mr. Big operation saved Knight's life, since MacDonald was planning to kill his old boss because he had not been paid for the murder. If Knight's life was indeed saved, he is now spending the remainder of it behind locked doors.

In other contract killings, the Mr. Big operation goes the other direction. The person hiring the killer makes the initial disclosure and then assists the undercover officers in getting confirmation from the person hired to do the killing. Iqbal Gill owned a blueberry farm in British Columbia's Fraser Valley. He took out a life insurance policy on his wife for $3 million and suggested they go for a walk. She was killed in a hit-and-run "accident." By the time Gill finished introducing Mr. Big to the participants in the scheme, a total of four people had implicated themselves. All pleaded guilty to charges appropriately reflecting their level of culpability.

In some cases, the person making the initial disclosure is not used as a way to bump other participants. Instead, the relationship with the Mr. Big team is put on a maintenance level while an entirely new Mr. Big operation is directed at identified colleagues.

Ronda Black's husband disappeared. She was told Mr. Big had a friend awaiting execution in Thailand who wanted a Canadian murder to confess to so he could be extradited to Canada and thereby avoid execution. Black disclosed that she killed her husband by stabbing him while he was asleep. She said she put him in the trunk of her car and, along with her year-old child, went to get assistance from a friend, Howard Steadman. She said Steadman had helped by cutting off her husband's hands and head before burying the rest of the body. The purpose of the dismemberment was to make identification difficult if the body was discovered. Black reported that the head had been buried separately after being shotgunned in order to eliminate the possibility of identification through dental records. The pair then parked the husband's car in a clearing beside a road in the mountains to make it appear as if he had gone hunting and gotten lost. Black told Mr. Big she did not know exactly where the pieces of her husband had been buried. It was dark and she was distraught. Between the time of the murder and the Mr. Big operation, relations between Black and Steadman had become strained, so police decided against using her to convince Steadman to show them the various places the body was buried. Instead they ran a separate Mr. Big operation on Steadman. He independently confirmed her story and helpfully showed where most of her husband could be found. Black went to jail for murder and Steadman for committing indignities on a body and being an accessory after the fact.

Earlier in the chapter, we saw how Dustin Moir's knowledge of how tree roots complicated grave digging enhanced the credibility of his disclosure about how he and his father, Jesse West, had murdered Chelsea Acorn. Strained relations between father and son caused the RCMP to run a sequential Mr. Big operation on West rather than using Moir for a bump. The two disclosures were consistent. After arrest, in the van taking them from the RCMP detachment to the courthouse, Moir told his father, "It's a freakin' family reunion in here, eh? . . . Some dads buy their kids a car. Mine sticks me in a fuckin' wagon full of bars." West replied, "You — if you'd stop the resentment . . . It wasn't all me. You had a part in it, you know." West's trial process flowed fairly smoothly, but Moir's became complicated because of debates about degrees of culpability.

Disclosures to Mr. Big generate leads to physical objects appropriate for forensic analysis, witnesses who can confirm the accuracy of components of the disclosure, and criminal colleagues who can confirm the essential features of the disclosure. Sometimes the validity of the disclosure is enhanced by an explanation about the absence of evidence. The disclosure to Mr. Big is verified by the explanation as to why particular evidence is missing.

Earlier we touched on aspects of the cases of Roy Niemi and Peter Fliss. In both these cases, police were puzzled. The victims appeared as if they had been sexually assaulted before being murdered, but the DNA evidence that usually accompanies a sexual assault was missing. Niemi and Fliss both explained this absence by telling Mr. Big they staged the sexual assault to lead the police astray.

Glenn Franz explained the complete absence of any sign of his ex-wife by telling Mr. Big that he'd thrown her head into the river and put her dismembered body into a manure storage lagoon for quick decomposition.

The most comprehensive case of validation by explaining the absence of evidence came in the disclosure made to Mr. Big by Dean Roberts. His disclosure explained the absence of an identifiable motive, the absence of forensic evidence, the absence of any sign of a struggle, and the absence of an explanation for the inexplicable. Roberts had appeared to be a model husband and father. He had no discernible motive when his wife was found strangled in her bed. There were no signs of struggle or forensic clues. The house had been set on fire. The Robertses had twin baby boys. One died as a result of smoke inhalation; the other had been strangled and discarded in the woods. The different treatment of the two children was inexplicable to police. Roberts's disclosure to Mr. Big did not give the police new leads to follow up for confirmation but provided verification through explanation. Roberts told Mr. Big that he had decided to kill his wife months before he actually did so — and that he had intentionally played the role of the perfect, loving husband in order to divert suspicion. He explained his wife's lack of struggle by saying that he had lulled her with a massage. While she was lying face down in bed and partly asleep, he'd slipped a rope around her neck and strangled her. She had no warning or opportunity for resistance. Roberts explained that he had strangled, transported, and abandoned one baby with the express purpose of puzzling the police. The strategy had been successful until Roberts explained it all to Mr. Big.

THE ANATOMY OF MR. BIG: A SUMMARY

This concludes our dissection of Mr. Big operations. We've laid bare the anatomy of Mr. Big. While each case is unique and some techniques have changed over the years, the structure of a Mr. Big operation consists of the following:

- Selecting an unsolved case (usually a homicide) in which a suspect has been identified but for which there are unanswered questions or inadequate evidence with which to ensure a conviction;
- Making the bump so that an undercover officer can introduce themselves to the suspect in a way that does not arouse the suspicions of a paranoid person;
- Conducting scenarios in which the undercover officer builds a relationship with the suspect and offers membership in a powerful criminal gang that values honesty and looking out for its members;
- Nudging the suspect towards disclosure by creating a simultaneous sense of imminent danger and opportunity;
- Having the suspect meet Mr. Big and get the opportunity and encouragement to make a detailed disclosure of his role in the crime, if any. This disclosure is ideally captured on video so that it can be viewed in court by a judge and a jury; and

- Following up on the disclosure to verify its accuracy and find confirmatory evidence.

While Mr. Big has retained the same basic structure over the past three decades, a lot of changes have been made. A Mr. Big operation today is much longer, more expensive, more sophisticated, and more reliant on psychology rather than implied coercion. It is much better suited to generate disclosures that are accurate and that will stand up in court. We'll look at what drove these changes in Chapter 10.

CHAPTER 6

Self-Accusation: The Power of Confession and Disclosure

As we examined the anatomy of a Mr. Big operation, one conclusion was inescapable. Calling on Mr. Big is time-consuming and expensive to police. These operations consume a lot of police resources. In addition to the time spent on the operation itself, the police officers conducting the Mr. Big operation can now expect to spend hours or days on the witness stand. During the voir dire hearing, their actions, not those of the accused, will be on trial. Every action during the operation is attacked as defence lawyers attempt to portray the undercover officers as unethical, unprincipled, or incompetent. The cost of a Mr. Big–generated disclosure raises a question: Why do police and prosecutors value these disclosures so highly?

To understand the value of a Mr. Big disclosure, we have to compare it with other types of evidence available to police. The Canadian legal system, in common with others descended from the British system, is called an accusatorial system. In this system, someone (normally a prosecutor employed by the government) goes before a judge or jury to make an accusation that the accused committed a criminal offence. If the accused does not admit to the accusation by pleading guilty, there is a trial. The prosecutor calls witnesses to present evidence. The accused challenges the accuracy or inferences drawn from this evidence. The accused can also call witnesses to present evidence. The judge or jury members are supposed to be neutral observers. They evaluate the evidence to assess whether the accused is guilty of the crime they are accused of committing. If not convinced "beyond a reasonable doubt," the judge or jury's legal mandate is to find the accused "not guilty." The onus is on the prosecutor to convince the judge or jury of the accused's guilt. The accused has no obligation to prove their innocence.

There are a lot of rules about what can be considered evidence in a criminal trial. The *Canada Evidence Act* has fifty-four sections. A textbook called *The Law of Evidence in Canada, 5th ed.,* is 1,704 pages long. The judge must use these rules to decide what evidence will be admissible in a trial. During a jury trial, debates about the admissibility of evidence occur without the jury being present in a voir dire hearing.

Despite the complexity, the types of potential evidence admissible in a trial for a serious criminal offence are limited. With eyewitness testimony, a witness says, "I saw the crime happening, and it was the accused who did it. I saw it with my own eyes." With forensic and physical evidence, blood, hair, saliva, semen, or other bodily substances have been found in suspicious places. Things such as fibres from a rug, the bullets found in a body, or pieces of clothing can constitute non-human forensic evidence. Forensic evidence is inanimate and cannot speak to the jury; to make it admissible, someone must testify about what it is, and where, when, and how it was found. Finally, evidence can come from witnesses who testify about the circumstances surrounding the case. For example, after seventy-seven-year-old Otto Loose disappeared, his car was found abandoned in a casino parking lot.

A short time later, his body — minus its head and hands — was found in the bush. Police established that Timmy Engel had withdrawn $10,500 from Loose's bank account using both a cheque and a debit card. This was deemed to be a suspicious circumstance. Most criminal cases are built on some combination of eyewitness testimony, forensic evidence, and circumstantial evidence. To convince a judge or jury of guilt beyond a reasonable doubt, a prosecutor will paint a picture by using each piece of evidence as a single brush stroke.

Eyewitness testimony, forensic evidence, and circumstantial evidence have three problems in common. They can be unavailable. They can be wrong. Different inferences can be drawn from the same piece of evidence. In this chapter, we'll set aside the question of the possibility of different inferences and focus on the potential for absence or error. We'll then look at how confessions and disclosures fill in evidentiary gaps.

Evidence can be unavailable. Some murderers kill their victim in front of numerous witnesses, don't wash the victim's blood from their hands, and have announced their hostility towards the victim. Such murderers are rare and easily caught. In most cases, evidence is harder to obtain.

Homicide is a personal act. Like sexual intercourse, it is usually done in private. Direct eyewitnesses are rare unless witnesses are also culpable, in which case they are usually not eager to be helpful to police.

We've seen examples of the remarkable lengths that killers go to in order to eliminate forensic evidence. Michael Bridges buried the body of his victim in another person's grave. Glenn Franz cut up his ex-wife's body and threw the pieces in a manure lagoon at a dairy farm. Other killers we've mentioned also worked hard to eliminate forensic evidence. David Lowe, the man who was nudged to disclose a murder because he couldn't sit with other members of the criminal gang for supper, was much better at hiding the forensic evidence than in keeping his mouth shut. When he murdered his business partner, he committed the act on a tiled floor sloping into a drain hole. The drainage was created to make cleanup of spillage behind a bar easier. Lowe reasoned that the arrangement would work as well for blood.

Circumstantial evidence can be missing for many reasons — including incompetence. Lancelot Skeith was hired to administer a vicious beating on a man suspected of dallying with the wife of Skeith's employer. Skeith beat up the wrong man. The mistake made it very difficult for the police to identify a reason for the attack.

Mr. Big is called in because there is a lack of sufficient evidence to complete painting the picture of guilt. An absence of eyewitness, forensic, or circumstantial evidence can be the result of planning, chance, or even incompetence on the part of the murderer.

Evidence can be unreliable. The hard truth is that all forms of evidence can be unreliable. In 2004, the Prosecutions Committee Working Group of senior prosecutors from across Canada issued a report on wrongful convictions. They reported most wrongful convictions were based on false eyewitness identification, inaccurate assessment of forensic evidence, or false confessions/disclosures. This covers almost everything available to prosecutors.

Understanding the potential problems with particular kinds of evidence is a learning process. A particular type of evidence will be believed to be valid and reliable until confidence in it is eroded by repeated examples of falsity.

An illustrative example is provided by the "crime" of being a witch. From AD 1500 to AD 1700, witchcraft was considered a common crime in Europe. About half a million people were convicted and executed for entering into a pact with the devil, killing babies, causing livestock to die, flying at night, and so on. There was a problem identifying witches. It was believed only witches could see the activities of other witches. This made coming forward as an eyewitness risky, so the justice system looked for other forms of evidence. One method considered reliable was called "watching." This was based on the "knowledge" witches used cats as intermediaries to communicate with the devil. The suspected witch would be tied to a stool with cats nearby. The judges watched. If a cat approached the person, it meant they were sending a message to the devil and were a witch. In the twenty-first century, this seems amusing. One envisions someone whispering, "Go away, kitty. Scat." It was not so funny for the unfortunate person tied to the stool. By the dawn of the eighteenth century, most people lost their faith in both the prevalence of witches and the reliability of watching for cats as evidence. The understanding of what was good, reliable evidence changed.

Eyewitness testimony seems compelling. When an alert, credible person says, "I saw him do it. It was him," judges and juries take the evidence very seriously. Bruce MacFarlane, who served as senior official with Manitoba Justice, argues that eyewitness testimony is powerful because it is "both honest and sincere." It can also be wrong. People make honest mistakes. Reliability varies depending on whether the person is identifying someone they know or a complete stranger, how long they saw the person, how close they were, what the lighting was like, how emotional or dangerous the situation was when the observation occurred, and so on. Research has also shown that people are more likely to misidentify someone from a different race. Identification can be based on changeable attributes such as clothing, headgear, or the state of cleanliness. Also, procedure influences results. If a witness is asked whether a person wearing handcuffs while in police custody is the person seen doing the crime, there will (almost) always be a positive identification. Mistaken identification will often result from a "lineup" or "photo-pack" if the suspect looks different than others in the comparison group. If the witness is told the guilty person is in the group, they will feel compelled to pick someone. When making an eyewitness identification, a witness might be scrupulously honest but still wrong. Their heart is telling the truth, but they can have lying eyes.

Forensic evidence can also be "wrong" or be wrongly interpreted.

Belief in what is forensically possible changes. In Chapter 3, we saw the wrongful identification of human hair contributed to the convictions of both Kyle Unger and James Driskell. At the time, police forensic experts believed they could "match" human hairs or other fibres with microscopic visual comparison. As it turns out, they were wrong. Just as the sociability of cats was discredited as evidence of witchcraft, much of the hair and fibre evidence used "scientifically" during the twentieth century has been discredited in the twenty-first.

Interpretation also matters. The results of accurate forensic analysis can be made inaccurate by imprecise presentation to a judge or jury. This was a common problem with testimony on hair and fibre evidence. The forensics expert would testify that one fibre "matched" another. The implication was they were from the same source, but this can be misleading. Thousands of identical rugs can be produced in the same factory with "matching" fibres. Similar problems can arise when a forensic expert testifies about blood evidence. When looking for blood at a crime scene, forensics experts will spray the area with a chemical called luminol. This makes blood fluorescent under ultraviolet light. The problem is that many metals and cleaning products produce the same results. Luminol testing is effective as an initial screening test, but slower, more expensive, and more accurate tests must be performed to follow up. If these additional tests rule out the presence of blood, there is no evidentiary reason to mention the false positive produced by luminol, but forensics experts testifying will often do so. This mention of a "presumptive positive" test for blood can create an evidentiary falsehood. Forensics experts are like every other expert. They have their own technical language, with precise meanings. It is easy for them to forget that non-experts will attach a different meaning to the same word.

Some forensics techniques have (thus far) stood up to scrutiny. Fingerprints, DNA, and measuring blood-alcohol levels from breath samples are technologies that are accepted as delivering valid and reliable results — when they are performed properly. False results occur when the staff in the crime labs don't do their jobs properly.

Sometimes flawed results arise from incompetence. In 2001, Gregory Turner was on trial for murder in Newfoundland. The forensics laboratory had reported finding a tiny amount of DNA material from the victim on Gregory's ring. At Gregory's trial, a technician at the lab admitted that she had likely accidentally contaminated the sample from other samples at her workstation. She said it was the third time she had made this mistake. Gregory was acquitted, but only because he had the benefit of an extremely competent and diligent defence lawyer.

Other flawed forensic results come from intentional error. Several forensics laboratories in the United States (including the one operated by the Federal Bureau of Investigation) were caught intentionally producing false forensics reports. Sometimes this is a response to overwork. It's quicker to make up a result than to run the test. Other times it is a way to achieve career goals. Promotion can follow "finding results." Very likely, the most common reason for intentional error comes from what is called "noble cause corruption." It is easy for the forensics expert to see their mandate as putting bad guys in jail rather than seeking the scientific truth. Sometimes people do this subconsciously. Dr. Itiel Dror of the University of Southampton in the UK conducted a study of consistency and bias by fingerprint experts. He found the experts' opinions often changed if they were provided with details of the crime before expressing an opinion.

The bottom line is that forensic evidence, when it exists, can be problematic. The 2004 Prosecutions Committee Report of the Working Group on the Prevention of Miscarriages of Justice concluded that "tainted, tailored and unsubstantiated expert evidence, couched in scientific terms and language, based on unreliable fact and ultimately debunked science has long been recognized as a leading cause of wrongful convictions."

THE POWER OF DISCLOSURE AND CONFESSION

We've taken this detour through eyewitness and forensic evidence to highlight a problem faced by police, prosecutors, judges, and juries as they determine guilt in serious criminal cases. There is a lot of uncertainty. Sometimes evidence does not exist — and sometimes it does not exist because of the active efforts of the perpetrator to conceal or destroy. Even where there is eyewitness or forensic evidence that appears reliable and powerful, it must be treated with skepticism. Eyes can lie. Mistakes can be made in interpreting the tales told by blood, hair, fibre, or other forensic evidence. Sometimes the police, prosecutors, and courts have to rely on expert opinion for the very first question as to whether or not a crime had been committed. In Ontario, a detailed review of the work of the province's most prestigious forensic pathologist concluded he was wrong in twenty of forty-five cases in which he concluded a child had died from homicide rather than from natural causes. In twelve of those cases, parents or other caregivers were convicted of killing a child who had died of natural causes. The difficulty and unreliability of other forms of evidence make a disclosure or confession attractive as evidence.

At one level, a disclosure or confession is no more than eyewitness testimony. A person says, "I saw the crime being committed. I recognized who committed it. It was I!" This eyewitness identification has a special credibility. Most people recognize themselves in the mirror. "It was me" does not allow for adding a cautionary note of "or someone who looked a lot like me." The confession or disclosure is based on self-identification. This is presumptively considered accurate.

In a disclosure generated by Mr. Big or a confession made to police under interrogation, the goal is more than an eyewitness identification. Detailed knowledge of the crime and the motivation for it can be uncovered. The statements of the suspect are deemed to be true if the person knows details that could be known only by someone present when the crime was committed.

The power of a confession or disclosure goes beyond self-identification and possession of privileged knowledge. It is a self-accusation and an active claim of ownership of the deed. This characteristic makes a confession or disclosure powerful even when details are lacking or wrong. A whispered "I did it" is usually convincing even if there is no verifiable detail, since it contains a moral claim to ownership of the deed.

A confession receives a privileged status if accompanied by a formal guilty plea. With this, the accused formally admits guilt. Any dispute between the prosecutor and the accused is confined to what punishment is most appropriate. It is different when the accused has disclosed or confessed guilt but pleads not guilty. With this, there is a trial. The admission becomes a piece of evidence presented by the prosecution and subject to challenge by the defence. In a strictly legal sense, it has the same status as other eyewitness or forensic evidence — but the prior admission has different consequences. It has a different effect on a jury. Bruce MacFarlane summed up its impact by saying, "Except in the rare situation where a perpetrator is actually caught in the act of committing the crime, a confession is regarded as the most powerful, persuasive, and damning evidence of guilt that the state can adduce."

The impact of confession or disclosure can be powerful enough to cause a change in other evidence. Researchers have shown that witnesses who provided alibis will often withdraw their willingness to testify or change their testimony if the suspect has admitted guilt. Controlled experiments verify the human tendency to respect confessions. In one experiment, subjects were asked to do a series of tasks. Working alongside was a collaborator of the researcher posing as another volunteer subject. The collaborator was accused of a theft that happened in an adjoining room. Ninety-five percent of research subjects were willing to verify the accused had not left the room. This dropped to 45 percent if the accused admitted guilt.

Other evidence can be affected by an admission of guilt. An experiment was conducted in which people witnessed a staged robbery. They were asked to identify the robber from a lineup that did not include the person who played the robber. Some correctly said that the robber was not in the lineup. Others demonstrated the fallibility of eyewitness testimony by making an identification. Two days later, the witnesses were told that someone had confessed. Sixty-one percent of the people who identified a different person changed their identification. Half of those who correctly said the robber was not in the lineup now confidently identified the "guilty" person. Researchers have shown knowledge that a confession or disclosure will affect the recognition of handwriting, the interpretation of polygraph tests, and even DNA test results. Evidence exonerating the accused degrades or disappears while evidence confirming the admission of guilt strengthens. This phenomenon has been called "corroboration inflation" by the leading authority on false confessions, Dr. Saul Kassin of the City University of New York.

Once someone has admitted guilt, the case is generally considered "solved." Except for efforts to verify the admission, investigations come to an end. Any discrepant evidence that might emerge is often dismissed as irrelevant. The negative impacts of a confession or disclosure can even affect the accused's own defence lawyer. When DNA testing provided a new standard for analyzing forensic evidence, there were exonerations of people who had been wrongfully convicted. In the United States, an analysis of 273 trials for these DNA-exonerated false convictions showed that the incidence of "bad defence lawyering" tripled when the accused had confessed. Confronted with a case in which their client has confessed, the defence lawyer's thoughts turn towards plea bargaining rather than acquittal.

A prior admission of guilt places the accused in a bind. Canadians have the constitutional right to avoid being forced to self-incriminate. A suspect who has disclosed to Mr. Big or made a post-arrest confession to the police has already done so. It is hard to get this genie back into the bottle and almost impossible without testifying. Deciding to "take the stand" in one's own defence is a major decision for an accused. It changes the order of the closing statements. It exposes the accused to cross-examination by the prosecutor. Guilty or innocent, this holds many risks for the accused, including simple physical exhaustion. When Glenn Franz was on trial for murdering his wife, he took the stand in order to recant his disclosure to Mr. Big. His cross-examination lasted twelve days. Most prosecutors don't take this long, but every accused wanting to recant their prior admission can expect a very rough ride from the prosecution. Regardless of guilt, not every defendant is capable of withstanding the inevitable assault on their veracity and character. It gets worse for the defendant; if they choose to testify, they face an uphill fight. Psychologists have demonstrated that people are more likely to believe statements admitting guilt over statements denying it. If both the admission and denial have equal intrinsic credibility, it will usually be the admission which is believed.

Mr. Big disclosures are valued by police and prosecutors because they solve crimes that have been unsolvable by other means. But there is more to the story. Mr. Big disclosures are valuable because they make conviction almost inevitable. They are the next best thing to the smoking gun in the hand of a killer at a murder scene. The author of a standard American textbook on evidence wrote, "The introduction of a confession makes the other aspects of a trial in court superfluous." A disclosure to Mr. Big has much the same effect. If a suspect discloses guilt to Mr. Big, they are going to jail for a long time. Almost all will be convicted. The legal process for the handful that are eventually acquitted will take years — and the person will usually spend most or all of this time behind bars.

FALSE DISCLOSURES: LYING TO MR. BIG

Disclosing guilt to Mr. Big or confessing to police after arrest is tantamount to the suspect putting the handcuffs on their own wrists. Despite these dire consequences, as we have seen, some people lie when they claim to have committed a murder.

There are both similarities and differences in the dynamics between false disclosures and false confessions. In this discussion, we will consider only confessions officially made to police during interrogations and disclosures made to Mr. Big. Disclosures to friends or family members who subsequently come to relay the information to police represent a different dynamic, while confessions to jail cellmates are less solid than the air they are written on. They will be ignored for the simple reason that most of these confessions were never made.

We'll begin by looking at false confessions in order to understand the basic psychological dynamics involved.

People confess to crimes that they did not commit. We don't know how often this occurs, but it happens. For example, Thomas Sophonow told two interrogating officers he murdered sixteen-year-old Barbara Stoppel in a Winnipeg doughnut shop. In actuality, when Barbara was being murdered, Thomas was in a Canadian Tire store buying gift Christmas stockings that he later distributed at a children's ward in a local hospital. In the United States, analysis of data from the National Registry of Exonerations reveals that in 13 percent of convictions in which the convicted person was legally exonerated, the person had, at one point, confessed to the crime.

One form of a false confession can be a guilty plea. Many people will confess to a crime by pleading guilty even if they are innocent or believe they are.

In the United States, the most important driver of insincere guilty pleas is coercive plea bargaining. As an example, let's look at the cases of two Hollywood actresses who perhaps went a bit too far helping their children get admitted into a prestigious university. Felicity Huffman and Lori Loughlin were among the rich and famous to be charged with using inappropriate means to bypass college admissions requirements. Huffman quickly pleaded guilty and received a sentence of two weeks behind bars. Loughlin insisted she was innocent. She argued that she thought she was making a legitimate and legal donation to the university but became the victim of a dishonest employee. The prosecutor's response was to increase the severity of the charges she was facing. If convicted, Loughlin would have faced up to twenty-five years in prison. She capitulated, admitted guilt, and pleaded guilty. In exchange for her compliance, she was sentenced to two months. Nobody will ever know whether Loughlin was factually innocent or not. The disparity in potential outcomes made it prudent for her to confess by pleading guilty.

In Canada, those accused of a crime obtain a lighter sentence in exchange for a guilty plea, but the discount is usually kept within the bounds of good taste. In Canada, the primary means for coercing guilty pleas is the passage of time and the increased use of remand (pre-conviction) custody. If a person is charged with an offence, they are either released on bail or kept locked up in remand. Time in remand is credited as "time served" when the sentence is finally imposed. Canadian courts are slow and have been getting slower. It is common for an accused to spend more time in remand waiting for a trial than the ultimate sentence would be. Pleading guilty becomes a mechanism to get out of jail immediately. Insisting on innocence means staying locked up. A false confession in the form of a guilty plea becomes a rational act.

Different dynamics are at play when someone makes a false confession during a police interrogation. This confession is not made to reduce the potential penalty arising from a finding of guilt or to get out of jail. Confessing a murder to a police officer while being interrogated in front of a video camera means spending a lot of time in jail. Even if the person is eventually acquitted, the process will be long, arduous, and expensive. Despite this, people still make false confessions.

If we go back several decades, the reason was easy to understand. From time to time, police literally beat a confession out of someone. Early studies of wrongful convictions were filled with accounts of people who confessed to murder to stop the infliction of physical pain. In countries such as Canada, the United States, and the UK, giving suspects "the third degree" has effectively ended. Courts have ruled that confessions obtained from torture or beatings were not voluntary. They are not admitted as evidence in court. As a result, police have (almost) completely stopped trying to get confessions this way. Physical beatings were replaced by psychologically informed techniques.

In 1947, a psychologist named Fred Inbau and a Chicago police officer named John Reid co-authored a book called *Criminal Interrogation and Confessions*. Subsequent editions have refined the approach, but the basic methodology remains unchanged. In addition to this textbook on interrogation, a company called John E. Reid and Associates provides training in the "Reid interrogation technique" across North America and around the world. The company claims to have trained over five hundred thousand police officers and security officials in its interrogation technique. There is no reason to doubt this claim.

The essential feature of the Reid technique is that it is not an information gathering exercise. Potential witnesses are interviewed. Suspects are interrogated. The interrogator starts with the belief that the person being interrogated is guilty. The objective is to generate a confession. The Reid technique is popular with the police because it is very effective at achieving this goal.

The Reid interrogation technique consists of nine steps or strategies designed to *maximize* the subject's perception that the case against them is overwhelming and to *minimize* their sense of moral culpability. The suspect is told they will inevitably be convicted and that the interrogator is offering the opportunity to explain why they committed a crime so that they can put their actions into the most advantageous perspective. The person being interrogated is told that it can be established that they have committed a monstrous act, but they have the opportunity to convince the world they are not a monster. This maximization/minimization approach is accompanied by wearing down the suspect with a very long, persistent interrogation. Exhaustion can lower a suspect's resistance and create a desire to get it over with.

The Reid interrogation technique and similar approaches are very effective at generating confessions. Sometimes they are too good. The innocent can be convinced to confess to something they did not do. Researchers have shown that young people and those with mental health or cognitive difficulties are particularly prone to making false confessions. Saul Kassin argues that innocence itself makes a person more likely to wind up confessing. Because they begin with the certainty of their innocence, they are more likely to waive their right of silence in order to cooperate with the police. The interrogation technique is so good at generating confessions that the innocent person can sometimes be convinced of their own guilt.

As courts forced police to stop getting confessions through physical violence and intimidation, Inbau and Reid showed the old techniques were not needed. A strategy based on psychology was as good at getting confessions as one based on the infliction of physical pain. It also generated "better" confessions with more details compelling to a jury. Other measures originally designed to prevent abuse also yielded unexpected benefits. Videotaping of interrogations was introduced to prevent violence and abuse. Police and prosecutors quickly discovered that videotaping also made the confessions more convincing for a jury. Watching the person confess is more powerful than hearing a second-hand report from a police officer or reading a signed statement.

When a person is being interrogated for a crime such as murder, their resistance must be overcome. It goes against their long-term interests to confess. It makes the confession hard to obtain but, if obtained, makes it compelling as evidence. This dynamic is different with a disclosure to Mr. Big. When a person tells Mr. Big he committed a crime, he does so with the belief that the disclosure will allow him to avoid the consequences of his act. He discloses to stay out of jail rather than confesses with the knowledge that his words will put him there.

This different psychological dynamic was not always appreciated by the police conducting early Mr. Big operations. People such as Clayton Mentuck or Jason Dix were presented with negative reasons to disclose. Clayton was told he was at physical risk if he did not disclose. Jason was told the criminal gang needed something to "hold over" him. These negative, threatening reasons were challengeable in court and were not particularly effective in generating a confession, let alone an enthusiastic and detailed one. Clayton told Mr. Big what he wanted to hear only when the positive inducement of a million dollars was added. Jason abandoned his efforts to join the putative criminal gang and went home. In later Mr. Big operations, the police aligned the reason for disclosing with the circumstances. Suspects are now given a positive reason for a full, honest, and detailed disclosure. The "dying guy" ploy and similar stratagems contain a built-in incentive to tell the truth, the whole truth, and nothing but the truth. It leads the suspect to draw maps to help police locate bodies, re-enact the crime, take undercover officers on "show-and-tell" trips to the crime scenes, and enlist the aid of collaborators to confirm their accounts. The suspect has a positive reason to make a detailed disclosure. Once their innate (and justified) paranoia about discussing their crime is overcome, the killer discloses with enthusiasm. The confession obtained through interrogation is obtained by overcoming resistance. The disclosure to Mr. Big is given with gusto.

The fact the person has a positive reason for making the disclosure to Mr. Big and usually does so with enthusiasm creates both a problem and a benefit for the police and prosecutors. As discussed in the introduction, motivations change abruptly when the person realizes Mr. Big was not his friend. This is the paradox of Mr. Big. A compelling reason to claim credit for the crime is instantly transformed into a compelling reason to deny. Almost as surely as day follows night, disclosure is followed by denial. While this creates a problem for police and prosecutors, the videotaped documentation of the disclosure undermines the credibility of denial. At trial, the accused and his lawyer will claim the disclosure was made because of fear and intimidation. In early Mr. Big cases, this claim sometimes had some credibility since the disclosure was "forced" out of someone who was reluctant. When the person is filmed enthusiastically disclosing detail after detail, claims of fearful compliance lack credibility.

The police will often complete the circle by using the video of the disclosure to Mr. Big to generate a more traditional confession. A core component of the Reid interrogation technique is to maximize the suspect's belief in the hopelessness of continued denial. Showing the accused a video of their disclosure to Mr. Big is a powerful tool in achieving this goal. People rarely feel like eating popcorn when watching themselves in that particular movie.

THE SPECIAL CONVINCING POWER OF MR. BIG

We've seen both disclosures and confessions represent a kind of self-accusation about a crime. In theory, in an accusatorial legal system, these admissions are just one piece of evidence that must be weighed alongside other evidence such as eyewitnesses, forensic analysis, and circumstances. In reality, a disclosure or confession is the thousand-pound gorilla. It overwhelms all other evidence. It can even cause these other kinds of evidence to be transformed to confirm guilt.

While Mr. Big operations and police interrogations operate with a different psychological dynamic, they share essential similarities. The results of both are incredibly powerful in the courtroom. Further, both techniques are designed to obtain admissions from someone police investigators already believe to be guilty. Only suspects experience the delights of an interrogation or have a chance to meet Mr. Big. When they use these techniques, the police have moved beyond information-gathering. They are setting out to gather proof to support a presumption of guilt. In the next chapter, we'll explore the basis of this presumption and its implications for a Mr. Big operation.

CHAPTER 7

Dogged Determination vs. the Disease of Certainty

As we saw in Chapter 5, there are four essential criteria before Mr. Big is called in. A serious crime has been committed or has likely been committed. The police have a primary suspect and have determined that the suspect might be susceptible to Mr. Big. Finally, the police do not have enough evidence to support a charge and conviction. This means before Mr. Big enters a criminal investigation, the police are quite certain their suspect is guilty. This presents a danger. Mr. Big is an effective tool for generating disclosures. If the police are certain of an innocent suspect's guilt, Mr. Big can transform an erroneous suspicion into an untruthful disclosure and possibly a wrongful conviction. As the sociologist W.I. Thomas once observed, "If men define situations as real, they are real in their consequences." Being defined by police as guilty can have the real consequence of going to prison.

Let's go back to the case of Kyle Unger. The police were convinced two people were involved because they believed one person could not have thrown Brigitte Grenier's body into the creek. From this definition of the situation, everything else followed. When the police interrogated Tim Houlahan, they introduced the idea of an accomplice. When Houlahan named Kyle, the police assumed the accusation was true. From there, the malignant effects of certainty prevented the police from accepting evidence that pointed to exoneration. When witnesses told police Kyle's clothing remained clean through the evening, the police theorized that he "could have" changed at a friend's house. When shown the jailhouse informant was not accessible to Kyle after the charges were stayed, the police theorized the disclosure "could have" happened at a different time. There was no evidence for these suppositions.

When investigating a homicide, police must narrow the field of potential suspects to keep an investigation manageable. To do so, they will develop theories about the crime and who committed it. Problems emerge when a confirmation bias causes them to ignore or explain away evidence undermining their theory. Certainty of guilt can even change witness testimony or forensic test results. This process is often called "tunnel vision."

The term "tunnel vision" describes one symptom of a deeper pathology. Everett Doolittle was the head of the Cold Case Unit for the Minnesota Bureau of Criminal Apprehension. Writing for the publication *FBI Law Enforcement Bulletin*, Doolittle called it "the disease of certainty." He said the disease is "fatal to investigations." Officers who are certain about their beliefs fall prey to tunnel vision. "Those who resist the disease [are often] ridiculed and ostracized for their . . . inability to see the truth."

In some cases, tunnel vision is understandable. When Erin Chorney disappeared, the police kept an open mind to the possibility that she was still alive but were certain about one thing. If Erin disappeared because she was murdered, the police were certain that Michael Bridges was her killer. Their certainty was demonstrated to be justified. Because the police were right, certainty was not seen as a pathology. It became the basis for dogged determination.

In other cases, certainty was understandable but produced less wholesome results. In Chapter 5, we touched on the ethical problems that arose when Mr. Big targeted two underage wards of the Alberta government. The police took this unusual step because they were certain the pair were guilty of two brutal murders. Even in retrospect, it is difficult to find fault with the RCMP for strongly suspecting the teenagers. They had escaped a custodial facility for young offenders to go on a wild crime spree. When caught, they were driving a stolen pickup truck down a major street in Edmonton at high speeds, shooting pedestrians with a pellet gun. The owner of the pickup truck and his tenant were found to have been brutally murdered that evening. It is almost inconceivable that the police would reach any other conclusion than the one they did — that the two teenagers were the killers.

Despite this understandable conclusion, there was a problem. There was no forensic evidence tying the pair to the killings. If they were guilty, there should have been. Sometimes a lack of forensic evidence results from careful advance planning or a diligent post-murder cleanup. Sometimes it results from the passage of time or the transportation of the body. In this case, none of these reasons was applicable. If the youths were the killers, the crime was opportunistic rather than planned. The arrest was timely and the bodies had not been transported. The cab of the truck and the boy's clothes should have been a veritable gold mine of forensic evidence, but there was nothing.

The police were confronted with two extremely unlikely possibilities. The first was that the boys had been completely successful in cleaning themselves and their clothing. There was no evidence that they had tried or were capable of doing so. The second possibility was that the unfortunate landlord and his tenant received two sets of unwelcome visitors the same evening. The odds of an acreage in Alberta being visited in the same evening by unrelated thieves and murderers are infinitesimally small. Both possible explanations were unlikely, but one had to be true. The disease of certainty ensured that the police desperately tried to gather proof for the first alternative while ignoring the second. Mr. Big was summoned. He did what he was invented to do. Disclosures were obtained, but after a lengthy voir dire hearing for one of the youths, the judge concluded that the "statements were made while he was functionally detained, subject to coercion by inducement, and in a circumstance where he believed that no harm and only good would come to him by confessing, all create a real prospect that his confession to Mr. Big was unreliable." The murder charges were stayed.

The police and prosecution were still certain of guilt. As we learned in Chapter 5, during the Mr. Big operation, one of the youths announced his intention to murder the husband of his adult lover. To keep the youth from acting, the Mr. Big operation brought in a putative "hit man" to divert the youth from possible action into fanciful planning and to keep the husband from harm without damaging the Mr. Big operation. After the murder charges were stayed, the RCMP's diversionary strategy was used as the basis of a new charge of counselling murder. It served as a substitute for the stayed murder charge. The youth was convicted by a jury, but the judge overturned the conviction, ruling the threat was juvenile posturing rather than an actual intention. The judge ruled: "At a minimum, however, the police were justified in exploring how serious NRR [the youth] was about his wish to see his girlfriend's husband killed." He went on to ask whether the undercover officers "merely provided an opportunity for NRR to offend, or rather induced the commission of the offence." The judge answered his question by saying the Mr. Big operation "offered NRR a low risk weapon, which he had not requested, with which to commit the crime. In this way, the police instigated the crime of counselling. The specific offence of counselling murder was brought about by the officers' conduct and would not have taken place without their involvement."

An even more graphic example of the dangers of the disease of certainty was provided by the case of Wesley Evans, which has sometimes erroneously been described as a Mr. Big operation.

In 1984 and 1985, two women were murdered in British Columbia. The police believed the crimes were committed by Wesley Evans's brother. Wesley was arrested on the pretext of a marijuana charge so he could be questioned about his brother's activities. Wesley was born with severe cognitive impairments, which were compounded by brain injuries. While being questioned about his brother, he gave a murky and confusing confession of guilt for the double murder. He was charged, tried, and convicted of murder based on this confession. Wesley's confession was exceptionally questionable. Upon being returned to the police cell, he was asked by an undercover officer if he had killed the two women. Wesley said he did not, but that he had confessed. The undercover officer asked why he confessed. Wesley replied, "Well they, they wouldn't give a rest until I confessed." He later expressed some puzzlement, saying, "You know, it's funny. I don't remember killing them . . . usually I won't forget somein like that." After Wesley spent five years in prison, the Supreme Court of Canada overturned the conviction and ordered an acquittal.

When Wesley returned home, people believed a dangerous murderer had been freed on a legal technicality. He was subjected to suspicion and scorn. The police began to receive reports of strange behaviour, so they put him under surveillance. No criminal activity was observed. Since ongoing surveillance was expensive and time-consuming, two undercover officers established a relationship so that Wesley would self-report any illegal activity. None was disclosed, but Wesley once said he wanted to kill an ex-girlfriend. The police did not take this seriously and nothing was done. Five months later, he said he would like to kill another person. This time the undercover officers encouraged him to start planning. He was then charged with two counts of conspiracy to commit murder. The judge hearing the case was unimpressed. As he threw the "case" out of court, the judge said, "I found it difficult to believe that these events took place in Canada." The disease of certainty produced pathological police behaviour.

THE DISEASE OF CERTAINTY:
MR. BIG DOES NOT GET A DISCLOSURE

In the case of the two Alberta youths, the police had good reason to consider them as the primary suspects in the murders. Their legitimately strong suspicion transformed into a certainty, but there was a gap in the evidence. Mr. Big got disclosures of guilt, but the result was unsatisfying. The question of which of the two unlikely alternatives was the truth remained unanswered, but only one alternative was ever seriously explored. If the murders were committed by someone else, it was the luckiest night of the killer's life. Who could have predicted that a couple of out-of-control, impaired youths would show up to divert the investigation? In the end, we have no idea who was responsible for the brutal killings.

The RCMP are careful to say that the Mr. Big operation can "clear" a suspect of suspicion. Sometimes it does. For example, a Mr. Big operation was launched to determine whether Douglas Holtham's lover was implicated in the murder of his family. The Mr. Big operation demonstrated that she was not. Darin Randle was suspected of killing his partner in a marijuana grow op and disposing of the body. He told Mr. Big that his partner accidentally shot himself and that he (Randle) burned the body to protect their illegal business from exposure. Randle was charged with committing an indignity to a body but was never charged with murder.

We don't know how many times a Mr. Big operation has the effect of clearing a suspect since, by definition, these cases rarely end up in court, although occasionally knowledge of cases in which someone is cleared is revealed accidentally. For example, the court decision declaring Clarence Smith's Mr. Big disclosure unreliable indicated that another suspect had been targeted by Mr. Big, but had been cleared by the operation.

The best illustration of the disease of certainty is *when the suspect refused to make a disclosure to Mr. Big but is still charged.* In the case of Jason Dix, Mr. Big's failure to get a disclosure was interpreted as confirming guilt. In the case of Craig Short, it was ignored.

In the fall of 1994, Jason Dix worked for a company that sold industrial scales. A paper-recycling company located near Edmonton purchased a scale and Jason worked on the installation. He became friends with an employee of the paper-recycling company named James Deiter. One Saturday morning, James and his supervisor, Tim Orydzuk, worked overtime repairing a machine. The plant was almost deserted. Late in the morning, the two stopped answering telephone calls. A few hours later, James's brother went to the plant to investigate and discovered both men were dead. They had each been shot in the head three times in an "execution-style" slaying, but the second person on the scene announced that the deaths were caused by electrocution. This diagnosis was accepted by everyone arriving at the site including emergency medical staff, RCMP officers, and occupational health and safety officials. As a result, the deaths were initially treated as an occupational accident rather than as a homicide, resulting in the destruction or contamination of any forensic evidence. The next morning, the medical examiner began the autopsies and quickly determined that the wounds were from bullets rather than by electrons. As a judge drily noted years later, "The nature of the investigation into the deaths thereupon took on a new character."

The police investigation quickly identified two people who seemed to be promising suspects. One had recently quarrelled with James. The other had a strange fixation on Tim's wife. Jason, who had gone drinking with James the night before the murders, was interviewed as a potential witness. His transformation into suspect began ten days after the murders. The RCMP enlisted the aid of an FBI profiler who opined that the killer would be someone "young, male, white, physically large, and self-confident." When hearing this hypothesized description, the RCMP officer who had just finished interviewing Jason said he'd just shaken hands with the man described. With this, Jason was transformed into a suspect. His statement was examined from this vantage point. It contained gaps. Jason was married but was having an affair. He had seen no reason to share this information with the RCMP. The addition of deceit to the profiler's guess transformed Jason into the primary (only) suspect. Interest in the two initial suspects disappeared. The police were certain Jason was the killer.

Investigators quickly turned to Mr. Big. The Mr. Big operation was up and running just over a month after the murders.

Jason was bumped with the offer of "under-the-table" construction work. This gradually transformed into service as a lookout as imaginary crimes were committed. By April of 1995, he was engaged in cash counting for the gang. On one occasion, he counted a million dollars supposedly being prepared for laundering purposes. Jason soon met Mr. Big in person, who offered up a dying cancer patient willing to take responsibility for the murders. Jason told Mr. Big that he would say whatever the gang wanted him to say, but that he had not killed James or Tim.

The Mr. Big team tried again. This time they moved from the positive incentive of the "dying guy" to a cruder, less reliable approach based on fear and intimidation. As described in Chapter 5, Jason witnessed what he believed was a murder. Jason met Mr. Big in person a second time. This time, Mr. Big demanded Jason confess to killing James or Tim so that the criminal gang would have something to "hold over" him in order to ensure silence about the "Whack at Yahk." A judge later characterized the two-day-long effort as "extreme pressure." The judge said Jason was "left with the impression" that he would be killed and that "several statements by operatives acting as gang members constitute clear threats." Despite this, Jason refused to say he'd committed the two murders. The Mr. Big operation came to an end. In the words of the judge, "It was determined that there was really not much else that could be staged once a murder had been staged and the hoped-for confession had not been obtained."

By this time, the disease of certainty had become entrenched. The Mr. Big operation was deemed a success since the police believed that Jason's willingness to participate in the activities of the putative criminal gang indicated guilt. His failure to call police about the "Whack at Yahk" was interpreted as showing a willingness to kill. The possibility he believed the threats to kill him if he "squealed" was discounted.

Jason's "failure" to disclose did not clear his name or cause the investigation to stop. Jason voluntarily submitted to two polygraph or "lie detector" tests. The specialist who conducted the tests reported that Jason "passed" the questions dealing directly with his participation in the murders, but the results were "inconclusive" for some peripheral questions. As a result, Jason's overall test results were labelled "inconclusive." Once again, it was impossible for Jason to convince police of his innocence.

In August 1995, Jason made a mistake. He read Edmonton's tabloid newspaper, the *Edmonton Sun*. It contained an American "true crime" article about a case in which someone had thrown the murder weapon into a creek. Jason mentioned this article in a telephone call to his wife. The police were listening and concluded he'd also thrown a gun into a body of water. The previous fall, Jason and his mistress stayed at a lakeside cabin. A police dive team began scouring the bottom of this lake. Officers searched the surrounding bush area with a metal detector. At this point, Jason got unlucky. The police found a buried toolbox containing four revolvers packed in grease. The guns had been stolen in Vancouver several years earlier. Subsequent investigations suggested that they had probably been buried sometime in 1990 (four years before James and Tim were murdered) by long-time criminals who were, by the mid-1990s, in prison for an armoured-car robbery. At the time of discovery, the RCMP believed one of the handguns must have been used in the murder of James and Tim. When their own forensics experts were unable to confirm this, the RCMP found a technician in a crime lab in Oregon who provided a verbal confirmation that one of the handguns probably fired the fatal shots.

The discovery of the hidden handguns and the dubious identification of the murder weapon were deemed sufficient to justify an arrest. Jason was arrested and charged with two counts of murder. He was subjected to an eleven-hour interrogation. He denied being the killer and invoked his right to remain silent over two hundred times. The interrogation was followed by a midnight excursion to the crime scene. Jason's four-year-old son was interrogated. Jason's cellmate for the first eight days of his incarceration was an undercover RCMP officer. The two talked, but Jason made no disclosure of guilt. When all these efforts to get a confession failed, Jason was transferred from the police holding cells to the Edmonton Remand Centre. After he arrived there, three inmates promptly came forward with claims that Jason had disclosed his guilt to them. All three received preferential treatment on their charges or sentence recommendations. A judge later pointed to the inherent implausibility of these jailhouse informant disclosures. Jason denied being the killer to Mr. Big even when threatened with death. He denied being the killer during a long police interrogation. He did not make any disclosures during eight days in a police cell with an undercover RCMP officer. He had not made any incriminating statements during months of wiretapped telephone calls. Despite this, he was supposed to have blurted out his guilt to three separate strangers within a few days of being locked up in the remand centre.

Jason went to trial for the two murders. It did not go well for the police and prosecutor. Partway through the trial, the prosecutor was changed. The charges were withdrawn. Jason sued. He claimed that the police and prosecutor had abused their office, committed negligence, and falsely arrested him. The judge hearing the lawsuit agreed. Jason was eventually awarded over $700,000 in damages and costs.

The failure of Mr. Big to obtain a disclosure also had no effect on police certainty in the investigation of Craig Short. Just after 7:00 p.m. on October 18, 2008, Craig left his house to watch a hockey game. After the game, he went to a bar for some drinks. When Craig returned home, his wife was dead in the backyard. Barbara Short had been beaten to death with a two-by-four piece of lumber. Neighbours had seen her alive at about 6:00 p.m.; Craig said she was alive when he left the house. The police believed that he murdered her between 6:00 p.m. and the time he left for the hockey game, and that Craig's evening on the town was intended to create an alibi. The timeline was unlikely but possible. The big problem for police was a lack of forensic evidence. Barbara's death had been messy. If Craig killed her, he would have had to clean himself and dispose of bloody clothes within a tight temporal window without leaving a trace of evidence in his house.

The tight time window and lack of forensic evidence notwithstanding, the police had reason to be suspicious of Craig. The Short marriage had not been a happy one. While there was no evidence of past physical abuse, friends and family testified that Craig often treated his wife in a way summed up by a judge as "rudely, crudely and generally displayed a boorish behaviour to her in public." Shortly before the murder, Craig tattooed the name of another woman on his arm. For her part, Barbara was having an affair and had hired a lawyer with instructions to file, but not serve, an application for divorce. After Barbara's murder, Craig acted unwisely. He asked a friend to destroy a letter sent to him from his wife's lawyer and attempted to destroy poems his wife had written describing her unhappiness in the marriage.

Craig also intensified the suspicions against him by trying to help solve the crime. He suggested his wife's lover might have been guilty. He also told police that when he first arrived home and went into the backyard, he smelled gasoline. This was confirmed by the ambulance personnel attending the scene. Craig said that the cap to a gas storage tank in the backyard was off. He told police that Barbara might have noticed someone stealing gasoline and been murdered by the thief. The police dismissed these two theories as attempts by a murderer to divert suspicion.

Once the police became certain of Craig's guilt, the investigation reached an impasse. Craig was seen as having a motive and a (limited) window of opportunity. His conduct after the murder was seen as suspicious. At the same time, the lack of forensic evidence created uncertainty about a conviction. Mr. Big was summoned. Craig was bumped and groomed to make a disclosure. Craig refused to disclose that he was the killer. He turned down the generous offer to have a "dying guy" take the blame for the crime.

The failure of Mr. Big to obtain a disclosure was ignored. He was prosecuted for Barbara's murder. A trial resulted in a hung jury. Prior to his second trial, Craig again did something stupid and self-destructive. He refused to pay his lawyer for his first trial. The lawyer attempted to quit but was ordered by the judge to carry on regardless of the prospect of payment. The judge also refused to admit as evidence text messages that showed Barbara and her lover had been planning to get together while Craig was at the hockey game. Evidence raising the possibility of the gas theft was also excluded. Craig was convicted of first-degree murder. He spent five years in prison waiting for his case to reach the Court of Appeal for Ontario.

The appeal court judges found that a lot had gone wrong during Craig's second trial. He should not have been forced to be represented by a lawyer who did not want to represent him. There was forensic evidence on Barbara's body that was consistent with a lover's visit. It had not been tested because it was deemed irrelevant to the police theory of the crime. The emails setting an appointment had been ruled as inadmissible, and the lover was not called to testify under oath. The judges noted that if the lover had visited Barbara after Craig had left for the hockey game, the police and prosecutor's theory became impossible. Despite this, Craig and his lawyer had not been allowed to raise the issue. Finally, the appeal court noted that there was significant evidence supporting Craig's original theory that his wife had surprised a thief stealing gasoline. Craig's conviction was overturned and a new trial ordered. In 2019, almost eleven years after Barbara was murdered, her husband was acquitted of the charge of murder.

When confronted with the horrible reality that his wife had been murdered, Craig Short made mistakes. He attempted to destroy evidence. He damaged his relationship with his lawyer by refusing to pay him. On some occasions, Craig was his own worst enemy. This does not change the fact that he did not kill his wife. What is more, he was almost as good as Sherlock Holmes in deducing what had happened the night Barbara was murdered. The "surprised gas thief" explanation of the crime appears to be true. Years later, it was established that a thief had been out stealing gasoline in the neighbourhood. This suspect died by the time Craig's theory was taken seriously, but before doing so he made disclosures of guilt to his wife.

Mr. Big worked hard to get a disclosure of guilt from Craig. He failed. Craig refused to allow Mr. Big's dying friend to take the blame for the murder and continued to insist that he was innocent. The possible implications of this refusal to disclose were ignored. At Craig's third trial, the prosecution did not introduce any evidence acknowledging the existence of the Mr. Big operation. Craig's lawyer attempted to have Craig's statements denying that he had murdered Barbara introduced as evidence, but the judge refused to allow these statements to be admitted after the prosecution argued that Craig could have been aware that Mr. Big was a police officer and could have been making a false denial. Craig's denials to Mr. Big were treated as hearsay and were not shown to the jury.

MR. BIG AND THE DISEASE OF CERTAINTY

We began this chapter by arguing that Mr. Big is usually dispatched to assist with a homicide investigation when the police are already confident that they know who committed the crime. Mr. Big's task is to obtain confirmation in the form of a disclosure. In the next chapter, we will look at some cases where a denial of responsibility for the killing *was accepted* by police, prosecutors, or the courts. In those cases, a protestation of innocence to Mr. Big had beneficial effects for the suspect. For Jason Dix and Craig Short, the disease of certainty and the tunnel vision it causes created a dynamic in which the denial to Mr. Big was either ignored or treated as evidence pointing towards guilt. Neither case was really a matter of Mr. Big having tunnel vision. Instead, the original investigating team that called for Mr. Big's help suffered from the disease of certainty. Denials made to Mr. Big did not cause this certainty to be questioned.

It is understandable that the police were suspicious of Craig Short. Sometimes husbands kill wives, usually when marriages are troubled. At the same time, the most common factors correlated with intimate partner homicide were lacking. There was no history of physical abuse. Most people do not go to murder as their first act of violence against a spouse. Craig Short was middle-aged. Most men who kill their wives are young. Craig was sober before going to the hockey game. Many domestic murderers are drunk or stoned. The Short marriage was troubled, but still intact. Half of male-on-female intimate partner homicides occur *after* the woman has left the relationship. The reality was that Craig Short did not fit the statistical profile of a wife killer.

It is even less understandable why the police became so suspicious of Jason Dix. He had no motive. There was no forensic evidence. He became a suspect because he fit a generic guesstimate profile provided by an FBI profiler. This kind of profiling has since been discredited, but Jason had the misfortune of being a suspect a few years after the movie *The Silence of the Lambs*. In the 1990s, FBI profilers were credited with almost supernatural powers. This profile, combined with the fact that one of the RCMP officers had just talked to him as a witness, made Jason a suspect. His natural desire to avoid talking about his extramarital sexual activities turned suspicion into certainty.

In retrospect, the police certainty about Jason's and Craig's guilt seems foolish. At the time, it was real. What accounts for this?

Almost a century ago, the Russian-American sociologist Pitirim Sorokin developed a theory that helps explain how certainty can become a disease. Sorokin argued that people have two ways of *knowing*. People can arrive at their knowledge from external sources. They *know* something is true because they have seen, heard, touched, smelled, or tasted things from outside of themselves. Knowledge is developed in response to people's observation and interpretation of sensory inputs. To arrive at this form of knowledge, people collect and evaluate evidence. Sorokin argued that another form of knowledge comes from within the person. The person *knows* something because they *know* it. When this form of knowledge is used to understand the relationship between humans and their gods, it is often called faith. When this form of knowledge is used by police to solve crimes, it is called tunnel vision.

Both Jason Dix and Craig Short were victims of police who used an internally generated form of knowledge in a criminal investigation. These officers were not trying to *frame* a suspect whom they thought innocent. They were attempting to find empirical verification for what they already *knew*. In so doing, they abandoned what Sorokin identified as the greatest virtue of the form of knowledge generated from empirical observation of the world outside of the individual — the ability to find truths through active doubt. When the police move from suspicion to certainty in a case, Mr. Big becomes more like a priest conducting a mass in order to affirm and strengthen faith rather than as part of a fact-finding investigative team.

CHAPTER 8

Black and White and Many Shades of Grey

I n the last two chapters, we examined the power of a Mr. Big disclosure and the pathologies created by the disease of certainty. In this chapter, we'll examine Mr. Big's ability to deal with nuance. Guilt can be more subtle than an absolute "guilty" or "not guilty." It matters what the charge is. A person may be guilty of speeding but not of dangerous driving. Speeding is a provincial traffic offence that results in a fine. Dangerous driving is a federal criminal offence that results in imprisonment. Precision in defining the charge can be as important as pronouncing guilt or innocence. Black and white is accompanied by many shades of grey.

In Chapter 2, we saw an example of the ultimate verification of a disclosure to Mr. Big. Michael Bridges showed where he hid Erin Chorney's body. There was no innocent way he could possess this knowledge, but the question remained: guilty of what? Bridges provided two versions of how he'd killed Erin. In the first, he pushed her. She fell, hit her head, and died. In the second version, Bridges said he strangled Erin with his hands. When this didn't kill her, he used an electrical cord. The murder was completed by drowning. While the passage of time made it impossible to determine whether Erin had been drowned, the evidence was more consistent with Bridges's second story than his first. Erin's body did not have a skull injury consistent with hitting her head. There were two broken bones in her neck consistent with strangulation. The electrical cord was still wrapped around her.

Michael Bridges was found guilty of first-degree murder, but this was not the only finding of guilt possible from his knowledge of where Erin's body was hidden.

Bridges might have told Mr. Big that Erin died of a drug overdose and he hid her body because he had supplied her with the drugs. Bridges never made this claim. There is no reason to believe this happened in Erin's death — but it has in other cases. If something like that had happened, hiding Erin's body would be an offence under section 182 of the *Criminal Code*. It is referred to as "committing an indignity" on a human body. This provision of the *Criminal Code* is in the section dealing with nuisances rather than homicides and carries a maximum sentence of five years. The typical sentence for this offence in these circumstances is between two and four years.

If the jury accepted Bridges's first version of events, he would have been found guilty of "manslaughter." This is defined in the *Criminal Code* as a culpable homicide that is not murder. A person causes the death of someone by committing an illegal act but did not mean to kill them. Shoving someone is an assault. Many people are shoved but few die as a result. If there is no intention to kill, there is no murder. The charge of manslaughter replaces it.

A murder must have a culpable act, a resulting death, and the added element of *intentionality*. Murder is divided into two categories: first-degree and second-degree. Murders become first-degree if the killing is premeditated or planned. It is also first-degree if death occurs unintentionally while the perpetrator is engaged in a sexual assault, kidnapping, hostage taking, hijacking, terrorist act, or intimidation attempt. Murder is also first-degree when the victim is a peace officer performing their duties, if there is complicity in a contract killing, or if it occurs as a result of the activity of a criminal gang or a campaign of harassment. The *Criminal Code* defines second-degree murder as any murder that is not first-degree murder. This means that the killing was intentional but not premeditated and did not meet any of the criteria listed above. A murder charge can be lowered to manslaughter if the homicide occurred in "the heat of passion caused by sudden provocation."

There is a grey area at the boundary between categories. Some manslaughters look a lot like second-degree murders and vice-versa. During an assault, was an intent to kill formed? There is also ambiguity at the boundary between first-degree and second-degree murder. When does intent to kill become a plan to kill? Logically, every implemented intent has an element of premeditation, even if just for a second. In criminal law, premeditation is usually based on a temporal gap between forming an intention and carrying it out. Sometimes there are clear indicators. Accepting a payment to kill someone, buying a weapon, taking out a life insurance policy on the future victim, or digging a grave in advance are all evidence of premeditation. Other actions are more ambiguous. Luring an ex-spouse to a meeting in a secluded area might be an indication of premeditated murder or it might be an innocent desire to have a private conversation. If premeditation is predicated on a temporal gap between conception and execution of murderous intent, how long must the gap be? One minute? One hour? One day? The grey answer is that a first-degree murder involves acts not performed in a continuous sequence.

Let's apply these black, white, and grey distinctions to the guilt of Michael Bridges. By telling Mr. Big where Erin was buried, Bridges established he was guilty of something. He gave no indication Erin died from an overdose or heart attack, so we'll ignore the possibility that his only offence was committing an indignity on her body. If Bridges's first story was accurate, he intended to shove, not to kill. This would normally be manslaughter, not murder, but by his own admission, Bridges was attempting to convince Erin to drop the assault charges against him. If cajoling had turned into intimidation, the fatal shove would be first-degree murder. Bridges's second story contained two strangulation attempts and a fatal drowning. One spontaneous strangulation attempt could be second-degree murder — unless it was part of a sexual assault or intimidation attempt. Either would transform the strangulation into first-degree murder. At trial, the prosecutor argued the variety of methods used to kill Erin demonstrated premeditation. When Bridges fetched the electrical cord, he was planning to kill Erin. When Bridges carried Erin to the bathtub and turned on the tap, he was planning to kill her. The prosecutor argued there was enough separation between these acts to constitute premeditation. Bridges's lawyer argued it did not. The jury agreed with the prosecutor.

There was another potential path to argue for second-degree murder. If Bridges killed Erin with the first strangulation attempt but was mistaken in believing she was still alive, the second strangulation and the drowning would not count. A dead person cannot be murdered. However, the second strangulation attempt and the immersion in the bathtub could be legally defined as attempted murders. It seems strange, but the Canadian *Criminal Code* allows for the attempted murder of corpses if the would-be murderer did not know the person is dead. In this case, there is no evidence that Bridges was wrong in believing that Erin was tough to kill, and, in any event, this argument would probably not have impressed most jury members.

The difference in the level of culpability inherent in different charges is reflected in different penalties. Committing an indignity to a body carries a maximum penalty of five years. Manslaughter carries a maximum sentence of life in prison, but there is no minimum penalty. In rare cases, a perpetrator completely avoids incarceration. The sentence for manslaughter usually ranges between two and ten years. Murder, whether first-degree or second-degree, carries a mandatory minimum sentence of life. The difference between degrees is in the parole eligibility. People convicted of second-degree murder are not eligible for parole for at least ten years, but a longer period of ineligibility can be imposed. Many Mr. Big cases result in parole ineligibility of fifteen to twenty years. Those convicted of first-degree murder are ineligible for parole for at least twenty-five years. At various points in time, there has been a "Faint Hope Clause" allowing for parole consideration after fifteen years. People convicted for murders occurring when this provision was in the *Criminal Code* are eligible for this consideration, while those convicted at other times are not.

SHADES OF GREY WHEN MR. BIG IS LED TO THE BODY

Many Mr. Big cases begin as missing persons investigations. By calling in Mr. Big, the police are not just gathering evidence to support a criminal charge. They are attempting to find out what happened to the missing person.

If a suspect accurately tells Mr. Big where the body was hidden, that suspect will be presumptively considered guilty of a criminal offence, but there is a wide range of outcomes possible. These cases provide a good test of Mr. Big's ability to deal with shades of grey and generate the information needed for nuanced assessments of culpability.

In Chapter 5, we saw how Howard Steadman became a Mr. Big target after Ronda Black said he helped dispose of her murdered husband's body. Steadman told Mr. Big the same story and took the undercover officers to the various locations where the body was buried. Steadman was charged and convicted of committing an indignity to a dead body but was never charged with murder. A similar result occurred when Darin Randle told Mr. Big his friend and business partner accidentally shot himself. Randle could not lead Mr. Big to the body because he had burned it and thrown the ashes into a garbage dumpster. Like Steadman, Randle faced only a charge of committing an indignity to a body. In both cases, the police and prosecutor accepted the disclosure of the lowest level of culpability.

After Neil Valliere's girlfriend abruptly disappeared, Valliere became the target of a Mr. Big operation. He admitted killing Helene Boivin and showed the undercover officers where he hid her body. Valliere told Mr. Big that a naked, hysterical, and knife-wielding Helene woke him after concluding her boyfriend was having an affair. Valliere told Mr. Big he feared castration and took defensive action. Valliere said the two fell to the floor in the struggle and Helene died. Valliere said he had accidentally broken her neck or crushed her larynx. Valliere folded his girlfriend's naked body into a packsack, carried her away, and buried her under a cement culvert. By the time Helene's body was discovered, her cause of death could not be established. Valliere was charged with manslaughter and committing an indignity to a dead body. The judge said "it is inherently unlikely that the events occurred as Mr. Valliere described them. That is so because it is unlikely that Helene Boivin behaved in the manner that Mr. Valliere says she did. It is so because he was physically stronger and larger than she was and should have been able to control her without difficulty, never mind without falling to the ground and causing her death, if that is how she died." But the judge also said Valliere had every reason to tell the truth to Mr. Big: because he was talking to someone leading a criminal gang, Valliere had no incentive to minimize his role in Helene's death. As he acquitted Valliere on the manslaughter charge, the judge said that if the legal standard was a balance of probabilities, he would have likely found Valliere guilty, but the circumstances of the disclosure created reasonable doubt in the judge's mind. If Valliere told his story as a confession to police acting as police, he would have likely been convicted of manslaughter. As it was, he pleaded guilty to committing an indignity to Helene's body and was sentenced to eighteen months in jail.

Allan Shyback also benefitted from disclosing to Mr. Big rather than confessing. Shyback strangled his wife, buried her in the basement of their home, and poured a new cement floor to hide the grave. While doing all this work, Shyback used kitty litter to absorb the odor of his wife's rotting body. He used her cellphone to create the impression she was still alive. Shyback told Mr. Big his wife threatened him with a knife while taunting that she could get away with murdering him. Shyback said that he lost control in the resulting struggle. At trial, Shyback claimed he'd acted in self-defence. The judge ruled strangulation was excessive for self-defence but said, "I am left with a reasonable doubt as to the intention of the accused. It is not clear to me that he was able to form the intention necessary for second-degree murder, in the reactive situation in which he was put and the evidence as to the short period of time that may have been required for death to occur." On the basis of provocation, Shyback was convicted of manslaughter rather than second-degree murder. He was sentenced to a total of seven years. The Crown appealed the sentence and was successful in getting it increased to ten years — which is what the minimum period of parole eligibility for a second-degree murder conviction would have been. The difference is that Shyback will serve a maximum rather than a minimum of ten years.

In the cases of both Valliere and Shyback, the presentation of their story to Mr. Big increased its plausibility for the judge. Both trials featured the unusual spectacle of the prosecution arguing against the credibility of the disclosure and the defence insisting the disclosure was true. In both cases, the ability of the defendant to direct police to the location of a hidden body ensured they would be found guilty of *something*, but they received a less severe penalty because their disclosure to Mr. Big allowed their lawyer to argue for a shade of grey rather than black or white.

Nathan Hale and James Kakegamic told a different story and experienced a different result. Both were the last person seen with a young Indigenous woman who abruptly disappeared. In Saskatchewan, Hale told Mr. Big he strangled a missing woman and directed the undercover officers to the body. Kakegamic told a similar story about a separate case in Ontario. When charged with murder, both claimed the woman died from alcohol poisoning. They claimed that they hid the body because of fear of a murder charge. Both were convicted of murder. The story told to Mr. Big was deemed more credible than the one they told in court. Ironically, if the women had died of alcohol poisoning rather than being strangled, concealing the body made it impossible for the medical examiner to confirm this as the cause of death. In the case of Kakegamic's victim, the passage of time was sufficient to make confirmation of one story or the other impossible. In Hale's case, the passage of time was compounded by the fact that he burned his victim's body.

Brian Casement led Mr. Big to the body of a young Indigenous woman he'd strangled and hidden. He told Mr. Big that he'd strangled the woman for entertainment but told the jury he'd lied to impress Mr. Big. In court, he said the woman had died during rough but consensual sex. Casement was convicted of first-degree murder.

Even where a suspect leads Mr. Big to a hitherto undiscovered body, the investigative technique can find shades of grey. Knowledge of where the body is buried signifies some level of guilt, but in cases where the suspect told Mr. Big a story consistent with accidental death, self-defence, or manslaughter, it tends to be accepted either by the police or the courts. The circumstances of the disclosure lend credibility to their claim of a lower level of culpability. On the other hand, if the suspect directs Mr. Big to a hidden body while telling a story consistent with murder, chances are excellent they will be convicted of murder.

SHADES OF GREY FOR INDIVIDUAL CULPABILITY

Killing someone is usually an act of individual initiative, but sometimes it is a group activity. In most of these cases, there is little doubt about the culpability of the group as a collective entity, but shades of grey exist about the role of each group member as an individual. Sometimes this distinction does not have any legal consequence; other times it matters. Sometimes Mr. Big is good at assigning the proper individual shade of grey, but in other cases, Mr. Big makes a difficult or confusing case even more complex. Instead of finding shades of grey, Mr. Big sometimes colours the case an indeterminate murky shade.

Mr. Big's difficulties in assigning the proper level of individual culpability to a group act arise from the paradox of Mr. Big introduced in Chapter 1. When talking to Mr. Big, the suspect can have an incentive to *exaggerate* their own personal role in the group crime. They sometimes want to be seen as bigger, badder, or more competent than they actually are. After Mr. Big is revealed as a police officer, the same person has a strong incentive to *minimize* their personal role. Everyone suddenly becomes a semi-innocent bystander.

Cody Bates, as we saw earlier, wanted to impress Mr. Big by turning bumbling incompetence into a claim to be a bad-ass killer. In court, the prosecutor agreed that Bates's disclosure contained lies and exaggeration. Bates pleaded guilty to manslaughter and was sentenced to eight and a half years. If the prosecutor had taken his disclosure to Mr. Big at face value, there is every possibility that Bates would have been convicted of first-degree murder and sentenced to life.

The paradox inherent in individual disclosure about group activity is compounded by legal rules around hearsay evidence.

The starting point for these rules is that the accused has the right to cross-examine those presenting evidence. When a person makes a videotaped disclosure describing their role in a crime to Mr. Big, the videotape is (usually) admitted in court as evidence against them. If this disclosure also implicates someone else, the right to cross-examine conflicts with the right to avoid self-incrimination. If there is a joint trial, the person who made the disclosure to Mr. Big cannot be compelled to testify because this would violate their right to avoid self-incrimination (remember the oath to tell the truth, the whole truth, and nothing but the truth). In theory, this can be resolved with a warning to the jury to treat the videotaped disclosure as evidence when considering the guilt of the person who was tricked by Mr. Big, but forget it existed when considering the co-accused implicated. Few people, however, are capable of this kind of compartmentalized thinking.

The conflict between the right of one defendant to cross-examine and the right of another to avoid self-incrimination can be addressed by having separate trials. This creates problems of delay and expense. Slight variations in testimony from one trial to the next create confusion and complexity. With separate trials, the person who made the disclosure to Mr. Big can be subpoenaed to testify (and be cross-examined) at his colleague's trial. This testimony cannot then be used against him in his own trial. This can create awkward situations for the court. For example, Neil Yakimchuk told Mr. Big that he helped murder Isho Hana in a dispute over drug sales turf. Yakimchuk told Mr. Big that three other people were involved in the murder. Yakimchuk was convicted of first-degree murder. The other three were tried separately so that Yakimchuk could be cross-examined when the video of his disclosure to Mr. Big was played for the jury. At their trial, Yakimchuk said he had lied to Mr. Big. The three were acquitted. Yakimchuk then successfully appealed his first-degree murder conviction by arguing the jury had not been properly instructed about the difference between first-degree murder and manslaughter. Yakimchuk told Mr. Big that he had fired shots into Isho's back but told the jury that an accomplice pulled the trigger. Yakimchuk claimed that his intention had been to scare Isho rather than kill him. As of the writing of this book, Yakimchuk's case has not yet been resolved — nine years after Yakimchuk made his disclosure to Mr. Big. Meanwhile, Yakimchuk is in prison for a separate first-degree murder he also disclosed to Mr. Big.

Complexities arise when the person who made the disclosure refuses to testify. Lancelot Skeith told Mr. Big he participated in a savage beating and a truck hijacking. Skeith named two accomplices. They were acquitted when Skeith refused to testify. A similar situation arose in the trial of Robert Bradshaw. His friend, Roy Thielen, told Mr. Big the pair committed two drug-trade-related murders. Thielen re-enacted one of the killings for Mr. Big. Thielen pleaded guilty to second-degree murder. At Bradshaw's trial, the video of Thielen's re-enactment was played to the jury. Thielen was called as a witness but refused to testify or submit to cross-examination. A contempt of court charge would have been futile since he was already in prison serving a life sentence. Bradshaw's conviction was overturned on appeal after the re-enactment was ruled to be inadmissible hearsay evidence. The Supreme Court supported the appeal court decision. At the time of writing, Bradshaw remains in jail while waiting for another trial — a full decade after his arrest.

The desire to find the exact shade of grey for each defendant in a group crime can introduce complexity into a simple case. Patrick Smith, Matthew Moreira, and William Cummins launched an unprovoked and vicious attack on two men coming out of a restaurant. One victim was killed when his head was stomped on. There were many witnesses to the crime, and much of it was caught on video. Afterwards, the three were filmed re-enacting the crime in an elevator by a security video camera. It was a black-and-white, open-and-shut case but for the motive and identifying who gave the fatal stomp. Mr. Big got a disclosure from Patrick Smith that, when compared against other evidence, exaggerated his role and downplayed the role of Moreira. The result was a legal gong show with Moreira's lawyer arguing in a voir dire that the disclosure be admitted as evidence and the prosecution attacking it as unreliable. In the end, the three were convicted without the Mr. Big disclosure ever being seen by a jury. Aside from complicating the trials, the Mr. Big operation's only contribution was to generate a newspaper headline that the police had taken a murder suspect to a strip club.

On the other hand, the almost inevitable courtroom finger-pointing at colleagues can sometimes be resolved by Mr. Big.

Jason Klaus was tired of waiting to inherit the farm from his parents. He enlisted the help of Joshua Frank to speed up the process. The pair spent the evening drinking together in the local bar. After bar closing time, Klaus drove Frank to the farm. Frank shot Klaus's parents and sister and the family dog. He then poured a jerry can of aviation gas into the house, lit a match, and departed in the Klaus family pickup truck. Klaus followed Frank. The stolen truck was abandoned. They threw the gun into a river, returned to their homes to get some sleep, and waited for the news of the house fire.

The pair almost got away with the murders. The fire was so intense the medical examiner could not detect they had been shot. Their mistake was killing the dog. Firefighters and police were puzzled why the dog was dead in the yard — killed by a gunshot. The tragic death of the family began to be viewed with more suspicious eyes. Mr. Big was summoned. Klaus was bumped, groomed, and nudged. He told Mr. Big how he and his friend had gotten away with murder. Mr. Big asked to meet the friend. Klaus made the introductions and asked Frank to tell Mr. Big everything. Frank obliged. The pair then re-enacted the crime for Mr. Big. The disclosures and re-enactment matched every known detail of the crime. They even showed Mr. Big where the keys from the stolen truck could be found in a field. After the two were arrested, Klaus confessed.

When their cases came to trial, both Klaus and Frank claimed they'd lied to Mr. Big. Each blamed the other for the killings. Klaus said he'd conspired with Frank to steal his parents' truck. He said he'd waited at the end of the driveway and had no idea that Frank had killed three people and a dog before setting the house on fire. Frank said they were on their way to buy cocaine when Klaus made an unexpected stop at his parents' house. He also claimed to have been oblivious to the murders and arson. In an added twist, Klaus claimed that he had been able to disclose details of the killings because his murdered sister's spirit had visited him. It would be an understatement to describe the trial judge as being skeptical about the pair's courtroom testimony. Both were convicted of three counts of first-degree murder. When they appealed, the Court of Appeal of Alberta described the evidence against them as "overwhelming." Their appeal was dismissed. Mr. Big not only solved the crime. He short-circuited the efforts by a pair of killers to blame each other by conclusively demonstrating that both were guilty.

THE ABILITY OF MR. BIG TO SEE SHADES OF GREY

The police investigative and court adjudication processes are designed to produce a choice from the binary options of "guilty" and "not guilty." This simplicity obscures a more nuanced complexity. In cases of homicide, the simple question of "Did the accused kill the victim?" becomes a complex exercise in assigning differential levels of moral and legal culpability. Police and the courts must assess factors such as intention, circumstances, the degree of individual responsibility for group acts, and so on — the many shades of grey between the black and white of absolute guilt and absolute innocence.

To assess how well Mr. Big deals with shades of grey, we've looked at two types of cases. The first was where someone led Mr. Big to a hitherto undiscovered body (or a piece of a body). The ability to locate the body establishes that the suspect has committed a criminal act, but this act can range from the concealment of an accidental death to first-degree murder. In these cases, Mr. Big is capable of a fair degree of precision in establishing the shade of grey. The suspect will likely be convicted of the crime they disclose to Mr. Big. If they tell Mr. Big they were at the lower end of criminal culpability, that is what they will be convicted of. If they tell Mr. Big they committed first-degree murder, they will receive a life sentence. Mr. Big and the courts take the accused at their word. Admitting limited culpability during a disclosure to Mr. Big rather than in a confession during interrogation strengthens the accused person's claim to the lesser charge. In these circumstances, judges point to the lack of incentive to minimize culpability as enhancing credibility.

The dynamic is different when Mr. Big assigns individual culpability for a group crime. In these cases, suspects tend to exaggerate their individual role when talking to Mr. Big. They reverse course during trial since they then have a strong incentive to minimize their role. In these cases, Mr. Big can create a legal quagmire as individual culpability is sorted out. The best way to resolve this conundrum is to extend the operation by having the first target bump colleagues. In the case of Jason Klaus and Joshua Frank, this resulted in mutually corroborating disclosures. In several cases, the Mr. Big operation brought the criminal colleagues together to compare recollections of the crime. Their privacy was violated only by a hidden video camera. These recorded conversations produce evidence effective in assigning both group and individual culpability.

These individual cases suggest Mr. Big operations are often effective in accurately assessing shades of grey but on occasion can hinder attempts to assign individual culpability to group crimes.

Each case is different, and it is difficult for police to predict how it will play out. For example, the RCMP likely expected Darin Randle to disclose he murdered his partner in the marijuana grow op. Instead, they learned that Dennis Cornish's dying moments were likely spent contemplating the favourite dictum of writer of Western novels Louis L'Amour: "a gun [is] . . . not a toy."

While individual cases reveal the strengths and weaknesses of Mr. Big at establishing shades of grey, a small, purposefully selected sample can be misleading. We don't know how representative these cases are. To obtain a rough assessment of the ability of Mr. Big to assess shades of grey, we can compare the type of convictions that result after people tell Mr. Big they have killed someone with what is known about the overall pattern of homicide convictions in Canada. Statistics Canada reports that of all Canadian homicides from 1998 to 2018, 38.5 percent were first-degree murders, 48.8 percent were second-degree murders, and 12.7 percent were manslaughters. In the Mr. Big cases that resulted in a conviction examined for this book, 50.5 percent resulted in a first-degree murder, 40.6 percent in a second-degree murder, and 8.9 percent in manslaughter. This crude aggregate comparison indicates guilty findings arising from a disclosure to Mr. Big are more likely to result in a first-degree conviction than is the case for Canadian homicides in general. The higher rate of first-degree murder convictions is likely at least partially the result of an in-built bias in case selection. By definition, Mr. Big cases were ones that the police had difficulty solving. Most murders become first-degree because of premeditation. Murders that are planned in advance are usually more difficult for police to solve than those committed in a (usually) drug- or alcohol-assisted outburst of spontaneous violence. Despite the challenges faced, Mr. Big appears to be at least as good at discerning shades of grey as is the Canadian justice system as a whole.

CHAPTER 9

Mr. Big Travels the World

In some ways, Mr. Big personifies the old slogan that the "Mounties always get their man." The phrase was created in 1877 by the editor of the newspaper in Fort Benton, Montana, to describe the capture of whisky smugglers. Like most slogans, it is incorrect. The Mounties don't always "get their man" (or woman): about a third of homicides in Canada remain "uncleared." The slogan signifies an attitude and builds an image. The RCMP was created in Canada and operates in Canada, but much of its image-creation was generated in the United States. The slogan signifying RCMP determination was launched by an obscure newspaper in a small Montana town and was nurtured in Hollywood. The reality of the RCMP stayed in Canada, but the image was international.

If Mr. Big is a quintessential personification of the quintessentially Canadian police force, how does he fare internationally? In this chapter, we'll look at the travels of Mr. Big. We'll look at how Mr. Big has fared in countries with a similar criminal justice system to Canada: the United States, the UK, Australia, and New Zealand.

MR. BIG LENDS A HAND TO THE UNITED STATES

The size and diversity of the American criminal justice system makes a definitive statement impossible, but Mr. Big does not appear to be utilized in the United States. As will be discussed in Chapter 10, some claim this means Mr. Big operations are illegal south of the 49th parallel, but there is a difference between not utilized and illegal. Most people don't pick their nose in public, but it is not illegal to do so. Mr. Big has been called upon to lend a helping hand to American law enforcement agencies, and the evidence he generated was welcomed in American courts.

At about 2:00 a.m. on July 13, 1994, an eighteen-year-old Canadian named Sebastian Burns called 911 to report "some sort of break-in" at the home of the Rafay family. Burns reported there was much blood present and that the parents of his friend Atif Rafay (also Canadian) appeared to be dead. The police in Bellevue, Washington, responded quickly. They discovered Atif Rafay's parents, Tariq and Sultana Rafay, were dead. They had been brutally beaten. Their daughter, Basma Rafay, was also badly beaten and died soon afterwards in hospital. These killings had been messy as well as brutal. The beatings created a lot of blood splatters, but none was on the two youths. The police treated Burns and Rafay as bereaved survivors and as potential sources of information. The pair were interviewed — not interrogated — at the crime scene and the police station. They reported they were university students who arrived at the Rafay home for a visit about a week earlier. They told police they went out for supper, a movie (*The Lion King*), and then to another restaurant and nightclub. Burns and Rafay said they returned home to discover the fate of the rest of the Rafay family. After the two youths gave their statements, they were taken to a motel to rest and recover.

Police began looking at the pair with suspicion because of their behaviour over the next two days. They seemed strangely cheerful.

Rafay refused to help contact relatives or begin funeral planning. The pair gave a third statement on July 14. That night, they changed their status from grief-stricken witnesses to prime suspects by boarding a bus and returning to Canada. When Bellevue police located the pair in Vancouver, detectives arrived a short time later. This time the police wanted a more intensive talk. Burns and Rafay refused to meet with them. They stayed in Canada rather than return to Bellevue for the funerals.

The Bellevue police asked the RCMP to investigate the financial status of the pair and to obtain DNA samples. The RCMP was even more obliging and offered the services of Mr. Big. This created a bit of awkwardness. Burns and Rafay were both Canadian citizens and the murders were committed in the United States. There needed to be a Canadian crime to investigate before the police could obtain the necessary warrants. This problem was resolved by investigating the potential violation of section 465 of the *Criminal Code*, which makes conspiracy to commit murder a Canadian crime if the conspiracy occurred on Canadian soil. With this, the location of the murders became irrelevant. Nine months after the murders, Mr. Big was ready to go.

The Mr. Big undercover officers bumped Burns by waiting outside a hair salon while he got a haircut. When Burns came out, the undercover officer said he'd locked his keys in his car and asked Burns for a ride to his hotel. Burns was obliging. During the short drive, Burns told the undercover officer he needed to raise $200,000 to finance a film. The undercover officer said he knew someone who might be able to help. The operation was on.

As Mr. Big operations go, this one went quickly. At his fourth meeting with the undercover officer, Burns revealed he was a suspect in the Bellevue murders and expressed an enthusiastic interest in making money from drug sales or money laundering. Burns said he would not have "any dilemma" about killing someone since "anything goes." Burns asked whether the imaginary gang's police contacts could get a status report on the investigation in Bellevue. A little over a week later, Burns met with Mr. Big in person. He was shown a fake memo from the Bellevue police department indicating his arrest was imminent. Mr. Big said his associates could destroy the evidence but needed to know details to ensure the job was done properly. After a little hesitation, Burns made a detailed disclosure to Mr. Big and the hidden video camera.

After Burns completed his disclosure, Mr. Big asked him to summon Rafay, who confirmed Burns's story. They gave a lot of details. Burns did the killing while Rafay watched. Burns complained the job "took a little more bat work" than expected. He explained he stripped off his clothes before the murders. After beating three people to death with a metal baseball bat, he took a shower and got dressed. This explained both the absence of blood on his clothes and the hitherto mysterious presence of blood from the dead members of the Rafay family in a shower stall. For his part, Rafay explained they committed the murders to inherit money. Rafay said he planned the murder of his parents and sister to "become richer and more prosperous and more successful" and that the killings were "a necessary sacrifice" in order to get what he wanted in life — most immediately, his parents' assets and insurance policies.

The pair were arrested by the RCMP. The case against them quickly got stronger. A friend testified he heard the pair planning the murders before they occurred and talking about them afterwards. The prosecutor in Washington state requested the two be extradited and Canada's federal justice minister signed an extradition order. It looked as if Burns and Rafay were destined for a quick and smooth ride to the execution chamber. At the time, people convicted of aggravated first-degree murder in the state of Washington were given a choice between a lethal injection and a hanging. If the condemned inmate refused to choose, lethal injection was the default option.

This potential for capital punishment created problems. Capital punishment was illegal in Canada. Lawyers for Burns and Rafay argued extradition to a trial that could result in an execution violated the pair's rights as Canadian citizens. The American prosecutor refused to take the death penalty off the table, and the British Columbia Court of Appeal ruled that this meant the two should not be extradited. The Supreme Court of Canada agreed. These appeals were based solely on the issue of the potential for execution — the Mr. Big operation was not challenged. As an aside, the Supreme Court of Canada judges mentioned the evidence "amply justified" extradition.

After the Supreme Court ruling, the American prosecutor capitulated by promising not to seek the death penalty, and the two were finally extradited. Burns and Rafay had been arrested on July 31, 1995; the Supreme Court of Canada issued its ruling on February 15, 2001. Burns and Rafay were not taken back to the United States until April 6, 2001. After their trial, they unsuccessfully argued at appeal that the delay denied them their right to a timely trial. But this gets ahead of the story.

The trial lasted eight months. There were thirty-five days of argument on pretrial motions. The cornerstone of the defence was an attack on Mr. Big. The defence lawyers argued Mr. Big was a strange and foreign intrusion into the American justice system who obtained false disclosures as a result of coercion and terror. To make this argument, the defence relied on two earlier decisions by American courts. In 1991, the Supreme Court of the United States ruled a confession made to an undercover police officer should be ruled inadmissible because it had been obtained by coercion. Oreste Fulminante had been suspected of killing his eleven-year-old stepdaughter in Arizona. He was later incarcerated for an unrelated offence in Florida. An undercover officer posing as an imprisoned member of the Mafia threatened to let the other prisoners know that Fulminante was a child killer unless he made a disclosure. The Supreme Court ruled that since Fulminante had legitimate grounds to believe the other inmates would kill him if they believed he was a child killer, the disclosure was obtained by coercion and should be rejected as evidence. The other case the defence pointed to involved a man named McCullah who was believed to have been involved in a drug-related killing. McCullah had messed up and killed the wrong person by mistake. A police informant who had once been a member of the drug gang took McCullah for a "long ride into the mountains" and told him the drug organization was planning on killing him for the mistake. The informant offered to intercede on McCullah's behalf but said he needed full details. An appeal court ultimately ruled that McCullah's resulting disclosure had been based on coercion.

Unfortunately for Burns and Rafay, in *Arizona v. Fulminante*, the Supreme Court of the United States had not banned the use of trickery or undercover officers. The court held that the totality of circumstances had to be examined to determine if a disclosure had been voluntary or coercive. There were a number of differences between the circumstances of the two Canadian youths and Oreste Fulminante. Burns and Rafay were not in jail at the time of their disclosure and could have broken off contact with the undercover officers at any time. They received no credible threats of physical violence. They were not cognitively challenged — Rafay was attending an Ivy League university. The trial judge ruled that the totality of circumstances made their disclosures voluntary rather than coercive. The videotapes of their disclosures were viewed by the jury. When Burns and Rafay argued they lied to Mr. Big because they were afraid of him, the members of the jury evidently concluded that they did not look very afraid. The two were convicted of three counts of aggravated first-degree murder. The admission of the disclosures and the convictions were upheld on appeal.

Sebastian Burns and Atif Rafay were convicted on May 26, 2004. They remain in a state of Washington prison. Their ongoing insistence that they lied to Mr. Big has attracted media attention, including two episodes on the Netflix series *The Confession Tapes*.

While the police in the United States do not make a practice of launching Mr. Big operations, they have happened almost accidentally. In 1991, an undercover officer in Wisconsin worked on a sting operation posing as a buyer of stolen property. James Albrecht became a supplier of stolen property. The officer learned Albrecht was a suspect in the 1985 murder of Michelle Koy and began to cultivate a relationship. The police nudged Albrecht by having an officer introduce himself and telling Albrecht that advances in DNA technology meant his arrest was imminent. This caused Albrecht to seek the assistance of the undercover officer. Eventually, in a telephone call recorded by the police, Albrecht explained he had been burglarizing Michelle's apartment when she came home. Albrecht handcuffed her to the bed but then decided on more drastic action. He stabbed Michelle and set the apartment on fire in an attempt to cover up the murder. Albrecht told the undercover officer he threw his bloody clothing into a dumpster and cleaned his knife with acid. After arrest, Albrecht waived his *Miranda* rights and provided a voluntary confession. At his trial, Albrecht's lawyer unsuccessfully attempted to have both the disclosure and the confession suppressed on the grounds that they had been obtained by "outrageous and oppressive police conduct rendering them involuntary." The jury took less than two hours to convict. The members of the Wisconsin Court of Appeals upheld the conviction, noting that "nothing about that deceit is inherently coercive or improper." Albrecht's conviction arose from an accidental Mr. Big operation. Despite its origins, it possessed all the essential elements of a planned Mr. Big operation and was unsuccessfully challenged using the same arguments typically made by Canadian defence lawyers.

One feature of Mr. Big operations that has been accepted by American courts in several cases is tricking the suspect into making a detailed disclosure with the promise of a criminal conspiracy to cover up their involvement in the murder. Two cases illustrate the acceptance of this tactic in American courts.

In 1996, Lisa Seabolt told her husband, Leonard Thomas, that she was going to get a divorce. Thomas responded by beating her to death, burning her body in a 55-gallon oil drum, and claiming that she'd run away with a boyfriend. Lisa's twin sister helped police gather enough circumstantial evidence to have Thomas charged with murder. Thomas hired a professional hit man to kill his meddling sister-in-law in order to remove her as a witness. Unfortunately for him, the hit man was an undercover deputy sheriff. Thomas was duped into providing a detailed disclosure of how he had murdered his wife and disposed of her body. Californian courts had no hesitation in accepting this disclosure as evidence.

An imaginary criminal organization was used to trick Werner Lippe into providing a detailed disclosure of how he'd murdered and burned his wife rather than pay child support and maintenance after a divorce. Werner was a very successful jeweller who counted Donald Trump and Yoko Ono as customers. He burned his wife's body in a barrel in his yard using a propane and oxygen torch normally used for melting platinum and gold. The police recruited a friend of Lippe's who was retired from the military to warn Lippe that police were going to review video from military satellites to reveal what happened. A picture of Lippe's house and yard taken from Google Earth was used to demonstrate the quality of images available. The friend claimed he had connections in the military who could remove any incriminating evidence before providing the video to the police, but they had to know exactly what they were looking for in order to provide this service. Lippe gave a detailed description of how he'd destroyed his wife's body. When confronted with this in court, he claimed he'd been lying. Lippe got twenty-five years to life.

The convictions of Burns, Rafay, Albrecht, Thomas, and Lippe demonstrate that Mr. Big and similar deceptive tactics are not illegal in the United States. The disclosures Mr. Big generated, in every known case, have been accepted as evidence and resulted in a conviction by a jury. These convictions have been upheld on appeal. Similar tactics in other cases have also been accepted. American law enforcement agencies have refrained from using Mr. Big, but there is no legal barrier prohibiting its use. In the United States, Mr. Big is a bit like a distant relative — rarely invited to visit but not turned away from the supper table if he drops by.

One possible explanation for the American police ignoring Mr. Big is that they don't need him to get a conviction in the type of cases that Mr. Big is used for in Canada.

When DNA technology was developed for use in forensic analysis, there was a round of exonerations of people convicted of homicide or sexual assault. DNA analysis would show, for example, that there was only a "one in seven million chance" that the DNA-bearing material found at the crime scene matched that of the person in prison. Accounting for differential population and crime rates, more wrongful convictions were found in the United States than in Canada. There are several reasons for this.

Law in most American states is more expansive in assigning maximum individual culpability in crimes committed by groups. If someone is killed during a robbery in the United States, it usually does not matter who pulled the trigger. In Canada, it does.

American prosecutors are more aggressive at using extreme differentials in potential outcomes to coerce plea bargains. If someone is looking at life imprisonment if convicted but only a year or two if they plead guilty, there is a strong incentive to plead guilty even if innocent. The existence of capital punishment in many American states plays a similar role. The threat of the death penalty is often used to coerce a guilty plea.

Finally, it often appears easier to get charged and convicted in the US on the basis of marginal evidence than in Canada. Many American wrongful conviction cases look like the case of Paul Creek without the appearance of Mr. Big. On Christmas Eve in 1991, Bill Palmer was strangled in his room in a low-rent residential hotel in Vancouver. Earlier in the day, Paul Creek went on a "liquor run" for him. Neighbours reported hearing a dispute about financial accounting, although the murder did not occur until later. Creek's palm print was found in Bill's room. The police suspected Creek but did not have enough evidence to justify a charge. In many American states, these facts would be sufficient for a conviction. As it turns out, Canada was no different. Five and a half years after Bill's murder, Mr. Big was called in. Creek disclosed killing Bill along with claiming responsibility for other crimes that appear never to have happened. The judge ruled the disclosure inadmissible, but the trial proceeded based on the original evidence. The jury was not told that a Mr. Big operation had been conducted. Creek was convicted of second-degree murder even though prosecutors initially believed there was not enough evidence against Creek to justify a prosecution. The Mr. Big operation served to justify the laying of charges. One reason for the absence of Mr. Big in the United States could well be that he's not deemed necessary in cases where the evidence is, objectively, quite weak.

MR. BIG VISITS THE UK

The UK is often described as another country in which Mr. Big operations are illegal. As in the United States, the UK should more accurately be described as a country in which Mr. Big is not used but appears to be legal, at least under restrictive circumstances. As we saw above, the most relevant American case revolved around the use of a Mr. Big operation conducted in Canada to solve a crime committed in the United States. The most relevant British case flips this relationship. A Mr. Big operation was conducted on British soil to solve a crime committed in Canada.

In 1995, twenty-two-year-old Stacey Koehler was an assistant manager at a KFC restaurant in Burnaby, British Columbia. On the evening of March 22, she left work and went home to her basement suite. She donned satin pajamas, opened a bottle of wine, and waited for her boyfriend to arrive. He was playing in a soccer game and the couple had a romantic evening planned after the game. Unfortunately, Stacey's boyfriend went to the bar with teammates rather than keeping his romantic rendezvous. In the early hours of March 23, the drunken boyfriend arrived at Stacey's suite. There was no answer when he knocked, and she didn't answer her phone. The boyfriend reached the drunken conclusion that she was with another man. He wrote "slut" on the frost of her car windshield and let the air out of one tire before deciding to confront Stacey. He smashed a window, climbed into her suite, and discovered her lying dead in a pool of blood. Stacey's throat was crushed and her head smashed in. The boyfriend immediately became the prime suspect in the murder investigation.

Michael Proulx worked at the KFC outlet. Like all employees, he was interviewed by police. Proulx told police he was home with his own girlfriend the night of Stacey's murder, but gave different friends different stories. Eventually, police received a call telling them about Proulx's many alibis. They began casting suspicious looks in his direction. Proulx responded by fleeing to Mexico and disappearing, and immediately became the prime suspect. The investigation was at an impasse for a few years until the RCMP received a call from a KFC manager. A man named Michael Proulx had applied for a job with a KFC franchise in the UK and listed working for the Burnaby franchise in his application. The RCMP checked out the lead and discovered this was the Michael Proulx they badly wanted to talk to. Proulx had made his way to Britain, found work as a bingo caller, and become engaged to one of the bingo players. After his engagement, Proulx got a job at a long-term care home for people with disabilities.

The RCMP asked the British police for permission to run a Mr. Big operation against Proulx. The British were incredulous at first. They became intrigued, then co-operative. They ended up enthusiastic. A RCMP officer experienced in Mr. Big operations travelled to the UK to serve as the primary undercover officer. He was assisted by British police officers who both played different parts in the drama and provided technical services. The operation was supervised by British authorities to ensure compliance with UK law.

As in Canada and the United States, suspects in the UK being interrogated by police have the right to be warned about the implications of confession. The rules governing pre-arrest trickery to obtain a disclosure are more restrictive than in North America. They represent a compromise between traditional British conceptions of "fair play" and a pragmatic understanding that trickery can be useful. Police can use trickery but when doing so cannot ask the suspect direct questions. The key legal decision outlining the opportunities and limitations of police trickery originated from an operation designed to capture house burglars. The police opened a store called Stardust Jewellers and spread the word that jewellery would be purchased with no questions asked. It quickly became a favourite destination of London burglars. After three months, the true nature of the store was revealed and several burglars were arrested. Their disclosures were valid because no questions were asked. The feature of the store making it attractive to burglars disposing of their ill-gotten gains also made it acceptable to judges.

The Mr. Big operation against Proulx was run under this "ask no questions" rule. The RCMP officer bumped Proulx by pretending to have inherited a senior care home in Canada. He asked Proulx for advice about running this kind of enterprise. Their meetings were held in seedy bars to establish a mood. Thoughts of criminality were introduced by talking about Mafia movies. Mysterious events occurred within Proulx's range of vision or hearing that caused him to accuse the undercover officer of being involved in a criminal gang. The officer smiled and modestly refused to comment. No questions were ever asked. The Mr. Big operation let Proulx reach his own conclusions.

As we saw in Chapter 5, one of the common Mr. Big scenarios involves a demonstration of violence against someone outside of the criminal gang to give the suspect moral permission to disclose past violent acts of their own. When the RCMP proposed this scenario, British authorities were shocked and horrified. Staged violence was not allowed. It would offend British sensibilities. The British authorities proposed an alternative strategy, and this time the RCMP was shocked. The British proposed using a "honeypot" scenario in which Proulx would be introduced to a flirtatious female undercover officer. The lure of implied sex had never been in the RCMP's Mr. Big toolkit, but they decided that when in Britain they should do as the British do. A casting call was issued to female British police officers. There was much discussion about looks. The consensus was that the flirtatious undercover officer had to be physically attractive enough to attract Proulx's attention and create desire but not be too attractive. Proulx was both "loser" enough and realistic enough to be suspicious of any beautiful woman purporting to be interested in him. The female officer was selected. Proulx fell hard for her. He told the Canadian undercover officer his new friend was "absolutely gorgeous" and that he had fallen in love. He was told not to expect sex on the first date.

After being groomed with the implied promise of sex rather than implied violence, it was time for the nudge. Proulx was asked to return to Canada to help manage the undercover officer's imaginary senior care home and to assist Mr. Big in establishing a chain of them. It was "understood" criminal activity would be attached. The British undercover officer smiled flirtatiously and nodded when

Proulx suggested she move to Canada with him while the Canadian undercover officer conned Proulx into making a disclosure.

In a normal Mr. Big operation, Proulx would be introduced to Mr. Big for the disclosure. In this case, the operation had to overcome both geography and the ban on direct questions. Proulx would have to make his disclosure while still in Britain before he could be extradited back to Canada.

Proulx and the Canadian undercover officer were placed in a room equipped with a hidden video camera. The phone rang. Proulx answered. It was Mr. Big. He asked for the undercover officer. Proulx listened to one end of the conversation. He heard his friend express great surprise with the words "from Burnaby?" A few exchanges later, Proulx heard the officer say, "She wa— she what? Is that right? [Laughter.] Oh, that's something, eh? No, he never, no, he never did, no." This was followed by: "Well that's something, isn't it? No, he never did. Uh, it's not something you say I guess on the first date, eh. Yeah. No, no, he never. Or I would have fuckin' told you, wouldn't I?"

When the call was over, the undercover officer reported Mr. Big had found some surprising news. Proulx asked, "Is it something to do with murder?"

The undercover officer replied by saying "could be." A few minutes later, Proulx was telling the officer how he murdered Stacey. The key corroborating detail came in his description of the killing. Proulx said he beat Stacey with a dumbbell he'd picked up in her suite. He said the dumbbell cracked and was bloody, so he threw it into a garbage dumpster. Fine sand had been found around Stacey's body and in her head wound. The sand matched that in other, intact weightlifting equipment in her apartment. Proulx initially told the undercover officer he had killed Stacey because her boyfriend owed him money. The next day, Proulx modified his story by telling the Canadian officer that the real motive was because Stacey's boyfriend had kissed his (Proulx's) girlfriend about a month earlier. He explained he was embarrassed by the triviality of the real motive but now wanted to tell the full truth.

Proulx was arrested and an extradition order was issued. His lawyer appealed the extradition order, arguing the disclosure would be inadmissible in a British court. The British judges hearing the case said this was the wrong standard:

> The general requirement of fairness in the admission of evidence in criminal proceedings may be expected to be reflected in any developed system of law. But it is a quite different matter to suppose that it will in its application involve throughout the civilised world the same results as would follow in England from decided authorities, whether under s.78 or under common law. Current English thinking and practice as to what is fair and appropriate cannot be transmuted axiomatically into the touchstone of the outer limits of civilised values.

The judges concluded that Canada's justice system was well-established and governed by rules about fairness that were valid even if different than those in Britain. The Canadian rules were not deemed to "outrage civilised values," so the disclosure to Mr. Big was admissible for the purpose of ordering extradition to Canada. With that, Proulx received a free airplane ride to Vancouver. Proulx pleaded guilty to second-degree murder. At the sentencing hearing, Proulx's lawyer presented a third explanation for motive. He told the court Proulx had gone to Stacey's home to ask her out for a date. Proulx's lawyer said, "On that evening, he couldn't handle rejection."

The British judges posed the question of whether the disclosure would be admissible in a British court in a trial for a crime on British soil, but because this was not the issue before them, they did not definitively answer the question. They said the introduction of this kind of evidence would face "considerable difficulties" but admissibility must be established on a case-by-case basis. The judges said the closest comparison was a 1994 case in which a woman had disappeared. A female undercover officer pretended to fall in love with the woman's husband. She agreed to marry him but said she needed to know what happened to his first wife since she was afraid his first wife would reappear after the marriage. The once and almost-future husband offered the necessary assurances to his new beloved. This disclosure was rejected as evidence in court because it both came from sustained direct questioning and was unverifiable against known evidence. The judges noted that neither of these objections applied to Proulx's disclosure.

The Proulx case reveals an interesting difference between British and North American cultural and legal sensitivities. In North America, deceptive violence is permissible, but the deceptive promise of sex is inconceivable as a means to gather evidence. In Britain, the opposite appears true. This difference does not directly address the issue of whether Mr. Big is legal in the UK. Because Mr. Big has not been used to solve a crime committed in the UK, no court has decided whether the technique is permissible or not. The conditions placed on the Proulx investigation and legal reasoning during his extradition hearing suggest that Mr. Big would face more restrictions in the UK than in Canada, but that careful and clever police could still use Mr. Big to generate an admissible disclosure.

MR. BIG GOES DOWN UNDER

In both the United States and the UK, Mr. Big appears to be legal. Despite that, the investigative technique has not caught on in these countries. Mr. Big had a different reception Down Under, in Australia and New Zealand. Police in those countries observed Mr. Big's effectiveness and embraced him. In Australia, the courts were as enthusiastic as the police. When convictions in the first four Mr. Big cases were appealed, the High Court of Australia voted six to one to endorse the admission of the disclosures. One judge wrote:

> Australian police services need not only to use the most modern technology but also new techniques of investigation found to be successful in comparable police forces overseas. Just as some criminals have become more sophisticated, so policing techniques must also advance to ensure that those who are suspected of crimes are rendered accountable for them before the independent courts.

Mr. Big first arrived in Australia in 2002. He arrived with a flourish, generating four disclosures in the state of Victoria. Two of these were in cold cases.

In 1982, six-year-old Bonnie Clarke was sexually assaulted, stabbed, and ultimately smothered in her bed. The police suspected Malcolm Clarke (no relation to Bonnie, despite the last name). Bonnie's mother ran a boarding house in which Clarke had once been a tenant. At the time of Bonnie's murder, he was living next door. The case remained at an impasse for two decades until the Australian police heard about Mr. Big. The second cold case was the murder of Belinda Romeo in 1999. She had been found strangled in her apartment. An ex-boyfriend named Lemaluofuifatu Tofilau was the primary suspect, but a case in which to convict Tofilau could not be made until he met Mr. Big. Both of these cases resulted in convictions after Mr. Big became involved.

Upon his arrival in Australia, Mr. Big also generated quick results in two fresh cases. Shane Hill told Mr. Big that he had killed his stepbrother over a dispute regarding their supply of heroin. Hill had attempted strangulation. When that method of homicide failed, he smashed in his stepbrother's head with a brick. After Hill's arrest, two family members came forward with reports that Hill disclosed his guilt to them as well. In the second fresh case, Matthew Marks told Mr. Big that he had beaten his great-aunt Margaret O'Toole to death. Marks was in severe financial trouble. His great-aunt had given him in excess of $60,000, but he wanted more and was impatient. Margaret made the fatal mistake of telling Marks that he was the primary beneficiary in her will.

Clarke, Tofilau, Hill, and Marks all unsuccessfully attempted to have their disclosures ruled inadmissible during their trials, but none argued that the disclosures were false or untrue. Despite the implicit concession that they had told Mr. Big the truth, the four argued the disclosures should be rejected because they were given involuntarily due to the trickery used by police. The appeal court judges were almost all profoundly unsympathetic to this argument. They ruled guile is not coercion. Just as the police looked to Canada while creating Mr. Big, the Australian courts relied heavily on Canadian case law to endorse its use.

Since 2002, Mr. Big has made regular appearances in Australian criminal cases. His highest-profile successes include ending the eight-year mystery surrounding the disappearance of thirteen-year-old Daniel Morcombe in Queensland. Brett Cowan led Mr. Big to Daniel's body and explained how he had raped and murdered the boy. Mr. Big also visited Tasmania, where Stephen Standage bragged to Mr. Big that he was "too fucking smart and too fucking careful" to ever be convicted for the two murders he'd committed. Standage was sentenced to forty-eight years in prison.

Mr. Big was a bit slower in getting to New Zealand, making his first appearance in 2007. In 1993, Balwinder Singh disappeared. His skeletal remains were found by forestry workers in 2005. Police suspected Paul Cameron, the son of Balwinder's girlfriend and possessor of a long history of activity at the fringes of the law. Cameron told Mr. Big he and a friend had a large marijuana plantation in the forest. Balwinder had showed other people the location, so Cameron shot him. He said his friend and partner ("mate") fled the scene, discarded the murder weapon, and never again spoke of the affair. After Cameron was arrested, he confessed to the killing but claimed he pulled the trigger accidentally. Follow-up investigation by police produced testimony from Cameron's ex-girlfriend and his pastor that Cameron told them about the killing. Cameron's mate testified he was in the car when he heard shots. He reported that Cameron came running from the forest and told him to drive. He told the jury, "All I know is three of us went into that forest and only two of us came out." Cameron's lawyer argued that unless it could be proven that the skeleton came from a person killed by gunshots, the jury had to acquit. The jury disagreed. At the resulting appeal, the appeal court ruled the disclosure to Mr. Big was not "inherently coercive."

Since Paul Cameron's conviction, New Zealand police have used Mr. Big to get convictions in several cases. We'll look at two of them.

In 2014, Kamel Reddy cleared up the mystery surrounding the 2006 disappearance of his girlfriend and her three-year-old daughter. Reddy told Mr. Big that he strangled his girlfriend with an iron cord and smothered her daughter with a pillow. He cleaned out their apartment and buried the two under a newly constructed highway bridge. Reddy took Mr. Big to the burial site and proudly posed for a picture while pointing to where the bodies were buried.

In 2011, Brett Hall disappeared. His body has never been found. Police suspicion settled on David Lyttle, the last person known to have been with Brett. His behaviour following Brett's disappearance included an unexplained drive to an isolated section of the coastline. The two were good friends until Brett hired Lyttle to build a house. Disputes emerged about the progress of the job and the use of money advanced for construction material. Six years after Brett's disappearance, Lyttle told Mr. Big he killed his friend after being accused of misappropriating money. He said he shot Brett in the head with a small-calibre gun and put a plastic bag over his head until breathing stopped. Lyttle said he dismembered Brett's corpse and buried the pieces along two different beaches. Lyttle pointed out the locations, but no body parts were found. After his arrest, Lyttle confirmed the details of his disclosure with a confession.

Lyttle's prosecution was a mess. His trial was delayed while New Zealand's highest court heard a different appeal about the legality of Mr. Big operations. When Mr. Big was reconfirmed as legal, the trial was repeatedly adjourned and postponed as a result of incomplete and slow disclosure of evidence to the defence. The problem appears to have been incompetence and a separation of functions. The officers running the Mr. Big operation had been kept separate from the main investigation to avoid creating bias or contaminating evidence. After Lyttle's arrest, this division remained. Efforts to gather material for disclosure were disjointed and incomplete. The courts said that the failures to properly disclose evidence were not deliberate but created more than two years of delay. The police were ordered to pay Lyttle and his family compensation for the expenses associated with these delays.

Despite the organizational difficulties, Lyttle's trial followed the standard script for Mr. Big cases. The prosecution showed the jury videos of the disclosures and the confession. The defence lawyer said his client had lied. The jury convicted Lyttle of murder. In the sentencing ruling, the judge said he believed Lyttle's description of the killing was accurate but dismissed his report of dismemberment and multiple burial sites as a fabrication. The judge suggested Lyttle simply buried the body and concocted the more elaborate story as a defence against the possibility that Mr. Big was a police officer. After arguing throughout the trial that Lyttle's disclosure was false, the defence lawyer argued at sentencing it should be believed because the killing had elements of self-defence and provocation.

MR. BIG AS A CANADIAN EXPORT

The success Mr. Big has enjoyed in generating disclosures has attracted attention internationally. In the United States and the UK, the approach has been deemed legal, but police have not embraced the tactic. For the British, it remains an "only in Canada, eh?" novelty. In Australia and New Zealand, Mr. Big has been embraced by police and authorized by the courts. The international reception of Mr. Big has been a bit like that of other imaginative Canadian creations such as hockey and snowmobiles: they are all exportable anywhere but become popular only in the limited number of countries that have the right environmental and cultural conditions.

CHAPTER 10

Mr. Big under Pressure: "Reining In" or "Getting Better"?

M r. Big made his crime-fighting debut in the early 1990s. He is
now pushing thirty. Like most people, Mr. Big has changed
over time. He grew up. He is more experienced, smoother, and
usually wiser.

Let's begin by looking at one example. Like many young men,
Mr. Big had a fondness for alcohol. In his case, it was not for
personal consumption. Mr. Big believed that demon rum created
loose lips. In two investigations, getting the target drunk was part
of the strategy.

In 1992, Brian Cretney made a friend while attending an alcohol
detox program. Upon completing their program, the two shared a
cabin in British Columbia. Both fell off the wagon. A short time
later, Cretney's friend abruptly disappeared. Four years later, the
RCMP decided Cretney should meet Mr. Big. The operation was
crude. Its main element was plying Cretney with booze until he
talked. The approved liquor budget for the operation was $1,500,
which bought a lot of bad hooch in 1996. The undercover officer

drank while driving with Cretney in order to remove suspicions that he was a police officer rather than a criminal.

In 1997, another heavy drinker, Thomas Griffin, was targeted by Mr. Big. In this case, the primary undercover officer used alcohol to escalate Griffin's comfort with disclosure. She would get Griffin drunk. He would disclose a little. The next day, when Griffin was sober, she would follow up on the disclosure ("That was some wild story you told last night . . ."). This alcohol-assisted pattern of drunken disclosure and sober follow-up groomed Griffin for a detailed, videotaped disclosure to Mr. Big that earned him a second-degree murder conviction.

By the end of Mr. Big's first decade, the RCMP decided that using booze as a tool in Mr. Big investigations was unnecessary, dangerous to the public, and liable to challenge by defence lawyers. When the Cretney and Griffin cases went to court, defence lawyers argued the disclosures were unreliable because of impairment. In both cases, the judges ultimately ruled the disclosures should be admitted as evidence, but they looked closely and suspiciously at the "get them drunk so they'll blab" strategy. Mr. Big case officers got the hint, and this approach disappeared from Mr. Big's repertoire. Undercover officers still have a beer or two with the suspect, but attempts to get the suspect drunk were replaced with efforts to keep them sober. Wannabe gang members were given lectures saying real criminals don't get drunk or stoned on the job. Many suspects had the cleanest and soberest period of their adult life while under the moral guidance of Mr. Big.

The interactive dynamics of learning from experience combined with challenges from defence lawyers made RCMP-led Mr. Big operations more closely supervised, longer, more expensive, and more sophisticated. As a result, the disclosures they generate are richer in detail, more reliable, and more persuasive to a jury. Occasionally other Canadian police forces try running a Mr. Big operation. The

Calgary Police Service has run solid and sophisticated operations, but some police forces, primarily in Ontario, have demonstrated there is no substitute for experiential learning.

When a Mr. Big case goes to court, the outcome usually rests on whether the videotaped disclosure is admitted as evidence. As we saw in Chapter 5, Liban Omar was able to convince the jury he had lied to Mr. Big. People with this kind of persuasive power are rare. The defence lawyer's best hope for an acquittal is to keep a jury from seeing the disclosure. This means the conduct of the operation will be intensely scrutinized. Undercover officers playing a key role in a Mr. Big operation can expect to spend more time on the witness stand being cross-examined than the accused. These attempts to have Mr. Big disclosures ruled inadmissible have failed in about nine of ten cases, but the knowledge that these challenges will be coming has caused the RCMP to refine their methods. Today's disclosures are better able to withstand a challenge and are more persuasive to a jury than in the past.

Let's look at one example. After a person tells Mr. Big they've killed someone, they will be convicted unless they convince a judge or jury that they were lying. They often claim Mr. Big lured them into compliance and that the disclosures were generated by fear. There is an intuitive plausibility to this claim. After all, the suspect thought Mr. Big was the powerful boss of a dangerous criminal gang. In some of the early Mr. Big operations, intimidation was used. People like Jason Dix, William Terrico, Wilfred Hathway, Alan Smith, and Clayton Mentuck had every reason to feel frightened of Mr. Big. Intimidation played a significant role in these Mr. Big cases, but the cases showed the limitations of intimidation.

In one sense, the Mr. Big operation directed at Jason Dix was a success. He was innocent and refused to admit to the murders. The problem was the main investigative team was so blinded by the disease of certainty that they did not consider the most probable implication of his stubborn refusal to admit to the killings. It was a no-win situation for Jason. If he made a disclosure of guilt, he would have been convicted. When he "passed" the test, the results were dismissed as unreliable. Further, the use of threats and intimidation traumatizes the innocent.

Terrico and Hathway did disclose guilt. In their cases, the violent and intimidating scenarios formed the cornerstone of their attempts to recant their disclosures. These attempts were unsuccessful, but the possibility existed that violent or intimidating scenarios could go "too far" and cause the dismissal of a *true* disclosure.

The cases of Clayton Mentuck and Alan Smith represent the worst of all outcomes. Intimidation helped generate an untrue disclosure. As we saw in Chapter 5, one reason for Clayton's disclosure was threats directed at himself and the undercover officer he thought was his friend. Alan Smith had a similar experience. In 2009, he was targeted by a Mr. Big operation conducted by the Durham Regional Police Service as they attempted to solve the 1975 murder of Smith's neighbour. This police force was inexperienced in conducting Mr. Big operations and the inexperience showed. When Alan refused to make a disclosure, the police and a prosecutor debated how far they could go in intimidating him. They inadvertently turned on the recording equipment in the room prepared for Alan's meeting with Mr. Big. The resulting video showed the police were willing to use coercion to get a disclosure. Alan duly provided a disclosure that contradicted many of the known facts about the case. He then spent five years in jail waiting for his day in court. After the trial judge watched the recordings of both the planning session and the disclosure, the disclosure was ruled inadmissible. The Ontario Ministry of the Attorney General changed the prosecutor. The new prosecutor called no evidence at the trial. Alan was acquitted, but he still spent five years behind bars.

The objectives of a Mr. Big operation should be to get a full, detailed disclosure from the guilty and no disclosure from the innocent. Intimidating the suspect does not help achieve either of these goals. If guilty, the suspect has no incentive to provide detail. The session with Mr. Big resembles a traditional in-custody interrogation and undermines the inner logic of the operation. It also undermines the disclosure's credibility in court and could allow the guilty to be acquitted. If the suspect is innocent, a fear-based approach subjects an innocent person to a very unpleasant experience and increases the possibility of a false disclosure.

These problems, arising from this early approach to Mr. Big operations, resulted in quality improvements.

The first was video-recording the final sessions with the person of Mr. Big and as many of the other scenarios as possible. Self-surveillance inhibits any police impulse to go "too far." Electronic recording also makes a good disclosure a much more powerful piece of evidence. The jury did not believe claims by Terrico and Hathway that they were terrified of Mr. Big because in the video they didn't *look* or *sound* fearful.

The other major change was providing a suspect with a positive reason for a truthful, detailed disclosure. Instead of telling the suspect that he needed to "prove himself" or give the gang something to "hold over him," Mr. Big offered a positive incentive. With the "dying guy" scenario or one of its spinoffs, a guilty suspect must give the fall guy all the details. A lack of detailed knowledge or inaccuracies makes the "dying guy's" confession useless or even harmful. This approach is not infallible, but the "dying guy" approach is much better than "brag for us" or "confess or we'll kill you." Positive reasons for disclosure have almost completely replaced the older, less effective threat-based scenarios. If Mr. Big reverts to the cruder methods, there is now a high probability the disclosure will be rejected either at trial or on appeal. For example, in overturning the first-degree murder conviction of Michel Laflamme, the Quebec Court of Appeal observed that when intimidating scenarios were introduced, "the undercover agents compromised their investigation, which was otherwise going well and having the desired effect, as it appeared that the appellant quickly felt trustful and wanted to become a member of the Organization." The promising operation was ruined by intimidating Michel.

MR. BIG ON TRIAL

In Canada, people have a constitutional right not to be forced into self-incrimination. Confessions must be voluntary. During the police investigation, voluntariness means the suspect has the right to remain silent during an interview or interrogation. The police can (and do) put *pressure* on the suspect to admit to guilt, but they cannot *force* the person to talk. The line between pressuring and forcing can be a grey one. Some things, such as torture, "truth serums," or threats to kill belong in the realm of force. Offering inducements is more ambiguous. If a police officer says, "Admit to the killing and we'll charge you only with manslaughter," any confession would probably be rejected as inadmissible. However, "We can't help you if you don't help us" is more likely to be admitted. When someone confesses guilt to the police during an interrogation, their lawyer will almost always argue that the confession should be ruled inadmissible because it was not voluntary. If the police have gone "too far" in the interrogation, the argument can be successful.

People suspected of crimes must be informed of their rights before being interrogated. In the United States this is provided in a *Miranda* warning, named after Ernesto Miranda, who was convicted of armed robbery, kidnapping, and rape. A 1966 Supreme Court decision overturned his conviction and entrenched the right to receive a formal warning from police. (Ernesto Miranda was convicted in a second trial.) In Canada, the right to be informed of the right to remain silent lacks a specific name but is as real as it is in the United States. Police interrogations conducted without a prior warning to the suspect will result in the confession being ruled as inadmissible.

At first glance, this combination of the requirement that self-incrimination be voluntary and that a warning be given before an interrogation makes a successful Mr. Big operation impossible. Even the least intelligent or most gullible suspect could figure out the implications of a crime boss giving a formal legal warning before a conversation. But Mr. Big is exempted from the warning requirement since the suspect does not know they are being questioned by a police officer or "person in authority." The legal logic is a person cannot be influenced by official threats or promises if they don't know the person questioning them is an official. It goes further. The courts have ruled limitations on threats or inducements apply only to "people in authority." Private citizens are free to do whatever it takes (subject to laws of assault, kidnapping, and so on) to obtain an admission of guilt. Because Mr. Big is not *perceived* by the suspect to be a person in authority, he is free to offer inducements and issue threats that would be illegal for a uniformed or self-identified police officer. Mr. Big operates in the grey area between the *reality* that Mr. Big is a police officer and the suspect's *perception* that he is not. This has generated some odd arguments in court wherein the accused claims he knew Mr. Big was a police officer. The prosecution responds with the question of why, if the suspect knew Mr. Big was a cop, did they admit guilt? The answers can get convoluted. Ronda Black claimed when she told Mr. Big she had stabbed her sleeping husband, she was both lying and knew Mr. Big was a police officer. She said her father was the real killer, but she claimed guilt in order to get charged. She said her intention was to provoke her father into making a voluntary confession and thereby "clear her name." She advanced this argument only after her father had died of cancer about a year after her arrest. Black's convoluted explanation failed to sway the judge. She was convicted of second-degree murder.

For two and a half decades, the arguments about the legality of Mr. Big were confined to trial courts and provincial appeal courts.

The Supreme Court of Canada generally refrained from hearing appeals on Mr. Big cases. On rare occasions, the Supreme Court was required to hear a Mr. Big case, but these cases did not address the operation's core legal rationale. We'll briefly review these cases.

In Chapter 5, we saw that Marven McIntyre was bumped by an undercover police officer with whom he once shared a jail cell. One judge at the Court of Appeal of New Brunswick said the nature of this initial contact meant McIntyre was still legally detained when meeting Mr. Big in Montreal several months later. In 1994, the Supreme Court wasted no time dismissing this argument. Its ruling was only five sentences long, including the succinct conclusion that "the appeal is dismissed." The Supreme Court unanimously agreed that "the accused was not detained" and "the tricks used by the police were not likely to shock the conscience of the community or cause the accused's statements not to be free and voluntary."

The next Mr. Big–generated conviction to reach the Supreme Court was that of Peter Fliss. This 2002 hearing did not deal with the legality of the Mr. Big operation but with a technical evidentiary question about a police officer's testimony. The Supreme Court upheld Fliss's conviction while describing the Mr. Big operation as "skillful police work."

The case of Cory Grandinetti was the next appeal of a Mr. Big case to make it to the Supreme Court. In 2005, his lawyer argued that because Mr. Big had claimed to have access to corrupt police officers, Mr. Big should be treated as a person in authority. The Supreme Court said Grandinetti "believed that the undercover officers were criminals, not police officers." Therefore, "When the accused confesses to an undercover officer he thinks can influence his murder investigation by enlisting corrupt police officers, the state's coercive power is not engaged. The statements, therefore, were not made to a person in authority." Grandinetti stayed in prison.

Until 2014, the results of the cases of McIntyre, Fliss, and Grandinetti, combined with the Supreme Court's refusal to hear appeals of other Mr. Big cases, indicate that Canada's highest court had no substantive concerns about Mr. Big. During this period, the accused who had disclosed guilt to Mr. Big and their lawyers regularly challenged the legality of the operation and the admissibility of the disclosure at trial or on appeal. More than nine out of ten challenges were unsuccessful. The successful efforts to have a disclosure to Mr. Big ruled inadmissible came in the following cases:

- In 1995, a British Columbia judge refused to admit the disclosure to Mr. Big made by Paul Creek about a 1991 homicide because of inconsistency and a lack of corroboration. As discussed in Chapter 9, Creek was convicted by the jury without knowing about the disclosure.
- In 2000, a Manitoba trial judge acquitted Clayton Mentuck because the disclosure to Mr. Big was generated by intimidation and the promise of a million-dollar wrongful arrest lawsuit. The judge ruled the threats and inducements made the disclosure unreliable.
- In 2000, a British Columbia trial judge refused to admit a disclosure to Mr. Big by O.N.E. that she pushed a man from a bridge in retaliation for an assault. The disclosure was deemed uncorroborated and internally inconsistent.
- In 2005, a British Columbia trial judge acquitted Clarence Smith on a murder charge because of a lack of corroborating evidence combined with Clarence's inability to separate truth from fiction.
- In 2006, a British Columbia trial judge acquitted Salvatore Ciancio on two counts of first-degree murder because his disclosures lacked corroborating detail.

This case was unusual in that the person making the bump and grooming Salvatore had already pleaded guilty to the murders but was temporarily released from prison to help with two Mr. Big operations against people he said were criminal colleagues. In the other case, Mark Therrien was convicted on five counts of first-degree murder.

- In 2007, a British Columbia trial judge acquitted M.(T.C.) on a murder charge. A drug dealer was shot on a Vancouver street, apparently as a result of a turf war. M.(T.C.) was at the scene. When he turned eighteen, he became the target of a Mr. Big operation. The trial judge pointed to inconsistencies in the disclosure and said guilt was not the "only reasonable inference from the evidence."

- In 2013, charges against NRR and ADS were stayed after an Alberta judge refused to admit as evidence disclosures made by the two youths when they were still sixteen. This case was discussed in more detail in Chapter 7.

- In 2014, an Ontario trial judge ruled Alan Smith's 2009 disclosure of guilt for the murder of his neighbour was inadmissible because it was obtained through threats and because the details were inconsistent with the known facts of the case.

In addition to these cases, Kyle Unger's disclosure to Mr. Big was ultimately shown to be false. As we saw in Chapter 3, this only happened after Kyle spent more than a dozen years in prison.

The most important predictors of whether a disclosure to Mr. Big would be accepted in the cases I analyzed was internal consistency and the extent of the corroborating evidence. If the disclosure of guilt was "all there was" or if, as in the case of both Clarence

Smith and Alan Smith (what is it about the Smiths?), the disclosure was incorrect in detail or outright fantastical, the accused had a reasonable chance of having his disclosure discounted. On the other hand, if the disclosure was corroborated, judges appeared reluctant to reject it based on how it was obtained. Arguments that the undercover officers were "persons in authority," that the disclosure arose from intimidation or inducements, that tricking the suspect was abusive, or that the accused lacked the social or mental capacity to protect their interests could be successful if *combined* with doubts about veracity, but judges were reluctant to exclude disclosures that appeared true.

The case of Nelson Hart caused the Supreme Court to conduct a detailed review of Mr. Big. As we saw in Chapter 4, there were ample grounds to suspect Nelson killed his two daughters, but nothing could be proven. A plausible alternative explanation also existed. The disclosure to Mr. Big did not really change this situation. It was possible that Nelson lied to Mr. Big and equally possible he did not. Further, Nelson was a bit pathetic. He was the kind of character who elicits sympathy so long as one does not have to spend too much time in his presence. He could be portrayed as cognitively challenged and socially isolated, while at the same time he possessed an interesting ability to mobilize people to work on his behalf. Finally, and perhaps most crucially, the Court of Appeal of Newfoundland and Labrador issued a split decision on the core issues of the constitutionality of Mr. Big as directly applied to the facts of the case. This meant that the Supreme Court had to address Mr. Big head-on.

In an interesting manoeuvre, the Supreme Court also agreed to hear the appeal of Dax Mack even though his conviction had been unanimously upheld by the Court of Appeal of Alberta. This case was discussed in Chapter 5. Mack was the landlord from Fort McMurray who caught his tenant stealing a piggy bank, shot him five times, and burned the body. Mack's case was everything that

Nelson's was not. Mack was not cognitively challenged or socially isolated. The Mr. Big team did not exercise a particularly strong influence on his life. There was a wealth of corroborating evidence. To paraphrase the old Roger Miller song, Mack was guilty just as sure as God made the little green apples. In normal circumstances, it is unlikely that the Supreme Court would have agreed to hear Mack's appeal. With Nelson Hart's case arriving from Newfoundland, Mack provided contrast. Whether planned by the Supreme Court or not, the court's decisions in the Hart and Mack cases provided balance. Nelson Hart served as the exemplar for when a disclosure to Mr. Big should not be admitted as evidence, while Dax Mack served as the ideal type for cases in which it should.

As was discussed in Chapter 4, Nelson's case was treated as a full-fledged trial of Mr. Big. The prosecutions branches of Canada, Ontario, and British Columbia joined Newfoundland in defending Mr. Big while a collection of organizations representing defence lawyers and human rights groups joined with Nelson's legal team in the attack. The prosecutors also weighed in on Mack's case, but the opponents of Mr. Big went silent. Good lawyers are not fools. They avoided arguing that Mr. Big generated false disclosures in a case where the disclosure was manifestly true.

Those attacking Mr. Big made a lot of different arguments, but their conclusions can be divided into two types: improve versus abolish.

The lawyers entrusted with the task of defending Nelson's interests argued for improvement. They asked for criteria for case-specific evaluations of Mr. Big disclosures, saying the primary criteria should be the specificity of disclosures and the degree of corroboration.

Those arguing for abolishment of Mr. Big claimed the operation was inherently abusive and corruptive to the legal system. The favoured approach to drive the stake through the heart of Mr. Big was to call for him to be considered a "person in authority." This would limit the use of inducements or threats. More importantly, it would require a suspect be given a formal legal warning before talking to Mr. Big.

The Supreme Court unanimously agreed to uphold the Court of Appeal of Newfoundland and Labrador's overturning of Nelson's conviction, although there was some disagreement on next steps. The Supreme Court stressed the importance of balance. It wrote that, on the one hand,

> To be sure, the Mr. Big technique has proven to be an effective investigative tool. It has produced confessions and secured convictions in hundreds of cases that would otherwise have likely gone unsolved. The confessions elicited are often detailed and confirmed by other evidence. Manifestly, the technique has proved indispensable in the search for the truth.

On the other hand, the Supreme Court acknowledged:

> But the technique comes with a price. Suspects confess to Mr. Big during pointed interrogations in the face of powerful inducements and sometimes veiled threats — and this raises the spectre of unreliable confessions.
>
> Unreliable confessions present a unique danger. They provide compelling evidence of guilt and present a clear and straightforward path to conviction. Certainly in the case of conventional confessions, triers of fact have difficulty accepting that an innocent person would confess to a crime he did not commit. And yet our experience with wrongful convictions shows that innocent people can, and do, falsely confess. Unreliable confessions have been responsible for wrongful convictions — a fact we cannot ignore.

The Supreme Court balanced the conflicting imperatives of punishing the guilty while avoiding wrongful convictions with two measures.

The first was to put the onus on prosecutors to convince the court the disclosure *should be* admitted as evidence rather than making the defence argue it *should not* be. This sounds like a hair-splitting, legalistic, quibbling change, but it has important implications. It makes the default position one of rejection. It's a bit like the difference between an automatic renewal (and automatic charge to your credit card) of an online subscription compared to a law saying the subscriber must authorize a renewal. The prosecutor must show that the Mr. Big operation was conducted properly and the disclosure is reliable. This means Mr. Big will be intensively scrutinized in every case.

The Supreme Court went on to say the first test of whether a disclosure should be admitted is reliability. A disclosure must be detailed and corroborated. The Supreme Court said only disclosures appearing to be largely true should be put in front of a jury or considered by a judge when making a ruling. If the disclosure could not be demonstrated to be reasonably reliable, it should not be introduced as evidence.

The Supreme Court added a second test for admissibility. If a disclosure appeared to be reliable, the Mr. Big operation itself needs to be examined. If the undercover officers threaten the suspect or offer too many benefits, the disclosure should be rejected. If the suspect is too stupid, socially isolated, or dysfunctional, the disclosure should be rejected. The Supreme Court acknowledged there is a grey area between police conduct that is clearly abuse and conduct that is not. The majority opinion said:

> It is of course impossible to set out a precise formula for determining when a Mr. Big operation will become abusive.

These operations are too varied for a bright-line rule to apply. But there is one guideline that can be suggested. Mr. Big operations are designed to induce confessions. The mere presence of inducements is not problematic (Oickle, at para. 57). But police conduct, including inducements and threats, becomes problematic in this context when it approximates coercion. In conducting these operations, the police cannot be permitted to overcome the will of the accused and coerce a confession. This would almost certainly amount to an abuse of process.

With the Hart/Mack rulings, the Supreme Court of Canada acknowledged Mr. Big was valuable and useful in solving serious crimes, but that he needed to be treated with caution. He is akin to tough towns in the American Old West in the 1870s hiring a gunslinger like Wyatt Earp or Wild Bill Hickok as their sheriff — useful in imposing order but sometimes a little too quick to pull the trigger. Useful but potentially dangerous.

How much did the Hart/Mack guidelines change the way Mr. Big operations are conducted? It appears the answer is "not much."

Mr. Big operations have changed since they first began in the early 1990s. There has been a process of continuous evaluation and improvement. It appears the Supreme Court guidelines represent a codification of the "best practices" for Mr. Big operations rather than a "reining in" of the technique.

Mr. Big cases can be divided into three groups based on their relationship to the Hart/Mack guidelines.

The first group is those in which both the Mr. Big operation and the complete trial-appeal process occurred prior to the Hart/Mack rulings. While researching this book, I identified seventy-three of these cases. Eight of these disclosures were rejected at the voir dire, trial by judge alone, or appeal court hearing. Sixty-five (89 percent) of the disclosures were accepted as evidence. Of these, one

(Kyle Unger's) has been proven to be a false disclosure resulting in a wrongful conviction. After the Hart/Mack rulings, some of these convicted murderers asked for a new appeal or review of their case. One of them, Wade Skiffington, has been successful in getting the federal Minister of Justice to review his conviction. Skiffington was convicted of second-degree murder in 2001 after telling Mr. Big that he shot his wife in 1994. He had been eligible for parole for four years prior to winning the review of his case, but he was turned down by the parole board because he had not demonstrated remorse by admitting guilt. In all likelihood, Skiffington's disclosure to Mr. Big would not have been admitted if the Hart/Mack rules were in place at the time of his trial since his disclosure lacked corroborative details.

The second group of cases is those in which the Mr. Big operation was conducted before the Hart/Mack rulings, but for which either the trial or the appeal occurred after the new guidelines were established. In these cases, either the trial judge or the appeals court assessed the Mr. Big operation against the new standard. Forty-one of these cases have been identified. Of these, thirty-one (78 percent) of the disclosures were ruled admissible. Seven disclosures were deemed nonconforming to the Hart/Mack guidelines. In two cases, prosecutors reached the same conclusion and stayed the charges. Finally, the Quebec Court of Appeal ordered a new trial for Alain Perreault, while saying his disclosure was corroborated by "a number of elements of circumstantial evidence" and was "rife with details and explanations. It is hard to imagine how a person who did not commit the murder could give them." The disclosure was admitted at a second trial, and Perreault was convicted of first-degree murder for a second time.

Some of these cases occurred long ago and usually involved cases that were cold when Mr. Big became involved. For example, the Quebec Court of Appeal applied the Hart/Mack criteria to the Mr. Big operation targeted at Michel Laflamme in 2007 in an attempt to solve a homicide that was committed in 1976. Two other Quebec appeal cases dealt with disclosures made in 2009 about homicides that happened in 1987. In these cases, the passage of time contributed to the decay of possible corroborating evidence. If nothing else, these cases show the wheels of justice can turn slowly in Canada. The longest-running court proceeding resulting in the "successful" appeal of a conviction based on a disclosure to Mr. Big came in the case of Andre Jeanvenne. In 2003, Andre disclosed to Mr. Big that he helped a friend commit suicide in 1983 and murdered a former criminal colleague in 2000. In 2016, the Court of Appeal for Ontario applied the Hart/Mack criteria to his disclosure and overturned the first-degree murder conviction resulting from his disclosure thirteen years earlier. It was the third time a conviction on this charge has been overturned on appeal. The majority of disclosures found to be non-compliant with the Hart/Mack guidelines came in cases that have been kicking around the court system a long time and arose from Mr. Big operations conducted before many of the modifications to Mr. Big procedures were made.

The third group of Mr. Big cases is those in which the Mr. Big operations happened after the Hart/Mack guidelines were implemented. In these cases, the police knew the standard against which their work would be judged. Either because fewer Mr. Big cases are now being conducted or because of the slowness of Canada's court process, not a lot of these cases have been decided. As of July 2020, there have been six of these cases. The disclosure to Mr. Big was accepted as evidence in four and rejected in one. In the final case, the prosecution obtained convictions without introducing the disclosure to Mr. Big.

The distinction between admissible and inadmissible disclosures following the Supreme Court's Hart/Mack guidelines is illustrated by the voir dire conducted for the trial of Garry Handlen, who was suspected of raping and murdering two twelve-year-old Indigenous girls in separate incidents. Kathryn Herbert was murdered in Matsqui, British Columbia, in 1975, and Monica Jack near Merritt in 1978. Kathryn's body was not discovered until two months after her death, while seventeen years passed before Monica's remains were found. Handlen was serving a twelve-year prison sentence for rape, so the Mr. Big operation did not begin until 2014. The passage of time degraded the evidence, including Handlen's memory. The Mr. Big operation had eighty-two separate scenarios over ten months and culminated with road trips to the crime scenes so Handlen could refresh his memory as he attempted to recall events four decades earlier.

The Hart/Mack rulings were issued halfway through the Mr. Big operation. The RCMP planned and began the operation without knowing what the new rules would be but conducted the later scenarios after seeing them. The judge deemed that Mr. Big's conduct met the criteria established by the Supreme Court, saying:

> I do not, however, see in the general relationship between the accused and the undercover officers a ceding of his will or autonomy. The accused appeared to see the organization as a good opportunity for himself and was willing to do what he thought would advance his interests within that organization. He did not lose his identity to the organization, and while he generally did what was asked of him, he made it clear that he would not do some things (e.g., traffic in drugs).

The judge said the Mr. Big team conducted the overall operation appropriately. The other test of admissibility was more problematic and nuanced. When measured against the known evidence, the disclosure about Monica's murder was corroborated well enough to be admissible, while the disclosure about Kathryn's was not. In Kathryn's case, the waters had been further muddied by television documentaries about the case. The judge said details known by Handlen could have come from the television broadcasts rather than from direct knowledge.

The prosecutor proceeded with the murder charge for Monica's death but not Kathryn's. As far as the jury knew, Kathryn never existed. Her murder and the disclosure to Mr. Big was not mentioned while the jury was in the courtroom. Handlen was convicted of first-degree murder and will die in prison (he was sixty-seven years old when he met Mr. Big). For Handlen, avoiding trial for Kathryn's murder had no substantive impact. For Kathryn's family, her murder will always remain officially unsolved.

The real impact of the Hart/Mack ruling on Handlen's case was in the intensity of examination Mr. Big was subjected to. The voir dire hearing into this Mr. Big operation began on January 24, 2017, and was not completed until April 17, 2018. The 164-page ruling was not issued until August 8, 2018. Two hundred and ninety-four days passed from Handlen's first contact with an undercover officer to his arrest. The process of deciding whether to admit the resulting disclosures at a trial took 562 days. Undercover officers were in contact with Handlen on eighty-two occasions during the operation, but 106 days were spent in court examining what happened. Every scenario generated 1.29 days of voir dire scrutiny.

The level of scrutiny in the Handlen case is not extraordinary in the post-Hart/Mack legal environment. Prior to the new rules, a voir dire ruling on a disclosure's admissibility typically ran between ten and thirty pages. The ruling on the Handlen voir dire was 164 pages. The decision on the admissibility of Robert Balbar's disclosure was 143 pages, while the decision on David Caissie's was 162 pages. Not every post-Hart/Mack decision is the length of a novel, but the length of both voir dire hearings and written decisions has increased significantly. We'll discuss the likely implications of this in the next chapter.

While most of the changes to Mr. Big operations have come from a combination of police learning and challenges to disclosures in court, the media and academics in Canada have also contributed changes in how the operations are conducted.

PUBLICITY AND MR. BIG

Mr. Big is an undercover police officer. The entire Mr. Big operation is based on deceiving and tricking the suspect. The probability of the suspect disclosing guilt would be exceptionally remote if the person realized the truth of what was happening. Because of this, it was assumed that publicity about Mr. Big would mean his demise. When the first Down Under Mr. Big cases were examined by the High Court of Australia, a judge wrote, "The particular technique of deception adopted in the present cases seems to have been imported into Australia from Canada. Since these trials, it has been reported in the media. Presumably, unless Australians suspected of serious crime are unaware of what is contained in the newspapers, it has a limited life expectancy."

The expectation that Mr. Big would be destroyed by publicity seemed like intuitive common sense. It was not true.

During Mr. Big's first decade, prosecutors often requested permanent publication bans on the details of the investigations. These were sometimes granted. Some published judicial rulings dealing with Mr. Big operations in the 1990s still have several paragraphs redacted. More than two decades later, the reader is confronted with a series of paragraph numbers followed by white space.

Media outlets fought these restrictions on publication. As a matter of principle, they argued court proceedings should be transparent so justice can be seen to be done. As a matter of commercial imperative, Mr. Big cases make great stories. The published accounts of Mr. Big's exploits attract readers to newspapers and viewers to television broadcasts.

The contest between transparency and the perceived need to protect Mr. Big's secrecy came to a head in the case of Clayton

Mentuck. He lied to Mr. Big, believing his life was in danger, and his disclosure was recognized as false by the judge. Clayton was acquitted. He was innocent in the eyes of the law, but he remained guilty in the eyes of the community. As far as most Manitobans were concerned, he "got off" — probably just because he had a good lawyer. Clayton's lawyer was excellent, but having a good lawyer does not make a person guilty. Clayton believed that if people knew why he lied to Mr. Big, he would be able to put the mark of Cain behind him. Clayton was a little naive in his belief. Just as the police overestimated the power of publicity to destroy Mr. Big, Clayton likely overestimated the effect publicity would have in clearing his name in the court of public opinion. Nonetheless, the lines were drawn: Clayton wanted the full story told and the RCMP wanted to keep it a secret.

The prosecutors asked for a publication ban on ten "hallmarks of the operation" such as the fact that Clayton had been given the opportunity to join an organized crime gang if he admitted to killing Amanda Cook; that he had been asked to make this disclosure to a "crime boss"; that he had been paid to perform duties such as picking up parcels from bus depot lockers and counting cash; and that he had met Mr. Big in a hotel room. The police argued the efficacy of future Mr. Big operations would be undermined if these details were published. The judge ruled the request for an ongoing publication ban had the potential to undermine confidence in the justice system. Without explanation, the acquittal appeared inexplicable. The trial judge ruled that "the right of the police to maintain investigative techniques in the name of the proper administration of justice does not bring a constitutional guarantee." Instead, Mr. Big should be subjected to "the penetrating light of public scrutiny." The prosecution appealed.

The case went to the Supreme Court of Canada. The *Winnipeg Free Press*, *The Brandon Sun,* and the Canadian Newspaper Association intervened to support Clayton's demand for publication of all the details presented at his trial. The Attorneys General of Canada, British Columbia, and Ontario joined Manitoba in arguing for partial secrecy. They argued details of Mr. Big operations should be available for publication in legal journals and law reports but not in newspapers or news broadcasts. The judge writing the unanimous opinion for the Supreme Court noted, "This would mean that lawyers, law professors and law students would be aware of the police practices, but not the general public." He described this prospect as "disquieting to say the least." The Supreme Court ruled Mr. Big needed to operate within the penetrating light of public scrutiny rather than lurk around in the darkness of secrecy.

The exception to the rule of full transparency is the identity of participating undercover officers. These officers use their own names while working, both to be able to respond to their name without hesitation and to minimize the damage if they encounter an acquaintance while with the suspect. As a result, publishing the names of the undercover officers puts both them and ongoing investigations at risk. This danger has become more pronounced with the rise of the internet and search engines. In the 1990s, a judicial ruling would often provide the name of the undercover officers with an accompanying ban on media publication of this identity. In the past decade, these officers have invariably been identified in court documents by their initials or a first-name pseudonym. This reduces the possibility of a suspect making an interesting discovery if he googles the name of his new friend.

Accessibility of information about Mr. Big operations has increased even further with the arrival of the internet. Simple searches can produce news stories, court decisions, and commentary about Mr. Big cases. There are even YouTube videos showing suspects making disclosures to Mr. Big.

When ruling in favour of transparency, the Supreme Court expressed skepticism this would seriously damage the viability of the operation, saying, "There are a limited number of ways in which undercover operations can be run. Criminals who are able to extrapolate from a newspaper story about one suspect that their own criminal involvement might well be a police operation are likely able to suspect police involvement based on their common sense perceptions or on similar situations depicted in popular films and books." The court predicted that "media publication will not seriously increase the rate of compromise."

The Supreme Court's crystal ball appears to have been accurate. Publicity has not prevented Mr. Big from racking up disclosures and convictions. Part of this is because publication does not equal readership. Contrary to the belief of the High Court of Australia, people suspected of major crimes are not often big readers of newspapers. But it's not only potential targets of Mr. Big operations who remain oblivious to his existence despite media coverage. In 2008, the RCMP in British Columbia commissioned a telephone survey about Mr. Big. Fifty-eight percent of respondents were not aware he existed, even though British Columbia was the birthplace, spiritual home, and most common location of the technique.

Ignorance of Mr. Big, despite media coverage, is only part of the explanation for his ongoing success. Most targets of Mr. Big are aware of the potential for undercover operations against them. Almost every suspect, at some point, accuses the undercover officer of being an undercover officer. The most effective reply to this accusation is turning it back by saying, "Maybe you are the cop." This non-denial has a soothing effect on suspicions. Many Mr. Big targets have been given explicit warnings about Mr. Big. They are all suspects in a murder case. Most have been interrogated by police. Some have been arrested and released. Some have undergone preliminary hearings. Some have even been tried and convicted but had their convictions overturned on appeal. These people have all had contact with a criminal defence lawyer. Their lawyer gave them three fundamental pieces of advice:

- Keep your mouth shut. Don't talk about the case with anyone.
- If you are arrested, keep your mouth shut. You cannot talk your way out of trouble during an interrogation. Anything you say will make your situation worse, so shut up.
- If you meet someone who seems to be a member of a criminal gang wanting to recruit you, this person is an undercover police officer. Keep your mouth shut. If you meet someone called "Mr. Big" or "the Boss," this person is a police officer. Keep your mouth shut. If you tell these people you killed someone, you have given yourself the ultimate Go to Jail card. You will not Pass Go, and you will not collect $200.

Many, if not most, Mr. Big targets received an explicit warning about Mr. Big from their lawyer. Most still make a guilty disclosure. A few talked to their lawyers during the course of the investigation and were specifically told their new friend was an undercover police officer. They still told Mr. Big they were guilty. In one case, a suspect told the undercover officer about a Mr. Big trial covered in the media, asking, "Who could possibly be so stupid as to fall for that?" A few weeks later, she told Mr. Big she and a friend killed her boyfriend. The power of Mr. Big obviously rests on a more solid foundation than simple ignorance.

Children want presents, so they believe in Santa Claus. They want candy, so they believe in the Easter Bunny. They want money, so they believe in the Tooth Fairy. Adults want to get rich, so they buy lottery tickets. Some base their retirement plans on the expectation they will win. People believe what they want to believe, regardless of any empirical facts that suggest implausibility. It's a form of the disease of certainty. Mr. Big works because some people want to be part of a powerful criminal gang offering wealth and acceptance. If a suspect wants this and is guilty, they will make a disclosure to Mr. Big. If the suspect wants this and is innocent, they may claim to have killed someone. Guilty or innocent, for people who become enmeshed in a Mr. Big operation, he is a combination of Santa Claus, the Easter Bunny, the Tooth Fairy, and the lottery ticket seller promising the winning ticket. That is why publicity has not killed Mr. Big.

"SHOCKING THE CONSCIENCE" OF UNIVERSITY PROFESSORS

In 2016, an article in the *Criminal Law Quarterly* began as follows: "In the '90s the RCMP came up with a method of undercover investigation currently not employed anywhere in the civilized world: Mr. Big." The third sentence of the article proclaimed that the first Mr. Big case was *Evans* conducted in 1992 followed by that of *Skinner*. This opening paragraph invites skepticism. As we saw in Chapter 9, Mr. Big has been employed in Australia and New Zealand. Almost everyone includes these countries in the "civilized world," however that is defined. Further, the cited cases of *Evans* and *Skinner* were not Mr. Big cases. Later in the article, the author claims, "Suspects' lives are taken away and given new ones, in a deity-like display of power." The article even claimed, "Sometimes the individual was asked to do (fake) drug trafficking, sell firearms, contract with killers, and forcibly collect debt." Two cases were cited in support of this claim. Mr. Big made no appearance — whether real, promised, or imagined — in either one of them.

If this was just one article in an academic journal rife with perplexing statements and mistakes of fact, it would not be worth spending time worrying about. However, a survey of Canadian academic output about Mr. Big reveals many mistakes, omissions, or distortions.* Straightforward errors are common. For example, an article in the *Manitoba Law Journal* pointed to two cases in which disclosures to Mr. Big were excluded as evidence after the *Hart* ruling. Neither were Mr. Big cases. Two Canadian law professors in an article published in the *Oxford University Commonwealth Law Journal* said, "Since *Fulminante*, U.S. courts have often excluded confessions made to undercover police that raised issues about voluntariness." They cite the ruling in *Burns* and *Rafay*. These disclosures were admitted, not excluded. Other errors are real, but more subtle. As we saw in Chapter 9, Mr. Big is not used in the UK or the United States. Fully half of the academic journal articles discussing Mr. Big state, without citation, that the technique is *illegal* in these two countries. One went to far as to say that there had been numerous cases establishing this illegality. "Not used" is different from "illegal." When researching this book, I contacted the lead authors of all articles claiming Mr. Big is illegal in these two countries to ask for the relevant statute or case law; only one responded. He dodged the question.

Others present information that is technically correct but misleading. Following the *Hart* ruling, an article in the *Manitoba Law Journal* called for a review of all past convictions from Mr. Big cases. The authors pointed to a 1990s review of spousal homicide convictions following a Supreme Court ruling creating an expanded definition of self-defence in spousal homicide cases where the killer was subjected to abuse. The federal government appointed a judge to review previous convictions against the new legal standard. The *Manitoba Law Journal* article correctly pointed out that the inquiry

---

* Exempted from the criticism that follows is an excellent article on the implications of the Hart and Mack decisions by Lisa Dufraimont of Osgoode Hall Law School and a number of articles produced by researchers at Saint Mary's University.

distributed 238 applications for review and received 98 responsess. That sounds like a significant number of injustices were found, but the authors neglected to report on the results of these reviews. The judge heading the inquiry recommended corrective action in only 7 cases. Only 3 involved the change to the self-defence law. The judge concluded most of the self-defence claims had no "air of reality." When the authors of the article presented applications as the equivalent of findings, they exaggerated the nature of the problem. Three people convicted when they should not have been is a serious issue — but it is much less significant in scope than the 98 implied in the article.

Many more examples could be provided. Errors happen and mistakes get made; notably, however, the errors and mistakes in academic articles about Mr. Big all point in the same direction. They support the abolishment or serious undermining of Mr. Big. For example, when the erroneous claim is made that Mr. Big is "illegal" in the UK and the United States, the implication is that it *should be* in Canada as well. A preconceived notion that Mr. Big is the personification of evil likely explains why so many factual errors survive the peer review process. Cognitive psychologists call this "confirmation bias." If a fact appears to confirm a person's viewpoint, it is more likely be accepted as true even if it is not. Many Canadian academics appear to *know* that disclosures to Mr. Big are false regardless of the empirical evidence. It is their own version of the disease of certainty.

For the first two decades of his existence, Mr. Big was ignored by Canadian academics. This changed with the publication of two journal articles in 2009 and a book the following year. There was a flurry of articles around the time of the Hart/Mack Supreme Court cases. The published articles on Mr. Big are listed in the Appendix. The book *Mr. Big: Exposing Undercover Investigations in Canada,* by Kouri T. Keenan and Joan Brockman, sets the tone for most academic analyses of Mr. Big. As a result, the book is referred to directly in the following discussion while the journal articles are not, since overall themes are more important than critique of individual pieces.

Other than the prevalence of unidirectional error and sloppiness, the Canadian* academic bias against Mr. Big shows itself in four major ways: selecting cases to talk about; ignoring the victims of crime; minimizing the culpability of those convicted or the evidence against them; and creating a curious and spurious moral equivalency between the actions of the undercover police officers and the target. Let's briefly look at each of these in turn.

Nobel Prize–winning economist Daniel Kahneman and his research partner Amos Tversky demonstrated that people's perceptions about the commonness of something are usually based on the *availability* of examples rather than actual statistical frequency. We believe that movie stars have numerous marriages because the lives of those who do are well-publicized. Canadian academic writing on Mr. Big focuses on the relatively small number of cases where false confessions were obtained. The operations against Kyle Unger, Clayton Mentuck, and Andrew Rose are portrayed as normal and typical Mr. Big investigations rather than the aberrant fiascos they actually were. The fact that neither Clayton nor Andrew was actually convicted as a result of the disclosure to Mr. Big is usually glossed over (Andrew was wrongfully convicted twice *before* Mr. Big appeared in his case, but not afterwards). By focusing on the handful of cases where a false disclosure was given while ignoring most other cases, these academics create a misleading perception of the frequency of false confessions. The general rule for Canadian academic discussion of Mr. Big cases is that the more obvious it is the person is guilty, the more the case will be ignored. This even shapes the discussion of the pair

---

* Academic writers in Australia and New Zealand tend to be much more supportive of Mr. Big.

of landmark Supreme Court decisions. The murky disclosure of Nelson Hart that was ruled inadmissible is profiled, while that of the unmistakably guilty Dax Mack is often ignored. On many occasions, the availability distortion is compounded with descriptions of false confessions that had absolutely nothing to do with Mr. Big.

In their book, Keenan and Brockman said they studied ninety-three suspects charged because of disclosures to Mr. Big and "established that eleven of the targets were Aboriginal and at least twenty-one came from economically disadvantaged backgrounds." They went on to operationalize the availability distortion by naming and describing a number of these "disadvantaged" individuals but did not do the same for any of the majority who were not. Successful entrepreneurs such as David Knight — who disclosed to Mr. Big that he hired a hit man to murder his wife in order to avoid the financial implications of divorce — are not named, described, or mentioned. More seriously, the victims remain unmentioned. Some people who go to prison because of Mr. Big are Indigenous or economically disadvantaged. So are many of their victims. The majority of victims in homicides solved by Mr. Big were female. Cynthia Burk, Monica McKay, Jocelyn McDonald, Daleen Bosse, Victoria Nashacappo, Olive Hill, Monica Jack, Chelsea Acorn, and Heather Hamill were all Indigenous women whose murderer would not have been sent to prison but for Mr. Big. They remain unnamed and unacknowledged in the academic condemnations of Mr. Big. While the racial or socio-economic status of some of the convicted is presented as an argument against conducting Mr. Big, the victims' status is ignored.

Keenan and Brockman acknowledge that Michael Bridges represents the "poster boy" for good Mr. Big cases. As was discussed in Chapter 2, Bridges showed the undercover officer where he had hidden Erin Chorney's body — in the grave of another person. Bridges first said Erin died after hitting her head while falling because he pushed her. Bridges subsequently disclosed he strangled Erin manually and then with an electrical cord before drowning her in the bathtub. Erin's body was found with the electrical cord tied around her. She had broken bones in her neck and no sign of a head injury. Despite this, Keenan and Brockman note that Bridges's lawyer argued at appeal the acknowledged killer "had exaggerated his confession." They conclude their discussion of the case by saying, "The question still remains, was this really a first-degree murder case?" A seemingly reflexive unwillingness to accept empirical evidence gets even stranger when Keenan and Brockman discuss the conviction of Patrick Fischer. They correctly note that the British Columbia Court of Appeal found there was no merit to his claim that he lied to Mr. Big and the Supreme Court dismissed his leave to appeal. Despite the conclusion reached by the trial judge, a jury, and the appellate courts, Keenan and Brockman express a preference for the opinion of someone else, saying, "Patrick Fischer's mother has been questioning the conviction of her son, alleging that the undercover officers induced him to falsely confess to a murder." A mother's love is a magical thing. It protected the baby Harry Potter from the evil Lord Voldemort. But the story of Harry Potter is a work of fiction. In real life, a mother's love for her child does not trump a corroborated disclosure of guilt. The presumption of innocence is very important in our legal system, but it is supposed to end with a conviction.

One common academic criticism of Mr. Big involves the undercover officers pretending to be members of a criminal gang acting like . . . members of a criminal gang. They have a beer with lunch rather than sipping tea. They use "extremely foul language." When trying to let a person suspected of murdering a woman know that a disclosure will not result in rejection, they speak about women in misogynist terms. They degrade women by having their meetings at strip clubs rather than in church. Many Canadian academics find this behaviour shocking to their conscience and demand that Mr. Big operations, if not abolished, be changed, so that the undercover officers prioritize "minimizing disrepute to the administration of justice through illegal or immoral behaviour on the part of undercover police." One academic wrote, "There has not been enough research done on what the effect of such operations are on the people who conduct them, but alienation of the suspects from the real world and their submergence into a fictive, rotten one must take a toll at least on the suspects." It is a curious kind of moral equivalency that finds the tactic of taking a suspect to a strip club to facilitate a disclosure of guilt more abhorrent and degrading to women than raping and strangling a twelve-year-old girl. The ends don't always justify the means, but an exclusive focus on the means trivializes the ends.

In objecting to the means by which Mr. Big obtains disclosures, academic critics often protest the cost of the operation. An abstract of an article on holding Mr. Big accountable states, "Such operations deserve scrutiny because of their cost and potential for wrongful convictions." Pennies are put before principles. Another writer complains that a Mr. Big operation "uses a large amount of the taxpayers' money to follow a single individual, and may produce highly unreliable evidence." Again, the complaint about cost comes first. In their book, Keenan and Brockman complain that the Mr. Big operation directed at Nelson Hart "ended up costing $413,000." This Mr. Big operation ended up generating more murk than clarity, but were the lives of Karen and Krista Hart so valueless that we should begrudge the spending of just over $200,000 each in an effort to find out whether they were murdered?

Does the peculiar certainty of the general opposition to Mr. Big by Canadian academics have any impact? Does it matter what is said in books that quickly go out of print and in the pages of academic journals few people read?

At the level of individual Mr. Big cases, academic opinion does not have an effect. Judges have served as effective gatekeepers against professors' opinions being presented as evidence. One psychology professor has repeatedly offered to explain to juries why Mr. Big disclosures should be viewed as false confessions. Voir dire hearings have been held to determine whether he can provide "expert" opinion. In these cases, the professor admitted to being willing to provide an opinion without knowledge of the particular Mr. Big operation being examined. With varying degrees of politeness, judges have told him that his opinions are not required by the jury.

An example of how preconceived biases could impact specific trials but for judicial vigilance came in the case of Robert Balbar, who told Mr. Big he murdered his girlfriend by hitting her head with progressively larger hammers until she died. Two psychologists appeared at the voir dire hearings to support the defence's argument. One testified that Balbar could not read. He was unable to explain how Balbar sent and received numerous text messages. He told the court Balbar scored 44 on a standardized IQ test, which, he said, placed him at the first percentile in intelligence. This would mean that of a hundred people picked at random, ninety-nine would have a higher IQ. Upon cross-examination, the psychologist conceded his statistical analysis was wrong. An IQ score below 45 would place Balbar in the lowest 1.3 people in a random sample of 10,000. The testimony of the other psychologist was similar. He reported Balbar scored between 37 and 48 on the IQ test. The prosecutor pointed out it was impossible for the test to produce a score of 37. The grading system did not go that low. It got worse. Under cross-examination, the psychologist admitted that the test contained questions designed to test whether the person was malingering by trying to get a low score. The psychologist admitted Balbar scored high on the malingering rating. He then dismissed these results by concluding the extraordinarily low IQ score "as reflecting his true/valid performance . . . rather than as reflecting poor test motivation or a conscious attempt to manipulate test results."

After spending five days of voir dire hearings examining the work of the two psychologists, the judge concluded, "The expert opinions of [the two psychologists] with regards to Mr. Balbar's intellectual capacity as expressed in their reports and their testimony in court do not provide the Court with reliable evidence in this regard." It's one thing for defence lawyers to fight hard for their client and mount any possible defence. That is their job. It is something different to see testimony from experts that is unreliable and which, if accepted as evidence, would produce an unjust outcome in a homicide trial.

In large part because of judicial gatekeeping, academic opinion masquerading as expert knowledge has had little effect on the adjudication of individual cases involving disclosures to Mr. Big. The effect has been more pernicious in the media. Reporters are not, and cannot be expected to be, experts in everything they must write about. They are too busy. As a result, when confronted with an unfamiliar issue, they turn to "experts" such as university professors. Because it is an article of faith in much of Canadian academia that the primary purpose of Mr. Big is to generate false confessions, this opinion becomes the prism through which many Mr. Big cases are reported on. It is difficult to find a news story that does not describe Mr. Big as "controversial" because it "can lead to false confessions." The many successes of Mr. Big remain invisible.

MR. BIG: IMPROVE OR ABOLISH?

As the Supreme Court of Canada articulated in its ruling on Nelson Hart, Mr. Big is both a valuable tool for solving terrible crimes that would otherwise remain unsolved *and* a technique capable of generating false confessions. It is like a hammer. You can use it to fix your fence. It is also capable of smashing your thumb. One way to keep your thumb intact is to throw away your hammer, but your fence would eventually fall down. Another approach is to learn how to use your hammer better and take more care when swinging at the nail. If you do this, you can keep both your fence and your thumb.

Mr. Big has changed a lot in his thirty years of life. Many of the features that made a false disclosure more likely have been eliminated or modified. There is more rigorous advance internal vetting of operations by the RCMP and dramatically more scrutiny by the courts. The police themselves, defence lawyers, prosecutors, and judges have all played a role in making Mr. Big a better user of the hammer. This was demonstrated with the Hart/Mack criteria for admission of disclosures established by the Supreme Court. These comprehensive guidelines did not really force much change in Mr. Big's practices: the improvements had already been made.

CHAPTER 11

The Future of Mr. Big

As 1990 turned into 1991, Catherine Carroll died a horrible death. The woman, from St. John's, Newfoundland, went to bed early rather than celebrate New Year's Eve. She woke to find someone in her bedroom. The man stabbed her fifty-three times.

Catherine's body was found on January 2, 1991, by her nineteen-year-old son, Gregory Parsons. Numerous witnesses said relations between mother and son were strained. The police learned Gregory was a member of a "trash" rock band which recorded a song called "Kill, Kill, Kill" that included the lyrics:

> Kill your fuckin' mother, kill your fuckin' father.
> Stab once, stab twice. Ha, Ha, Ha, Ha.
> Kill your parents.

On January 10, Gregory was arrested and charged with murder. Three years later, a jury convicted him. The conviction was overturned on appeal. The appeal court judges ruled playing "Kill, Kill, Kill" to the jury was more prejudicial than probative. Gregory had not written the song, and a fellow band member described it as "more of a joke than anything." Despite this, the song was admitted as evidence of Gregory's guilt. The closing statement of the prosecutor was also problematic for the appeal court judges. She told the jury:

> In spite of what I expect is your instinctive reluctance to find or to believe that Greg Parsons is guilty, you have to ask yourselves the following question, **if Greg Parsons didn't cause his mother's death who did?***

The judges of the appeal court did not think highly of this question, saying, "The obligation of the Crown in any criminal case is to prove the guilt of the accused beyond a reasonable doubt; there is no onus on the defence to prove anything, and no obligation to suggest that the crime was, or may have been, committed by someone else." Shortly after Gregory's conviction was overturned, new DNA technology revealed the skin found under Catherine's fingernails belonged to someone other than her son. While dying, Catherine managed to scratch her assailant. With this, she saved her son from the possibility of spending decades in prison. The prosecutors agreed Gregory was wrongfully convicted at his trial. The Newfoundland government held an inquiry, and Gregory was paid compensation. While Gregory was cleared, Catherine's killer had avoided justice.

The DNA under Catherine's fingernails was eventually linked to one of Gregory's friends, Brian Doyle. This gave the police a strong suspect, but it did not prove Doyle was the killer. In 2002 — twelve years after Catherine's murder — it was time for Mr. Big. Doyle offered to kill the imaginary wife of the undercover officer.

---

* Emphasis added by Supreme Court of Newfoundland and Labrador, Court of Appeal. Case reference *R v. Parsons*, 1996 CanLII 11073 (NL CA).

When he met Mr. Big, Doyle said he was drunk and stoned that fateful New Year's Eve. He'd broken into Catherine's house through a basement window, took off his clothes, and entered her bedroom. Catherine woke up and, confronted with her son's naked friend, ordered him to leave. He left the bedroom, got a small kitchen knife, returned to the bedroom, and stabbed Catherine fifty-three times. He had a shower, got dressed, and left. Doyle took the knife with him and hid it. Twelve years later, he showed Mr. Big where he had hidden the knife. It was still there. After finding out that Mr. Big was an RCMP officer, Doyle pleaded guilty to second-degree murder and was sentenced to life in prison with no possibility of parole for eighteen years.

In this case, traditional investigative methods produced the conviction of an innocent person. New DNA technology cleared him. The combination of DNA technology and Mr. Big sent the right person to prison.

This case demonstrates the power of a well-run Mr. Big operation. It also shows all investigative tools available to law enforcement agencies are capable of producing wrongful convictions. Catherine Carroll's murder became a case involving Mr. Big, but Gregory Parsons was wrongfully convicted before anyone in Newfoundland — including the RCMP — had ever heard of him. Witnesses can be mistaken or can lie. Eyewitness identification can be mistaken. Forensic evidence can be wrong or misleading. Even good forensic techniques such as DNA testing can be performed sloppily, producing inaccurate results. As with other investigative techniques, Mr. Big is not immune to the possibility of error. Had Catherine Carroll's murder been committed a few years later, a Mr. Big operation would likely have targeted Gregory Parsons. It is not inconceivable that he would have made a false confession. With this not-unreasonable counterfactual scenario, Mr. Big could have helped send the wrong person to prison rather than ensure the right one got punished.

While every investigative technique creates the possibility of error, very few people believe that police should stop questioning witnesses, trying to find eyewitnesses to crimes, or conducting forensic analysis. Reasonable people believe that process improvement and caution while interpreting results make more sense than abolition of investigative tools. The real and potential problems with Mr. Big have, by contrast, often generated a different reaction. For example, after the Supreme Court ruled on Nelson Hart's case, a columnist writing in the *National Post* described Mr. Big as providing "cash rewards for confessions. Police pretending to be violent thugs, capable of beating the living daylights out of anyone who stands up to them." The columnist proclaimed that Mr. Big "relies on coercion, inducements and threats. As such, it should be stopped."

So why do real or imagined problems with Mr. Big result in calls for abolition regardless of his overall record of success?

In part, it's likely because Mr. Big is based on trickery and deceit. We don't like being tricked and lied to, so we have a visceral reaction against government operations based on unseemly acts. Our aversion to "unscrupulous" measures can be overcome when they are seen as necessary. In 1929, US Secretary of State Henry Stimson shut down the United States' program for breaking the codes in diplomatic telegrams sent by other countries. He explained, "Gentlemen do not read other's mail." That was when his country was at peace. In the 1940s, Stimson served as Secretary of War. In that time of peril, he was converted to the necessity of spying through code-cracking and interception of communications. We have a similar reaction to Mr. Big. When feeling safe and comfortable, people look askance at police strategies based on deception. When confronted with the reality of a horrible crime and a dangerous criminal, we demand they solve the crime and throw the perpetrator into jail. One reason jury members rarely appear shocked or horrified by Mr. Big tactics is because the opening phase of every homicide trial begins with a detailed description of the crime. They see crime scene photos. They hear testimony about the autopsy results. In the context of the horrible, painful reality of what it actually takes to kill someone, people on juries don't find it particularly shocking that the police might lie to the suspect in order to get a disclosure.

There is another aspect of Mr. Big that has only been indirectly alluded to so far in this book. Mr. Big evidence is different than other forms of evidence in that it inherently puts the accused in a very bad light. An eyewitness identification proven to be a mistake or a forensic test proven to be sloppily done does not discredit the accused. A disclosure to Mr. Big is different. Even if the disclosure is false, the accused is seen willingly (usually enthusiastically) telling Mr. Big they killed someone so they can join a criminal gang. The legal term for this is that the evidence is prejudicial. We are supposed to convict for the commission of specific, proven illegal acts rather than on the basis of whether the accused is a bad person. Convictions should be for crimes, not character. The reason Mr. Big disclosures are examined so carefully before being seen by a jury is because the only people who make a disclosure to Mr. Big are those who want to have a career in crime. This makes them disreputable. However, it is not unreasonable to expect that those who have crime as a career aspiration are *more likely* to commit homicide than those who would rather work as a teacher, sales clerk, construction worker, or server in a restaurant. The prejudicial effect of a Mr. Big disclosure is not entirely irrelevant.

A suspect telling Mr. Big that they did the dirty deed falls in the category of "post-event behaviour or demeanour." Judges will properly warn jurors to be careful about inferring guilt based on how someone behaves after a crime has been committed. Some people are demonstrative in expressing their sorrow. Others are not. Innocent people run from crime scenes sometimes, not just guilty people. Many people are guilty of discreditable behaviour and will lie to police to conceal this rather than to avoid getting caught for the homicide. People will even sometimes lie because they are innocent. Disclosures of guilt to Mr. Big are viewed differently than other types of "suspicious" post-event behaviour. There is good reason for this. These disclosures are different than running in panic from a crime scene or lying to police to conceal an affair.

Let's look at segments of the disclosure Dean Roberts made to Mr. Big. Roberts's case was discussed in Chapter 5 when we looked at how an explanation about the lack of forensic evidence can serve as a corroboration of the disclosure. In this transcript, Mr. Big is identified as "G" while Roberts is "D":

> G [Mr. Big]: Yeah, the thing is, like I've been in there?
> D [Roberts]: Okay, um, I know enough about you to—
> G: Put me away.
> D: Naturally.
> G: That's fuckin' a lot of concern to me.
> D: You know that I am presently under investigation by the police in Cranbrook.
> G. For what?
> D: For the murder of my wife.
> G: Aahhh, no.
> D: She was killed two months ago?
> G: Ya.
> D: And ah, they haven't figured out who did it, so naturally, I'm on the list, with about ah, 17 other people.
> G: So.
> D: So I was the one who did it.
> G: Really?
> D: Ya, I did.
> G: Are you shittin' me or what?
> D: No, I'm not.
> G: You fuckin' did your old lady?
> D: . . . No lic [sic]?

G: No way! You serious?

D: I'm very serious.

G: No way! So you can do it then.

D: Yes, I can do it.

G: How'd you do it?

D: Strangled her in her sleep.

G: Fuck, that takes guts.

D: Hell no, fuck that. It took me four months. I had thought of everything, I tried three times, to ah, put together some kind of a poison out of by-product and I had found what, larkspur and ah, monk's root, which are natural um, plants in the Kootnay's [sic] that are poisonous by nature, and I put some of it in the soup and she got really sick once, and she got kind of a mild . . . It wasn't strong enough. Umm but I was trying the easy way, nothing bloody, nothing you know. Thought about a way to ah, torch the house and keep her in it. Umm, thought about a way to sabotage her truck, but none of those are guaranteed.

G: Why did you want to do it?

D: Pardon?

G: Why did you want to do it?

D: I hated her.

D: . . . take care of me but ah, I was still pretty cramped. And before I could, I met her, got married and had twins, like ah, nine months after—

G: Ah, fuck.

D: Right away.

G: That's a tie-down, eh?

D: She brought in the marriage, ah, a one-year-old boy, who's the one that is still alive now. Who's not mine. Um, she was just turning really violent and really, she was psycho.

G: Really? So did you just fuckin' do her in her sleep?

D: Oh, I put two hundred grand on her.

G: Oh, you insured her?

D: Ya.

G: (laughs) Right on.

D: And ah—

G: So why are you hurtin', hurtin' for money?

D: Because they won't release it until they ah—

G: Oh, really?

D: And I'm going to do that just after Easter. Because all I have to do that, is take a polygraph.

G: Think you can beat it?

D: Absolutely.

G: How?

D: Polygraphs are based on emotions, not based on truth.

G: You have no emotion over it?

D: Not if I can fuckin' sit there and do it, I'm not—

G: . . . do it?

D: See ah—

G: Did you do it in the bed, or what?

D: Ya, our bed. Ah, we put all the kids to sleep, it was Monday night, it was expected for me to go out visit my friends, that was normal, so ah, it worked out that she was really bagged, because ah, I kept her up late the whole night before and I went to work for a longer day than usual, so she was just exhausted. She went to sleep early, and I just started giving her a massage . . .

G: (laughs)

D: Ah relaxing her, her neck and her shoulders, and in the process of giving her the massage, I manoeuvered the rope underneath her neck, and double-knotted it, and put my knee into the back of her head.

G: Really.

D: And that's how the killing was done.

A little later in the session, there is this exchange:

D: . . . And then I took one of my twins, and strangled him, put him in a bag, set the house on fire and left.
G: Took one of your twins?
D: Ya.
G: How old is he?
D: He's one year.
G: (laughing) Wow, what did you use for that?
D: Just another piece of rope.
G: Oh, really. Was he fuckin' . . . where?
D: He was in a room. I wanted him out of the house, just to cause a distraction. If there's a child missing, the police would focus on that, not on anything else.
G: Oh, so you took the kid out?
D: Ya, I took him out and through [sic] him out into the bush.
G: (laughs) Fuck me!
D: That's what I mean, anything is possible if you thought out.
G: Ya, okay, so then, you did what?
D: I took him, dropped him off in the bush, and then I arrived at my friend's house where I was expected to be.
G: Oh, you, you just did one kid, or what?
D: Ya, ya, then I set the place on fire.

This conversation took place two months after Roberts's wife and two sons died. It is post-event behaviour of a different order of magnitude than failing to shed tears at the funerals. After his arrest and conviction, Roberts claimed his disclosure was a lie. The UBC Innocence Project at the Allard School of Law has taken up his case to no avail. One reason is that the disclosure was so prejudicial that it revealed a truth.

WILL MR. BIG SURVIVE?

As we saw in Chapter 10, many people (including the police) thought that the publicity would kill Mr. Big. It did not. Mr. Big survived quite nicely even though his tricks were regularly reported in the media.

Some hoped or feared the Supreme Court would drive a stake through Mr. Big's heart with its ruling on Nelson Hart's conviction. As it turned out, the decision codified existing best practices for Mr. Big. The practices in some early Mr. Big cases that were rightly criticized as increasing the potential for false disclosures had long been eliminated. Undercover officers no longer used a "get them drunk to get them to talk" scenario. Threats to the suspect or creating reasons for him to brag were gone from every properly conceived and supervised operation. Positive reasons to provide truthful disclosures were now standard practice. The level of inducements had been restrained. Because Mr. Big case managers had already responded to both the lessons they learned on their own and the challenges raised by defence lawyers, the probability of false disclosures had already been lowered. As a result, the Hart/Mack criteria did not present a threat to Mr. Big's crime-solving ability.

Despite all this, the future viability of Mr. Big is threatened. The reason is paradoxical. Scrutiny of Mr. Big by the courts in response to defence lawyer challenges was the most important driver of improvements to the technique. Now the intensity of this scrutiny has the potential to kill Mr. Big. An increase in scrutiny preceded the Hart/Mack rulings, but the reversal of onus intensified the trend. As we saw in Chapter 10, the length of voir dire hearings sometimes exceeds the length of the operations. Undercover officers end up spending more time on the witness stand describing, explaining, and justifying every action and utterance than they spend investigating crime. This dramatically increases the cost of Mr. Big operations and diverts police officers away from conducting investigations. Shedding light on Mr. Big operations is a bit like a person getting sunshine. Getting some sun creates a nice tan and helps your body create more vitamin D. Getting too much gives you sunstroke and can even kill. There are signs that the level of scrutiny faced by Mr. Big in the courts has gone from healthy to pathological — from suntan to sunstroke.

Mr. Big is in danger of being smothered under the weight of the scrutiny he faces. This comes from a pathological risk aversion on the part of the justice system. There are, in fact, no real consequences for police or prosecutors if a homicide case is not solved and a killer is not put in jail. Life goes on for everyone except the victim. Nothing happens when nothing happens. It is different with the conviction of an innocent person. That has consequences. The most severe are faced by the poor person imprisoned for something they did not do, but when wrongful convictions are discovered, fingers are pointed, blame is assigned, compensation is (sometimes) paid, and careers are (sometimes) ruined.

As a society, we have a legitimate desire to catch and punish those responsible for terrible crimes such as homicides *and* to avoid convicting the innocent. There is an inherent tension between these two important goals. By improving investigative techniques and maintaining a healthy skepticism, we can minimize the potential for wrongful convictions, but the only way we can be *certain* that innocents are never convicted is to convict nobody. Few of us would want to live in a society in which murderers are never brought to justice.

Our approach to dealing with violent crime comes down to the relationship between doubt and certainty we are willing to accept in each case. There should always be some doubt, since failure to doubt means succumbing to the disease of certainty. But how do we quantify how much doubt we should accept while still convicting? The legal standard is "reasonable doubt." This sounds imprecise, but a wise judge once told me he had a simple way of operationalizing the concept. If he found himself struggling over deciding someone's guilt, the question answered itself. He had reasonable doubt and needed to acquit.

If the standard of a complete and absolute elimination of doubt would mean all guilty would avoid punishment, the standard of reasonable doubt means some guilty will go free. In 1765, the famous British legal writer William Blackstone attempted to quantify this by saying, "Better that ten guilty persons escape than that one innocent suffer." This is properly described as stressing the importance of avoiding convicting the innocent, but it is not an open-ended commitment. Others have proposed various numerical ratios to express a different balance. One of the signers of the US Declaration of Independence, Benjamin Franklin, said it was better a hundred guilty go free rather than one innocent person be convicted. This is moving towards a standard of absolute certainty. At the other end of the spectrum are the nineteenth-century "Iron Chancellor" of Germany, Otto von Bismarck, and the twentieth-century communist revolutionary Che Guevara, both of whom said it was better ten innocents be convicted than one guilty person avoid punishment.

For what it is worth, my personal opinion is that Blackstone got the numbers about right. Franklin's formulation would mean almost every murderer would avoid punishment while the Bismarck/ Guevara formulation is that of a police state. Mr. Big's record suggests he is much closer to Blackstone than either of the extremes.

The most troubling prosecutions Mr. Big was involved in are Kyle Unger (1991); Jason Dix (1996); Clayton Mentuck (1998); Andrew Rose (1999); Alan Smith (2008); Craig Short (2010); and Larry Darling (2013). An ongoing examination could well add Wade Skiffington (1999) to this list. The year in parentheses is the year the suspect met Mr. Big. All these cases except for that of Larry Darling have been discussed in some detail in this book.

The first thing revealed by this list is that five of these eight problematic cases occurred in Mr. Big's first decade. The following two decades added only three cases to this list. Problematic cases have become less frequent.

The second feature of this list is that the investigations, as a whole, were characterized by the disease of certainty on the part of police and a degree of obsessiveness on the part of prosecutors. There were many problems in these investigations over and above the production of false disclosures to Mr. Big. Jailhouse informants, bad forensics, and dubious witnesses were features of these cases. Indeed, in two of the eight cases, about the only thing that did not go wrong was Mr. Big generating a false disclosure. Both Jason Dix and Craig Short were prosecuted despite telling Mr. Big they had not committed the murders. Craig was even convicted. Kyle Unger and Clayton Mentuck were introduced to Mr. Big only after a charge had already collapsed in court. Problems arising from the disease of certainty went even further with Andrew Rose. He was convicted twice before Mr. Big appeared in his case. After these convictions were overturned upon appeal, Mr. Big was used in the third failed attempt to get a conviction capable of withstanding appeal.

The legitimate criticisms directed at some early Mr. Big operations have generally been addressed by the RCMP. Mistakes are more likely when a police force inexperienced in the technique gives it a try. Two of the three most problematic Mr. Big investigations in this century were conducted by police forces other than the RCMP. The biggest challenge in avoiding bad results from Mr. Big is not in the conduct of the operation but in the use of the result. Some disclosures to Mr. Big cannot be corroborated — the case of Nelson Hart was a classic example of this. The problem did not lie in the conduct of the Mr. Big operation but rather in the murkiness of the results. At the end of the day, both possible explanations for the deaths of Karen and Krista Hart had a reasonable degree of plausibility. Reasonable doubt existed as to whether their deaths were an accident or murder. In our system of law, the correct outcome in the face of this doubt was acquittal.

As Mr. Big operations have gotten better, they have become longer and more expensive. If the end result is murky — a disclosure of guilt inconsistent with known facts or (as in the case of Nelson Hart) unverifiable — prosecutors face both pressure and a temptation to proceed with prosecution. This propels the prosecution forward. Let's look at one example of how this can work. In all the Mr. Big cases reviewed for this book, the conviction based on the least amount of evidence appears to be that of Paul Creek. He gave Mr. Big a guilty disclosure and was convicted even though the trial judge refused to admit the disclosure as evidence. Whether or not he lied to Mr. Big, Creek's disclosure played no role in the jury's guilty verdict. Without the Mr. Big operation, Creek would not have been charged. The British Columbia Prosecution Service had concluded there was insufficient evidence to proceed. After the disclosure was ruled inadmissible, the prosecutors still proceeded. Creek was ultimately convicted on evidence previously deemed insufficient to justify a charge.

Most of the time if a disclosure is ruled inadmissible at a voir dire, the charges against the person are stayed or withdrawn. However, charging a suspect based on an uncorroborated disclosure and relying on the voir dire process to sort it out is problematic. It is very expensive and time-consuming for the justice system. More seriously, it is very expensive and damaging for the accused. If someone is charged with a homicide, the cost to them is enormous even if the charges are eventually withdrawn. They will spend significant time in jail waiting for their day in court. They will be bankrupted by the cost of their defence and unemployment. Very likely, their family will be torn apart. Their reputation will be permanently damaged, as many people believe a charge means guilt. There is also a less quantifiable, but tremendous, cost to the victim's family and friends. When the suspect is charged, they are assured the guilty person has been caught and will be punished. Whatever psychological comfort this gives is then taken away. Most believe the suspect is guilty and has "gotten away" with the murder of their loved one.

The major remaining problem with Mr. Big is not in the conduct of the operations itself. By and large, the operations are conducted about as well as we can expect in a world wherein perfection is unattainable, but problems still remain in the treatment of questionable disclosures. Some of these are weeded out without the suspect being charged. This number could be higher than we think because, by definition, the public should never hear about these cases. There are also signs that the Hart/Mack criteria are contributing to a more rigorous examination of the disclosures by prosecutors. In the wake of these decisions, charges against two accused were stayed because the prosecutors decided the disclosures would not meet the new standards rather than proceeding so that a judge could make this controversial decision for them.

The goal should be that no disclosures to Mr. Big are ruled as inadmissible or unreliable by a judge. With this, the certainty of an appropriately rigorous examination of the Mr. Big operation causes the police and prosecutors to screen out cases where reasonable doubt exists *before* charges are laid.

A CLOSING OBSERVATION ON MR. BIG

This book is dedicated to the memory of the victims of homicide whose killers were convicted because of Mr. Big. The long list at the front of the book is incomplete, but it represents the best compilation possible given the fragmented record-keeping in our justice system and police reticence in talking about Mr. Big.

Some of these victims were killed in "high-profile" homicides that shocked and horrified a city, province, or country. They were "sympathetic" victims — small children brutally beaten, girls and young women savagely sexually assaulted before being murdered, or middle-class suburban people not normally expected to be the victims of a homicide. If we look at the victims in the highest-profile, most problematic Mr. Big cases, we tend to see "shocking" homicides. Clayton Mentuck and Kyle Unger were accused of raping and murdering teenage girls. That's not supposed to happen in rural Manitoba. Alan Smith and Craig Short were accused of killing respectable married women in suburban homes. That's not supposed to happen in Ontario. Jason Dix was accused of execution-style murders of two men working overtime on a Saturday morning. That's not supposed to happen in Alberta. Andrew Rose was accused of murdering two young German tourists. Visitors to Canada are not supposed to be treated that way. When these "shocking" homicides are committed, we, the public, put tremendous pressure on the police to make an arrest and on prosecutors to get a conviction. We insist justice be served. Our pressure can help create an injustice.

The majority of Mr. Big cases are not high profile. These homicides "shock" nobody. Many of the female victims were treated as disposable and expendable by our society while they lived because of their race, class, or means of earning their income. In death, they are often ignored. Many of the male victims are not sympathetic figures. There are a lot of drug dealers among the victims in Mr. Big cases. They were feared and despised by our society in life. In death, they are often viewed with an attitude of "good riddance to bad rubbish." There is no great public clamour for the killers of the "expendable" or the despised to be caught and punished. The media coverage in the majority of Mr. Big victims is shocking in its absence. Often, the homicides only make the news because of the novelty of Mr. Big's involvement. We, as a society, just don't care much about many of these killings.

But here is the thing. None of these people deserved to be murdered. Even the drug dealers should be able to practise their trade without being shot — let alone having their bodies dismembered afterwards. All these homicide victims left behind family members devastated by their deaths and friends who miss them.

Equality before the law is usually interpreted to mean people guilty of crimes should be treated equally regardless of their income, social status, power, race, gender, or any of the other criteria we use to assign worth to people. The concept should also apply to the determination with which we seek some measure of justice for the victims of criminal acts. The poor, powerless, or unsympathetic are just as dead after a murder as the rich, powerful, or sympathetic. They deserve equal effort in bringing their killers to justice.

Mr. Big, as practised by the RCMP and other police forces in Canada, represents a commitment to this conception of equal justice. Mr. Big operations are long, difficult, and expensive. They consume a lot of police time to conduct and even more to defend in court. In the majority of Mr. Big cases, the police were under no particular public pressure to find the killer. As a society, we didn't care that much. The victims were remembered only by a small group of family members and friends . . . and the police. Mr. Big's demonstrated commitment to bringing the killers to justice long after society has forgotten about their victims makes him a personification of the highest ideals of our system of justice.

APPENDIX

A Note on Sources and Further Reading

The primary source of information about Mr. Big cases for this book came from the legal decisions dealing with Mr. Big cases. These include decisions in voir dire hearings, written decisions in judge-alone trials, sentencing decisions, and appeal court decisions. The decisions on cases discussed in this book can be easily accessed by going to www.canlii.org and searching for the case by the last name of the accused. In some cases, the information contained in the legal decisions was enhanced by accessing other court documents or media coverage about the case.

Four book-length discussions on Mr. Big in general or on specific cases were published before this book.

Mr. Big: Exposing Undercover Investigations (Fernwood Publishing, 2010) by Simon Fraser University criminologists Kouri T. Keenan and Joan Brockman is a head-on attack on Mr. Big. Because it was published a decade ago, the case references are older. The book was released before the Hart/Mack Supreme Court decisions formalized the legal criteria for admitting Mr. Big disclosures as evidence in court cases.

The best existing case study of a Mr. Big investigation comes in *To the Grave: Inside a Spectacular RCMP Sting* (Great Plains Publications, 2006) by *Winnipeg Free Press* reporter Mike McIntyre. This book does an excellent job of capturing the feel of a Mr. Big operation by making extensive use of the actual transcribed dialogue between Michael Bridges and the undercover officers. *Real Justice: A Police Mr. Big Sting Goes Wrong: The Story of Kyle Unger* (Lorimer, 2015) by Richard Brignall is written for adolescent readers but provides a good, clear, accurate account for adults as well. *Mr. Big: The Investigation into the Deaths of Karen and Krista Hart* (Flanker Press, 2015) is co-written by former CBC reporter Colleen Lewis and Jennifer Hicks, the former wife of Nelson Hart. It provides an interesting perspective into the Hart case but is frustratingly silent on what caused Jennifer Hart to change from an advocate proclaiming Nelson Hart's innocence into someone calling for justice after his eventual acquittal by the Supreme Court.

As we've discussed, Mr. Big is no stranger in Canadian academic journals.

"Hart and Mack: New Restraints on Mr. Big and a New Approach to Unreliable Prosecution Evidence" (*The Supreme Court Law Review: Osgoode's Annual Constitutional Cases Conference* 71, 2015), by Lisa Dufraimont of the Osgoode Law School at York University, provides an excellent analysis of the implications of the Hart/Mack Supreme Court decisions.

Researchers at St. Mary's University in Nova Scotia have produced some useful and interesting articles on Mr. Big's ability to produce false disclosures. These are as follows: "Using the 'Mr. Big' Technique to Elicit Confessions: Successful Innovation or Dangerous Development in the Canadian Legal System?" by Steven M. Smith, Veronica Stinson, and Marc W. Patry (*Psychology, Public Policy, and Law* 15(3), 2009); "High-Risk Interrogations: Using the 'Mr. Big Technique' to Elicit Confessions" by Steven M. Smith, Veronica Stinson, and Marc W. Patry (*Law and Human Behaviour*

34(1), 2010); "Shocking the Conscience: Public Responses to Police Use of the 'Mr. Big' Technique" by Christina J. Connors, Nakita Archibald, Steven M. Smith, and Marc W. Patry (*Journal of Forensic Psychology Research and Practice* 17(1), 2017); and "The Mr. Big Technique on Trial by Jury" by Christina J. Connors, Marc W. Patry, and Steven M. Smith (*Psychology, Crime and Law* 25(1), 2019).

As was discussed in Chapter 10, other Canadian academic articles about Mr. Big should be read with some caution as advocacy against Mr. Big appears to be as prominent as analysis. These articles include "Deceit, Betrayal and the Search for Truth: Legal and Psychological Perspectives on the 'Mr. Big' Strategy" by Timothy E. Moore, Peter Copeland, and Regina A. Schuller (*Criminal Law Quarterly* 55(3), 2009); "The RCMP's 'Mr. Big' Sting Operation: A Case Study in Police Independence, Accountability and Oversight" by Kate Puddister and Troy Riddell (*Canadian Public Administration* 55(3), 2012); "What Is Voluntary? On the Reliability of Admissions Arising From Mr. Big Undercover Operations" by Timothy E. Moore and Kouri Keenan (*Investigative Interviewing: Research and Practice* 5(1), 2013); "Opposing Mr. Big in Principle" by David Milward (*UBC Law Review* 46(1), 2013); "R. v. Jeanvenne: 'Mr. Big' False Confession Jury Charge Comes to Ontario" by Arghavan Gerami (*Criminal Law Quarterly* 60, 2014); "R v Hart: A New Common Law Confession Rule for Undercover Operations" by Chris Hunt and Micah Rankin (*Oxford University Commonwealth Law Journal* 14(2), 2014); "Motive to Lie? A Critical Look at the 'Mr. Big' Investigative Technique" by Adriana Poloz (*Canadian Criminal Law Review* 19(2), 2015); "'Boys, You Should All Be in Hollywood': Perspectives on the Mr. Big Investigative Technique" by Elizabeth Sukkau and Joan Brockman (*UBC Law Review* 48(1), 2015); "The Hart of the (Mr.) Big Problem" by Adelina Iftene (*Criminal Law Quarterly* 63, 2016); and "Beyond Finality: R v Hart and the Ghosts of Convictions Past" by Amar Khoday and Jonathan Avey (*Manitoba Law Journal* 40(3), 2017).

The article by Everett Doolittle on the disease of certainty can be located in the *FBI Law Enforcement Bulletin* at leb.fbi.gov/articles/perspective/perspective-the-disease-of-certainty. It's worth a read.

There has been more research exploring why people give false confessions than on why people give true ones. The research on false confessions is vast. For an overview, I suggest a series of summary articles by Saul Kassin: "The Psychology of Confession Evidence" (*American Psychologist* 52(3), 1997); "On the Psychology of Confessions: Does Innocence Put Innocents at Risk?" (*American Psychologist* 60(3), 2005); and "False Confessions: How Can Psychology So Basic Be So Counterintuitive?" (*American Psychologist* 72(9), 2017).

The best treatments of wrongful convictions in Canada are "Wrongful Convictions in Canada" by Kent Roach (*University of Cincinnati Law Review* 80, 2012) and "Convicting the Innocent: A Triple Failure of the Justice System" by Bruce MacFarlane (*Manitoba Law Journal* 31, 2006).

The story of the knight and his wife can be read in *The Fabliaux: A New Verse Translation* by Nathaniel E. Dubin, translator (Liveright Publishing, 2013).